Soviet and East European Studies

RUSSIAN PEASANT ORGANISATION
BEFORE COLLECTIVISATION

Soviet and East European Studies

FIRST BOOKS IN THE SERIES

A. Boltho, *Foreign Trade Criteria in Socialist Economics*
Sheila Fitzpatrick, *The Commissariat of Enlightenment*
Donald Male, *Russian Peasant Organisation before Collectivisation*
P. Wiles, *The Prediction of Communist Economic Performance*

RUSSIAN
PEASANT ORGANISATION
BEFORE
COLLECTIVISATION

A STUDY OF
COMMUNE AND GATHERING
1925–1930

BY

D. J. MALE

CAMBRIDGE
AT THE UNIVERSITY PRESS
1971

Published by the Syndics of the Cambridge University Press
Bentley House, 200 Euston Road, London N.W.1
American Branch: 32 East 57th Street, New York, N.Y.10022

© Cambridge University Press 1971

Library of Congress Catalogue Card Number: 70-123662

ISBN: 0 521 07884 9

Printed in Great Britain by
Alden & Mowbray Ltd
at the Alden Press, Oxford

CONTENTS

Contents

PREFACE

The commune was the institution through which the majority of Russian peasants held land until mass collectivisation in 1930. In pre-revolutionary years it had also been responsible for the administration of local affairs and distribution of taxation. After the revolution these latter functions were nominally transferred to rural soviets. In the event many communes remained the effective organs of local government until their dissolution with collectivisation. The two-fold nature of the commune, as land holding organ and unit of local administration, and its response to the pressures for change in the late 1920s, is the subject of this study.

The commune is seen as an institution based on equalising re-distribution of member households' land. There is a scarcity of basic quantitative data about the commune, as well as qualitative descriptions of its working. Once the general physical nature of commune land holding has been described, the book attempts to demonstrate that communes differed very considerably in physical layout in different areas of European Russia. Thus while we talk of 'the commune' for lack of adequate area studies, generalisations should be received with great caution. Moreover, there was probably not a hard and fast line between commune membership and holding land individually. In the light of these warnings, the book goes on to look at the organisation of the commune for both land holding and local administration.

External pressures for change from the government are seen in the attempt to develop a system of rural administration in the rural soviets, and in the attempt to change forms of land holding, in the end by collectivisation. The attempts to strengthen rural soviets are briefly described, and the relationship between them and the communes is viewed from the points of view of physical area covered, functions envisaged in legislation, actual relationships and finance. The debate on land holding before the decision to collectivise is reviewed in so far as it touched on economic performance and social differentiation within the commune. Up to 1929, reforms in land holding were largely in land use measures designed to alleviate the more inefficient aspects of communal holding. The collectivisation campaign cut across existing institutions, including the communes.

This can be seen as a particular case in the general problem of land reform in a developing country. It expresses in institutional form the Soviet problem of an industrially-oriented party holding power in an agrarian country, and reflects the continuity of Russian themes in Soviet times.

My interest in these themes was originally aroused by the late Professor Alexander Baykov, who supervised in its early stages the Birmingham University Master of Commerce thesis on which this study is based. My thanks are due to Professor I. S. Kuvshinov of the Timiryazev Agricultural Academy, Moscow, for permitting me to study in his department when I was a British Council exchange research student. Most of the work on early drafts was done at the Department of Soviet Institutions, Glasgow University, where Mr J. Miller spent much time in giving extremely helpful and patient guidance. Professor Alec Nove was kind enough to make suggestions on rewriting the typescript. My greatest debt is to Professor R. E. F. Smith of Birmingham University, who took over supervision after Professor Baykov's death. His wide knowledge of the Russian peasantry and feeling for the essential problems involved have made me conscious of the inadequacies of this work, but his patience and stimulation have encouraged me to continue the work to this point. Finally, I thank Miss Jean Fyfe of 'Soviet Studies' for typing the bulk of the original manuscript under difficult conditions, and those who have helped in the preparation of the later stages.

Lichfield, March 1970   D.J.M.

INTRODUCTION

I THE SETTING

The commune was the institution through which the majority of Russian peasants held land until mass collectivisation in 1930. In Tsarist times, it had also been the lowest level in local administration, distributing taxation and other obligations between member households. After the revolution, these latter functions were nominally transferred to the newly-formed rural soviets. In the event, many communes remained the effective organs of local government until their dissolution with collectivisation. The two-fold nature of the commune, as land holding organ, and unit of local administration, and its response to the pressures for change in the later 1920s, is the subject of our study.

In pre-revolutionary times, the commune had been a far from static institution. The method of redemption payment after the abolition of serfdom in 1861 had reinforced communal tenure, with its equalising redistribution of land between member households. In the immediate pre-revolutionary years, government policy favoured industrial expansion, and encouraged peasants to break away from the inefficiency of the commune and consolidate their land into individual farms. How far this process had gone by the revolution is a matter for debate, but by the beginning of our period most peasants in European Russia were once more in communes.

We start in 1925, because by then the policy of exhorting the peasantry to 'enrich yourselves', and of attempting to encourage peasant production by a great measure of freedom, was well-established. It also marks the beginning of serious concern about the local soviet network, and of attempts to enliven the rural soviets. Our study covers the commune from a time when the peasantry was virtually unfettered by the government, through increasing pressure for change in the countryside as a result of both economic and political decision, to the end of the commune under mass collectivisation.

Introduction

Such a study may be viewed in several perspectives. In the most general, we are dealing with one aspect of a problem common to all industrialising countries. The question of land reform, and of adapting peasant institutions based on subsistence, or near-subsistence, farming to the demands of an industrialising economy is a pressing one in many countries. The problem of integrating the peasantry, forming the vast bulk of the population, into an economy committed by its leaders to industrialisation lies at the root of this study. Viewed in the perspective of peculiarly Russian conditions, we see a concrete example of the influence of specifically Russian conditions on the Soviet revolution. The commune not only survived, but gained in strength in the face of the system of rural soviets, developed by a government whose long-term aims could not be reconciled with the existing organisation of the peasant economy. The conflict reached its crisis with the decision of the government to abandon attempts to stimulate peasant production by economic means, with their potentially anti-socialist consequences in the development of prosperous 'farmer' peasants, and to achieve the necessary conditions for rapid economic growth by 'running the countryside'. The conflict between the commune and the soviet network expressed in institutional form the problems of an industrial party holding power in an agrarian country.

The focus of our study is on the commune as a unit of local administration, functionally based on a particular system of land holding. The emphasis is thus that of a political scientist, rather than of a sociologist or social anthropologist, if labels have to be affixed. Our choice of focus has been largely governed by the materials available. At this time there was much work on studying other problems related to the peasantry, especially social stratification. The continuing existence of the commune was admitted by all commentators, yet very few serious studies were published. In part this may have been due to the risk of being accused of Social Revolutionary influence if one studied the commune. There is a dearth of basic quantitative data, and such statistics as there are need to be treated with caution. The dynamics of social interaction within the commune is a field where there is practically no reliable material. In this study, we use materials which go some way to

2

clarifying the pattern of communal land holding, and also materials which illuminate somewhat the local government functions of the commune at this time. However, generalisations made in this study are not based on a rich fund of knowledge of particular local situations, but on what were seen as problems by those who wrote and spoke at the centre. This will be tested as far as possible against what we have been able to discover of the local situation.

In the second part of our introduction we will describe the general features of communal land holding. This is a preliminary to an attempt to give some precision to the concept of the commune in our first chapter. There is a great need for study of the commune to be firmly rooted in a geographical context. The variety of economic and natural conditions under which 'the commune' existed suggests that there were great local variations. It is possible to show this in terms of physical layout, as our review of land holding by area will show. Lack of materials make it impossible to extend this to deal with the commune's social organisation by area, but enough evidence is available to sound a warning note against generalisation. In the light of the subsequent political discussion, it is worth emphasising that a peasant household was not necessarily either a commune member, or an individual peasant completely hived off from the commune. While the commune was basically an institution for arranging communal holding of arable land, there was not a hard and fast line between those who were and were not members of the commune when it came to fulfilling other functions.

When we consider the internal organisation of the commune, it will be evident that there were internal pressures for change. There were those who wanted to leave the commune entirely, probably for economic reasons. The commune was not geared to production for the market. There was a greater number of households who wanted the communal holding to be rationalised. The fragmentation of large households into smaller units, and the return of young men from the war, led to conflict between the older heads of households and the younger members who had traditionally no part in the work of the commune gathering. These internal pressures for change in the commune were reflected in the external pressures from the government.

Introduction

The nature of these external pressures is the theme of our third chapter. Here we first of all turn to the work of local administration performed by the commune, and the resulting conflict between the rural soviet and the commune, reflecting a broader conflict of values and aims. There was comparative consistency in the aims of the government here. The need was to strengthen the rural soviet so that it could take over all governmental functions from the communes. This end was encouraged by an increasingly hard line towards the commune as an agricultural institution. In the second section of this chapter we trace this process from the arguments based on ideology to the actual land use measures which were undertaken. Here the question of social differentiation within the commune was seen as crucial at the centre and we must question the reality of the approach used. We finally try to examine what happened to the commune during the collectivisation campaign, and find that it was largely ignored by those conducting the campaign, who imposed a completely new system of agricultural organisation in the collective farms.

Before setting out on these tasks, we may sound a warning against two dangers. We talk here about the commune and local administration. The word 'administration' has connotations of officialdom, of a certain order and formality in the conduct of affairs. We must remember that at this time the points of contact between the peasantry and central government were largely confined to collection of taxes and grain. The commune was probably freer than under the Tsarist regime, where the attempt was made to turn it into a formal unit of administration. The setting up of the rural soviet network meant the commune was absolved from being the point of contact between central government and the peasantry. The soviets became the executors of unpopular policy, thus absolving the commune from one of its, to the peasantry, least liked functions. This may well have been a factor strengthening the peasant outlook. Organisation of the commune's affairs was usually informal in the extreme. From accounts in the twenties, it seems that the atmosphere had changed little from the time when Korovin painted his picture 'At the mir' in 1893 (hung in the Tretyakov Gallery). The men of the village are not gathered in a hall with carefully laid-out benches facing a plat-

4

form with table and decanter of water. They are in a loose group in the middle of the village street. The older men sit on a log, the elder stands in the middle, mopping his forehead, whilst a man who addresses him is addressed simultaneously by two other peasants. The rest of the group argue among themselves. The ideas of orderliness and discipline which the Bolsheviks brought to the revolution and tried to instill into the administrative apparatus of the country would obviously be difficult to transplant from town to country.

Another danger is to talk of 'the peasantry' as a homogeneous group; it is more dangerous still to talk of 'peasant demands'. Just how far peasants were socially stratified is a difficult question to resolve, and lies outside the scope of the present work. It would seem that, in the face of government pressure, a certain community of interest was found. The wishes of the peasantry did not find any formulation in articulate demands, which is hardly surprising. Rather these are to be inferred from the reaction of the peasantry to demands made upon them. Once the Bolsheviks embraced the Social Revolutionary policy of granting the peasantry land held by the former land-owners, they received a large measure of support. In fact the Bolsheviks were only making law what had been accomplished in any case during 1917. While this aspect of government policy was accepted by the peasantry, it was clear they did not accept the political and social context in which it had been made. For those at the centre, the 1918 law on land was the beginning of the building of a socialist state. For the peasant, it was an end in itself. It meant that he was given more land, and that he was freed of the obligation to the landlord. Families could afford to divide up their holdings now that they had more land. Economically, the implication for the government was that the peasantry would support the government by increasing output. The peasant probably saw this as an opportunity to produce for his own needs, with no landlord to bother him. In the event neither compulsion nor adjusting prices provided sufficient incentive for the peasantry to increase output to the extent required. Socially, the central government looked for an alliance with the peasantry, who would gradually learn the advantages of such co-operation. For the peasantry, the implication was that the land had been transferred to his possession. Social responsibility in land holding had never been very clear in the commune, where holding of a particular piece of land tended to be for a brief period, and was not seen as extending beyond the constraints of fellow villagers. Politically, the peasantry saw the new system of local soviets as an irrelevance. The rural soviet received papers from the centre couched in a language and spirit alien to the peasant. The questions discussed were either remote from the peasant, or, where they concerned the village, involved unpleasant matters such as taxation. The administration and peasantry were worlds apart, and it is with this problem that we are concerned here, at the 'grass roots' level. Maurice Hindus quoted a Russian peasant remarking to a party agitator: 'This world revolution's got stuck in the mud of our Russian roads.'[1] This study sets out to give a little more light on the way this happened.

2 DISTINCTIVE FEATURES OF COMMUNE LAND HOLDING

In its layout of fields, the commune resembled the pre-enclosure English village with its open field system. A map of a Russian commune and an English village would show a similar arrangement of strips and fields, with each household having a number of strips in the various courses of the rotation. The three-field system seems to have predominated in areas of redistributable land holding in Russia. However, while the physical configuration was similar, the distinctive feature of the Russian commune was periodic redistribution of these strips to adjust for changes in size of household. This probably originated in the eighteenth century in response to the system of *per capita* taxation, and was reinforced by the system of redemption payments after the ending of serfdom in 1861. The commune was essentially concerned with the holding of land rather than with the working of the land. Work was done largely by individual households on their own allotted land, although there were occasional obligations to work for the commune, such as in scything meadows. While there were other important functions connected

---

[1] Maurice Hindus, *Red bread* (Jonathan Cape, London and New York 1931), p. 38. Hindus's books are invaluable for conveying the atmosphere in a central black earth village. See also *Humanity uprooted* (1929) and *Broken earth* (1926).

with local administration, such as allocations of taxation, as far as the land was concerned, the commune basically arranged the equalisation of holding, and rotation of crops. Redistribution was on the basis of a number of strips allocated to each household in each of the rotations.

The main features of communal holding may now be outlined. While the basic field system was of three crops, winter, spring and fallow, each field was not always divided immediately into strips. While I have no direct description of a field-pattern in this period, Danilov has provided the following general description.

Each of the fields [*polei*] of the rotation was divided into *yarusy*, according to the distance of this piece of land from the settlement. *Yarusy* in their turn were divided into *kony* [or *gony*] – pieces of land equal in fertility. In each *kon* the member [household—D.J.M.] received his share – the strip [*polosa*]. In very large communes with many households the fields were first divided between tens, or hundreds, of households, then by separate households.[1]

Thus, each area given over to a specific crop was subdivided according to distance from the village and this subdivision was in its turn divided into areas of equal fertility. On this division the pattern of strips was imposed. The rarity of descriptions of this complicated process is noteworthy. Perhaps it was not practised in this manner, or, equally likely, urban observers noted only the obvious small plots without enquiring as to the subtle processes which led to them.[2]

Excessive intermingling of strips, with each household having a large number of strips, was the major problem in areas of dense agricultural population in relation to the land available. This was especially so in the north west and north and, to a rather lesser extent, in the Black Earth regions. A report of the People's Commis-

---

[1] Danilov, *Istoriya SSSR* (1958), no. 3, p. 104. Danilov's is the most important Soviet work on problems of land holding in the 1920s, and contains much archival material and reference to sources not readily obtainable in this country. While it came to the present writer's notice after the bulk of material had been collected, quotation is made from it where it would not otherwise have been possible to elaborate a point.

[2] The English terms for subdivision of a field, into furlongs (block system), and selions, or acres (strips) were similar, but it would be misleading to equate exactly with Russian terms as the means of deciding the subdivision differed.

sariat of Agriculture summarised the position thus: 'In non-black earth regions, there are 50–80 strips per household. In the black earth regions and wooded steppe, 20–30 strips per household. The problem is minimal in steppe regions.'[1] A similar conclusion was reached by a sample survey in 1925, which suggested that the proportion of households having land in 40 to over 100 separate places was 52·7% in the north west, 81% in the north, and 15% in central guberniyas.[2] By contrast, in the south eastern areas not more than 5–10% of households had more than 25 strips in 1925.[3]

An excessive number of strips per household gave rise to a number of problems. One of these was the narrowness of the strips. In Ivanovo-Voznesensk guberniya strips were between 7 and 14 ft wide, and 70 and 1400 ft long.[4] In Vyatka guberniya strips were scarcely as wide as this. They were so narrow in parts of Kostroma guberniya that it was difficult for a harrow to pass along them, and it was said to be impossible in Gvodsk uezd of Leningrad guberniya. There were similar complaints in the Central Black Earth and Ural oblasts.[5]

This multitude of small strips meant that a substantial area of agricultural land was lost to cultivation. In 1925 this was estimated as high as 7% of arable land.[6] The closeness of strips was a disincentive to use improved techniques, for apart from the temporary nature of tenure, weeds were easily blown from one strip to the next.

Little is known precisely of the economic effect of the large number of strips per household. There is some indication in the figures for the production of flax in the Smolensk and Tver areas given in Table 1; we have no comparable figures for a grain area.

Under conditions of farming with a large number of strips, the smallest households at times had to decline using their share of land

[1] Narodnyi Kommissariat Zemledeliya, *Materialy po perspektivnomu planu razvitiya sel'skogo khozyaistva RSFSR* (Moscow, 1928), p. 157.
[2] Yakovlev, *K voprosu sotsialisticheskogo pereustroistva sel'skogo khozyaistva* (based on Worker-Peasant Inspectorate research of 1925, published by them in 1928), p. 87.
[3] Gurov 'Predvaritel'nye itogi zemleustroistva', *Na agrarnom fronte* (1925), no. 10, p. 77.
[4] See below, p. 37.
[5] Danilov, *Istoriya SSSR* (1958), no. 3, p. 104, quoting Ts GAOR i SS, f 478, op 59, d 559, ll 7, 47.
[6] Gurov, *loc. cit.*

Table 1[a]

Strips per household	Costs of production (izderzhki proizvodstva) per hectare of sown area (rubles)	Yield (centner per hectare)	Cost (sebestoimost') per centner	Difference between price (45 r. per centner) and cost (sebestoimost')
1–10	135·9	3·3	29·1	+15·9
11–25	164·9	2·6	41·6	+3·6
25+	198·0	2·7	49·0	−4·0
	160·8	2·9	37·7	+7·3

a Danilov, *loc. cit.* p. 104. Source: Ts SU SSSR, *Sel'skoe khozyaistvo SSSR, 1925–8* (Moscow, 1929), pp. 454–5. There is a problem with this table, for the second column, divided by the third, should come to the figure in the fourth column. Apart from a possible error, the explanation may be that the costs in the second and fourth columns have a different basis – different Russian words are used – not apparent in Danilov's quotation.

as it was uneconomically small; they had either to rent it out to those with neighbouring plots, or themselves rent additional land.

Distance from house to plots and between plots was a problem which was more prevalent in the south, where villages tended to be large, centred on sources of water. As we have seen, number of plots per household was not great in this area, but distances between house and plot of 10–15 km were not uncommon. In Samara guberniya, 12% of households in a sample of hamlets had land at a distance of less than 3 km, 33% at over 10 km, and a significant number at 45–55 km.[1] Even on land where land use measures had been undertaken, it was estimated that distance remained a problem over 70% of the area.[2]

For the economic effect of distance, we must again turn to Danilov's research in archival materials. He quotes research in three volosts of Balashovsk uezd, Saratov guberniya, by the Guberniya Land Board on the eve of land use measures being undertaken in 1927.[3] This showed that costs of fieldwork doubled when the dis-

[1] Yakovlev, *K voprosu*, p. 88. Sample of 329 hamlets.
[2] Gurov, *Na agrarnom fronte* (1925), no. 10.
[3] Danilov, *Istoriya SSSR* (1958), no. 3, pp. 107–8. Ts GAOR i SS, f 3983, op 1, d 45, ll 157, 162, 163, 165.

tance to carry loads increased from 1·4 to 9·2 km. Sown area fell, so that of peasants with an allocation of equal size, those with plots 9–10 km distant could only sow half the area of those with a distance to plot of 1·4 km. Amounts of fixed and working capital of the more distant households was one third less than the nearer ones, due to high costs. Investment in agriculture was 28·6% of expenditure on production for the further away, 44·1% for the nearer. Earlier research had shown that land use measures in 323 households in Samara guberniya between 1920 and 1924 had, by decreasing distance alone, saved 20·4 working days per household, allowing an increase of sown area of 4·9 acres per household.[1] Distance of land from home could depress the position of a peasant in a large commune, compared with a peasant with an equivalent holding in a smaller commune. Thus, in these volosts of Saratov guberniya, the position was as follows:

Area of commune	Percentage of 'poor peasants'
2,700 acres	25
2,700–27,000 acres	35·8
27,000+ acres	49·8

This obviously assumes some definition of the land of a poor peasant external to the commune, and does not necessarily suggest increased polarisation in the larger communes, although fuller evidence might well suggest that this was so. A curious example of a reversal of this process was shown in a so-called 'class-oriented' approach to distribution in Bashkiria. In one village, the poor peasants received land up to 5 km away, and the richest the land furthest away.[2]

The sum of evidence on distance between home and plot suggests that Maynard's estimate that 'a man had to walk on average 1260 miles in the agricultural season to get round his own strips'[3] might well have been a conservative one.

[1] Danilov, *loc. cit.* p. 113, quoting Spektor, *5 let zemleustroistva v Samarskoi gubernii* (Samara, 1925), p. 11.
[2] Speaker at Central Executive Committee of the USSR. Ts IK SSSR, 4-yi sozyv, 4-ya sessiya Dec. 1928, Bulletin 16, p. 7.
[3] Maynard, *The Russian peasant and other studies*, p. 182.

Introduction

Finally, in this brief outline of the characteristics of communal land holding, we must make some estimate of the number and size of communes. This showed considerable regional variation, as one would expect.[1] Most of the information available concerns size in terms of household or population: there is even less information available about areas of agricultural land per commune, and the two measures need not of course be uniformly correlated.

There appears to have been no published census of the number of communes. The only figure which the present writer has found was a statement by Milyutin that there were 319,000 land societies.[2] There must be an element of doubt about the accuracy of this figure, as he also gave a figure of 40,000 collective and state farms and 211,000 fully enclosed farms and farms with fields only enclosed. He gave no date. In January 1928 there were in fact 33,000 collective farms in the USSR. The figure for the RSFSR was 22,000. There were approximately 3,000 state farms at the time in the USSR.[3] The figures were thus either completely inaccurate for the RSFSR, or a slight exaggeration of the USSR. As communal holding was largely confined to the RSFSR, it would not matter greatly if this were an error confusing figures for the RSFSR and USSR. The figure for households in enclosed farms presumably refers to the RSFSR – inclusion of the Ukraine would increase this considerably.

Confidence in the figure of 319,000 communes is increased by a reference to the fact that in 1925–6, 34,385 'land unions' had undertaken land use measures – that is 12% of all 'unions'.[4] If we assume that 'unions' meant communes, we have a figure of 288,000 for the RSFSR. The discrepancy with the Milyutin figure could be explained by rounding – one per cent less, and the figures would have tallied very closely.

There is still the question of date, and we can but assume that the

[1] Details of size in particular areas will be given in the following chapter, and the relationship in size of the commune to other administrative units in chapter 3.
[2] Speech at Central Executive Committee of the USSR. Ts IK SSSR, 4-yi sozyv, 7-oe zasedanie, April 1928. *Sten. Otchet* p. 724, and 4-yi sozyv, 4-oe zasedanie Dec. 1928. Bulletin 12, p. 21.
[3] Tsentral'noe Statisticheskoe Upravlenie SSSR, *Narodnoe khozyaistvo SSSR* (1933), p. 130.
[4] Narkomzem., *Otchet za 1925–6* (Moscow 1926), p. 27.

Introduction

figure was for the year in which he was speaking. On these assumptions, the following table may be drawn up for the RSFSR:

Number of communes	Number of peasant households[a] – all forms of holding	Area held communally – acres, 1 January 1927[b]	Commune size	
			Households	Area
319,000	17,552,000	555,000,000	app. 50	1,740 acres

[a] Tsentral'noe Statisticheskoe Upravlenie SSSR, *Sel'skoe khozyaistvo SSSR, 1925–8* (1929), p. 16, Table 3.
[b] *Itogi desyatiletiya sovetskoi vlasti v tsifrakh, 1917–27*, pp. 120–1. Quoted by Carr, *Socialism in one country, 1924–1926*, I, 214.

If we accept Milyutin's rather low figure for households in enclosed farms, average size of commune would be 53 households. If one allowed a figure of one million households in enclosed farms, size of commune would fall only slightly to 50 households.

This can be only a very rough guide to the number and size of communes. Size of commune varied over time. The number of households was increasing, with the break-up of large households as more land became available. A countervailing tendency was the land use measures which split up large communes into smaller units. We have no evidence how far these balanced out. Regional variation was in any case so great as to make a figure for average size of commune for the RSFSR no more than a guide when we come to discussing particular areas.

PART I

THE COMMUNE: ITS FUNCTION AND ORGANISATION IN ITS AGRICULTURAL PERSPECTIVE

LAND HOLDING IN EUROPEAN RUSSIA
IN THE 1920s

I INTRODUCTORY

We are largely concerned with the commune as an organ of local self-government. It is not possible to examine these aspects of the commune's work without considering in some detail the land-holding basis on which the Russian commune was founded. In fact it is part of our task in this section to show that the phrase 'Russian commune' hides a wide variety of types of organisation of agricultural holding. The only factor in common is the strip system with open fields, with the land held, but not worked, in common by a number of households.

There is sufficient information on the characteristics of land holding in particular areas to give at least some idea of the way in which communes varied in their physical configuration. A variety of factors led to these characteristics, and it would be a rewarding task to investigate in detail the weight of various influences which have led to a given pattern of settlement. This is the province of the geographer, and cannot be attempted by the present author. None the less, these factors in particular areas will be mentioned in a general way.

The next step would be to describe differences in commune life to which these physical and economic factors gave rise. Here we face a lack of any widespread systematic study of the organisation and working of actual communes. At this stage, it is only possible to sound a warning against generalisations about 'the commune'. We have sufficient evidence to show the considerable variations in physical configuration of communes, not only in different agricultural regions of the country, but within guberniyas and within okrugs. The rest of the study will, for lack of more adequate sources, discuss the commune as a single institution. There were many common problems encountered throughout the country, but this approach to the commune is made reluctantly, for the lack of more detailed evidence.

In this chapter, we are concerned to establish how the commune fitted into the prevailing pattern of land holding in certain broad economic areas, and showing, in a general way, how the characteristics of the commune in that area were related to the physical, economic and historical characteristics of that area. There is a great need for a systematic review of land holding in the years before collectivisation. This would be of great value in, amongst other things, helping to explain something of the nature and working of the commune. All we can offer here are some pointers for more systematic study when fuller data become available.

There is a difficulty in defining areas. The areas used here are those suggested by Gosplan, and modified to some extent by Baranskii in his *Economic geography of the USSR*.[1] They have the virtue of dividing the bulk of the RSFSR into main economic areas, but these do not always correspond with administrative divisions. In discussing particular areas, we often have to rely on handbooks issued on the basis of administrative areas. Administrative and economic area boundaries were frequently changed in the twenties, so the broad areas used in section 4 of this chapter are intended as general guides to an overall pattern. It would be useful to relate characteristics of communes to more carefully defined agricultural economic regions. This is done here in specific cases, but fuller information is needed for anything approaching a satisfactory synthesis of these elements.[2]

There is some consolation that this lack of reliable statistics is by no means confined to the Soviet pre-collectivisation period. Fifty years previously, Mackenzie Wallace found the same problem:

though the imperial administration has a most voracious appetite for systematically constructed statistical tables, no attempt has yet

[1] Baranskii, *Ekonomicheskaya geografiya SSSR* (Moscow, 4th ed. 1926). He lists eleven areas on pp. 21–2, but modifies these in his treatment of south east European Russia and North Caucasus, in the detailed area analysis.

[2] A model study of the patterns of land holding of communes in pre-revolutionary Russia is P. N. Pershin, *Zemel'noe ustroistvo dorevolyutsionnoi derevni* (Nauchno-Issledovatel'skii Institut Sel'sko-khozyaistvennoi Ekonomiki, Moscow and Voronezh, 1928). He confined himself to land holding, and did not venture to discuss the influence of this on the commune as a social organism.

Map 1. Administrative divisions and census regions, 1926. Based on a map reproduced in F. Lorimer, *The population of the Soviet Union* (League of Nations, Geneva, 1946), facing p. 44.

been made to throw light on this important subject. In spite of the systematic and persistent efforts of the bureaucracy to regulate minutely all departments of the national life, the rural communes, which contain about 5/6 of the population remain in many respects entirely beyond its influence and even beyond its sphere of vision.[1]

Although so much of the public debate in Russia in the ensuing half century concerned the peasantry, much the same could have been written in 1925. There was a legal provision that all communes should be registered,[2] but even if this was observed, the resultant statistics were not published. One can imagine that most communes were not particularly interested in making the sort of return required.

2   LAND HOLDING IN THE RSFSR IN THE 1920S: BACKGROUND

It is no part of our purpose to give any review of the development of communal land holding in Russia. None the less, the situation in the mid-twenties must be set in the perspective of the changing pattern of land holding of the previous half-century.

The Stolypin reforms of 1906 had been designed to encourage a strong individual peasantry based on enclosed farms. The essence of the reform was that ownership of land was to devolve directly onto the householder where this was requested. In communes that did not redistribute periodically, the land was declared as having passed from communal holding to individual. In a commune where redistribution was practised, any householder could claim at any time that the land which he was entitled to use be transferred to him in individual ownership. He had the right to claim the land in a single location, and the commune was bound to grant this request at a time of general redistribution, or if more than one fifth of households in the commune requested separation into consolidated plots. The whole commune could transfer to enclosed forms of holding by a majority of two thirds of householders.

How far this process had gone by the time of the revolution is very

---

[1] Mackenzie Wallace, *Russia* (1st ed. 1877). Here quoting from Popular edition with an autobiographical memoir (1886), p. 126.

[2] RSFSR Land Code, 1922, S.U. 1922, no. 68, art. 201.

much a matter for debate. At the highest estimate, just over half of peasant households were holding land in private hereditary tenure. Robinson[1] puts the figure at 7·3 out of 14 million households. This is similar to Pershin's estimate that 51% of households were holding land at the beginning of 1917 on the basis of private tenure, and 49% communal.[2] These figures greatly exaggerate the extent to which communal holding had decayed in this period. There is general agreement that, up to 1st January 1916, 2,478,000 households left the commune and secured their land in personal ownership. Of these, 470,000 were in communes not practising redistribution. This was 24% of householders in European Russia.[3] Of this number, it would appear that by no means all concentrated their land into enclosed farms. Only 1·3 million households were involved in such a change, so that by January 1917, only 10·5% of all peasant households had been settled in new individual enclosed forms of holding.[4] Within this broad summary of the position, there is room for much debate over the details. Among the main sources of confusion are the extent to which statistics prepared by land officials artificially exaggerated the numbers leaving the commune, and the numbers who left as a result of pressure from officials rather than a wish to leave.

After the revolution there was a rapid return to the commune. The reasons for this are far from clear. In the first place, this may be in some cases purely a statistical movement – households which never left the commune, but were counted as transferring, could again be counted as commune members without fear of pressure from above, and the post-1917 statistics may to some extent have merely corrected the Tsarist inaccuracies. There is little doubt that in many areas communes were broken up under considerable

[1] G. T. Robinson, *Rural Russia under the old régime* (Longmans, N.Y., 1932), chapter XI.
[2] P. N. Pershin in *Krest'yanskaya sel'skokhozyaistvennaya entsiklopediya* (Moscow, 1925), III, 324.
[3] P. I. Lyashchenko, *History of the national economy of Russia* (Macmillan, N.Y., 1949), p. 748. The same figures are used by Robinson and Pershin.
[4] P. N. Pershin, *Uchastkovoe zemlepol'zovanie v Rossii: khutora i otruby i ikh rasprostranenie za desyatiletie 1907–16 i sud'ba vo vremya revolyutsii (1917–20)* (Voronezhskii Sel'sko-khozyaistvennyi Institut, 1921, Novaya Derevnya, Moscow, 1922), p. 7. This figure is accepted by Robinson, and Owen in *The Russian peasant movement 1906–17* (Owen, King, London, 1937), p. 82.

pressure from officials, and once this pressure was gone, the
peasantry would return to these communes.

Two main reasons suggest themselves for the return to the commune after the revolution. First, in a time of disorder in the countryside, in an atmosphere of spontaneous appropriation of the landlord's land, those peasants with a conspicuously larger share of
land who had detached themselves from their fellow-villagers by
consolidation, would be under strong pressure to forgo those
marks of affluence and separateness by which they had attempted to
distinguish themselves from the rest of the community. In the
extreme case, the Committees of Poor Peasants used direct force.
There would probably be a difference here between those areas
which had, on the whole, gone over to enclosed farms by whole
communes, and those where individual households had separated
from communes. However, even in the first case, an influential
minority of peasants could probably have forced the hand of the
commune, and a time of revolution gave an opportunity for different voices to be heard. While return to the commune could thus
have been a result of pressure on the richer peasantry by the majority,
a second factor was also at work. This was that the peasantry needed
some form of communal organisation in the face of a revolution
which, it soon became apparent, had long-term aims which were
not attractive to the peasant, and short-term ones which involved
strong pressure to hand over grain surpluses. Without wishing to
advance the 'mystique' of the commune, it would seem that in a
time of uncertainty there would be a tendency for the process of
social differentiation of the peasantry to halt, and for there to be a
seeking of common ground among all peasants in the face of alien
pressures. With the return to the more settled conditions of the
New Economic Policy, and after the 1922 Land Code allowed
freedom of form of land holding, there were renewed movements
from the commune.

The move away from the communes during the Stolypin period
had been highest in areas where enclosed forms of holding were
already strongest, apart from certain areas where it had reached its
peak.[1] The movement against enclosed holding after the revolution

[1] See Pershin, *Uchastkovoe zemlepol'zovaniye v Rossii*, p. 9 (map 2), p. 20 (map 3) – how-

did not reverse the pattern completely. The movement was indeed greatest in the south and south east, but in the north west, it was only slight, and in the west, the proportion of enclosed holding actually rose (see Table 1.1).

Table 1.1   *Weight of enclosed holding*[a]

	1916 (percentage)	1922 (percentage)
Samara guberniya	19	0·1
Saratov guberniya	16·4	Negligible
Stavropol' guberniya	24·9	0·4
Don oblast	10·4	0·06
Areas later forming Central Black Earth oblast	4·1–10	0·1–0·2
Moscow guberniya	9·3	3·3
Petrograd guberniya	28·7	22·7
Pskov guberniya	17·6	15·1
Vitebsk guberniya	28·7	Rose
Smolensk guberniya	15·9	Rose

[a] Table constructed from materials in V. P. Danilov, *Istoriya SSSR* (1958), no. 3, referring to *Materialy po zemel'noi reforme 1918 g.*, Vypusk 1, Moscow 1919, pp. 9–10, and Pershin, *op. cit.* pp. 8, 335-45, and Ts GAOR i SS, f 478, op 59, d 559, ll 4569; f 4085, op 9, d 195, l 1. Unstated whether percentage of households or areas.

In the south east and east, the movement towards enclosed holding before the revolution reflected the development of grain production for the market, and in these areas the government put strongest pressure on the communes. These factors no longer applied after the revolution. In the north west and west, enclosed holding was more suited to the prevailing economy based on livestock production than the commune method of holding. We will below have to examine more closely the nature of the commune in these areas.

The general picture of land holding in European Russia by the time the Land Code was enacted in 1922 was that, while communal holding predominated, fully enclosed farms were stronger in the west and north west than elsewhere. Farms with fields only enclosed were stronger in the south east than elsewhere. Whether a majority of peasants held their land in enclosed holding in any area is difficult to establish, and we will consider the point in individual areas.

ever, the figures given there suggest some confusion between total enclosed holding and households transferring 1907–16.

Land holding in European Russia in the 1920s

What weight, then, did communal holding have in the RSFSR? There is no lack of any very general statements to support the view that, over the RSFSR as a whole, communal holding predominated. The sort of statement that 'the commune accounted for 99% of peasant land holding' is common.[1] There are general observations based on statistics which are not easily accessible, thus 'In the huge majority of cases in large villages there is communal form of land holding. It nearly always means compulsory three-field rotation. For many years peasants with initiative have struggled against these antiquated ways of cultivation.'[2]

The most definite indication of the scale of communal holding in the RSFSR was that in 1927, 222 out of 233 million hectares were farmed on the basis of redistributable holding and common crop rotation. Fully enclosed farms accounted for 2 million hectares, farms with fields only enclosed, 6 million, and collectives, 2 million hectares.[3] This is of course no indication of how active the commune was in these areas.

Communal holding thus predominated at the start of our period in 1925. In that year a report on land use measures by the Agricultural Inspectorate of the People's Commissariat of Worker–Peasant Inspection came to the conclusion that:

in 92% of all the area subject to land use measures the old communal-interlocking order remains, with its redistribution and compulsory rotation...that is land use measures have liquidated the negative side in the organisation and life of the peasant household only to a negligible extent. As a result, no more than 4% of the land subject to land use measures has been turned over to a multi-course system. The commune is a brake on the development of agriculture, and the Ministry of Agriculture should help the depopulation of the com-

---

[1] Smirnov, *Na agrarnom fronte* (1926), no. 11–12, pp. 131 ff. Speaking on behalf of Soviet of People's Commissars of RSFSR at Agrarian Section of Communist Academy.

[2] Gurov, 'Predvaritel'nye itogi zemleustroistva', *Na agrarnom fronte* (1925), no. 10, p. 77. Based on research by Agricultural Inspectorate of Worker-Peasant Inspectorate, inspecting land use measures by People's Commissariat for Agriculture in following areas: Tatar-Bashkir Republics, N. Caucasus krai, Urals oblast, Novgorod, Gomel, Yaroslav, Tver, Ryazan, Vologda, Saratov, Sumara, Tambov and Kursk guberniyas. No further details.

[3] *Itogi desyatiletiya sovetskoi vlasti v tsifrakh, 1917–27*, pp. 100–1. Quoted by Carr, *Socialism in one country, 1924–1926*, I, 214.

mune into settlements, and farms with only fields enclosed, or to wide fields.[1]

The effect and extent of land use measures will be discussed in chapter 4: our immediate task is to establish how far this predominance of the commune varied between areas and what differences there were in communal holding between areas.

3 SOME GENERAL STATISTICS

Before discussing the pattern of land holding by individual areas, we may note two sources which break down land holding in much of the USSR by area. There are several rather unsatisfactory features about the following tables, but as they are the only attempts at this kind of break-down the present writer has been able to find, they are quoted in full. Both sources are for 1922, but are sufficiently disparate to suggest they were based on different samples. In particular, they have only three areas in common.[2]

Before discussing the implications of these tables, certain points must be made about their quality. Three points should be made about the two latter tables, which refer to the same data. Firstly, the table referring to percentage of land held by given forms contains percentages for categories not mentioned in the table on size of holding. This would suggest that the former table is not derived from the latter, but that both are from a common source. Comparison of the sets of figures suggests that the figures for collective farm society for joint working of the land (TOZ), land organs, and 'institutions' may be included under other categories in the former table. For most areas, it is a tenable hypothesis that they are included in the commune figures. In the north west and west, it would seem that the absolute figures for communal and enclosed farms of both kinds contain the land organs, TOZ, and Institution percentage figure, with most going to the commune. In the figure for Belorussia this would be so if the percentage figures for these three categories were distributed between commune and fully enclosed farm, most

---

[1] Zasedanie Kollegii NKRKI RSFSR. 2 June 1925, *Vyvody i predlozheniya selkhozinspektsii po materialam obsledovaniya zemleustroistva. Prilozheniye k Protokolu*, 18, p. 2.
[2] Moscow Industrial, Central Landworking, and Belorussia.

Table 1.2

Area	Rural societies	Collective farms		Peasant farms			Institutions	Land organs
		Communes	Artel	Only fields enclosed	Fully enclosed	State farm		
Far north	98.7	—	0.1	0.7	0.3	0.1	0.1	—
Lake	68.9	0.1	0.1	6.1	4.0	0.7	—	20.1
Moscow Industrial	90.7	0.1	0.3	2.5	1.7	1.1	0.4	3.2
Central Landworking	90.5	0.1	0.1	—	0.1	5.6	—	2.6
Urals	95.8	0.3	0.4	0.3	0.8	0.6	0.1	1.7
Lower Volga	98.0	0.2	0.5	0.2	0.1	0.9	—	0.1
Malorossiya	90.0	0.2	0.3	1.8	2.1	3.0	0.1	2.5
Novorossiya	82.2	0.2	0.9	0.1	3.5	6.8	—	6.3
South west	93.4	0.0	0.1	0.8	0.8	3.6	—	1.3
Belorussia	63.5	0.2	0.5	3.8	20.7	2.0	0.1	9.2
South east	95.4	0.4	0.3	0.2	2.1	0.7	0.1	0.8
West Siberia	89.3	0.4	0.7	5.8	0.6	1.6	—	1.6
Sast Siberia	96.0	0.1	0.1	—	0.4	1.0	0.1	2.3

Percentage of land held by:[a]

[a] Ts. V. Chernyshev, *Sel'skoe khozyaistvo dovoennoi Rossii i SSSR* (Moscow–Leningrad, 1926), p. 50. Malorossiya = Ukraine. The term 'rural societies' is the administrative term used for commune at this time (cf. glossary). He does not quote his source for this table, neither does he indicate whether this is sample material.

Table 1.3

Percentage of land held by:[a]

Area	Commune	Collective farms			Peasant farms		State farm	Institutions	Land organs
		TOZ	Commune	Artel	Only fields enclosed	Fully enclosed			
North (excluding Far north)	92·7	5·3	—	0·2	0·9	0·6	0·2	—	—
North west	57·0	3·4	—	0·3	6·7	5·2	0·8	0·1	26·6
Belorussia	55·2	1·5	0·3	0·3	2·6	22·6	1·8	0·1	15·6
West	68·7	5·3	0·3	0·5	4·1	13·7	1·2	0·2	6·0
Moscow Industrial	87·2	2·3	0·1	0·4	2·4	2·0	1·1	0·4	4·1
Central Landworking	93·0	—	0·1	0·4	0·1	0·3	4·0	—	2·1
Volga-Kama	95·5	—	0·1	0·3	0·2	0·2	0·3	0·6	2·8
Urals	96·3	—	0·5	0·1	0·3	0·4	0·6	—	1·8
Bashkir ASSR	92·9	—	0·6	0·7	0·7	4·1	0·3	—	0·7
Volga (Lower Volga – no data)	97·6	0·2	0·2	0·5	0·2	0·1	0·9	—	0·3
Don and N. Caucasus	94·9	0·3	0·4	0·4	0·2	2·3	0·5	0·1	0·8
Mountain Autonomous oblasts	98·4	—	—	0·1	0·1	0·1	0·8	—	0·6
Ukrainian SSR	91·3	0·1	0·2	0·3	1·0	1·0	3·1	—	3·4
Crimean ASSR	73·0	—	0·3	0·7	—	6·7	13·7	—	5·6
Kirgiz ASSR (Orenburg guberniya)	96·2	—	0·1	1·0	0·1	0·1	1·6	—	1·0
Siberia	No data								

[a] *Narodnoe khozyaistvo SSSR* (Tsental'noe Statisticheskoe Upravanie SSSR), 1925, p. 145. Based on a sample survey. It is not clear what the basis of sampling was. See note to Table 1.4.

Table 1.4 ᵃ *Number of units in sample, and average amount of land held by each type of holding*

Area	Commune		Collective (commune)		Artel		Farm with only fields enclosed		Fully enclosed farm		State farm	
	No.	Desyatinas	No.	Desyatinas	No.	Desyatinas	No.	Desyatinas	No.	Desyatinas	No.	Desyatinas
North (excluding Far north)	1,483	270·8	1	107·0	14	70·4	394	10·1	161	15·9	14	50·6
North west	3,145	165·9	4	72·0	37	68·1	5,690	10·9	2,707	17·5	43	166·7
Belorussia	1,582	172·4	10	153·3	21	79·3	2,885	4·4	10,422	10·7	27	327·4
West	1,981	266·2	23	115·3	56	74·4	2,722	11·4	8,719	12·0	56	163·3
Moscow Industrial	5,294	223·0	25	82·6	125	44·3	4,165	7·7	2,082	13·0	113	132·4
Central Landworking	2,199	903·9	18	96·3	113	88·5	71	18·5	405	14·5	189	449·2
Volga-Kama	1,615	296·6	7	90·4	15	83·7	82	9·8	57	21·7	6	253·2
Urals	661	2039·2	22	297·4	15	134·7	325	11·7	151	38·1	20	453·7
Bashkir ASSR	321	862·5	7	257·3	15	129·5	122	17·0	641	19·2	3	355·4
Volga (Lower Volga – no data)												
Don and N. Caucasus	77	2647·9	12	258·3	51	199·2	213	18·5	29	54·0	24	667·8
Mountain Autonomous oblasts	327	5633·3	25	313·7	36	192·7	122	39·8	103	43·3	15	694·8
Ukrainian SSR	50	2312·3	—	—	1	99·0	—	—	3	45·3	2	452·0
Crimean ASSR	1,011	1443	9	321·1	47	110·6	1,568	45·0	463	34·4	90	551·6
Kirgiz ASSR (Orenburg guberniya)	252	977·7	8	333·3	31	83·4	—	—	175	129·8	51	903·4
Siberia	114	2715·5	3	144·8	9	348·9	1 No data	40·0	6	58·0	4	1285

ᵃ *Ibid.* p. 143. The following figures appear in the text, but would seem to be misprints: Don and N. Caucasus – consolidated homestead, 433·5 desyatinas; Ukrainian SSR – farms with only fields enclosed, 4·5 desyatinas, fully enclosed farms, 344. An argument against this is that by moving the decimal place, the figures are not then to one decimal place, as are the others, and that a simple misprint cannot be the answer. Whatever the reason for this, it would seem that moving the decimal place and rounding gives a more reasonable figure.

going to the commune. Volga figures could not be explained by any such redistribution. There the latter, absolute, figures suggest a higher percentage of artel (4·0%) and state farm (6·0%) than in the percentage-holding table. In this area in the latter table addition of land organ and TOZ to commune figures gives but 90% communal land.

This redistribution of the figures for TOZ, land organs and institutions may be a satisfactory explanation, apart from the Volga area, especially as the TOZ did not necessarily involve any consolidation of plots, and could reflect the prevailing pattern of holding in an area. (Many collective farms at this time were not consolidated – see below, p. 229.) The same could be true of the category of 'land organ' land. However, this coincidence in many of the areas may be fortuitous; since the figures must add up to 100, the proportion of communal holding will inevitably be less in a table with more non-communal categories, and, as the sums are very small, coincidence of certain categories in Tables 1.3 and 1.4 may not be significant. It is only supposition that the categories of the latter table contain those in the former not mentioned in it.

Secondly, the basis of the sample is far from clear. It would seem that the basis varied from area to area. Thus with the Ukrainian SSR it is claimed that 91% of land was held by communes, on the basis of 1,011 communes, while for Moscow Industrial Area, 5,294 communes are the basis for the 87% of land claimed to be in communal holding, yet obviously Ukrainian SSR was a far larger area, and a larger size of commune there could not explain the difference.

Thirdly, there are some rather strange figures. The figures for communal holding seem exceptionally high in the Ukraine, Belorussia, North west, and West areas in all the tables. This is especially so in the Ukraine and Belorussia where most sources suggest there was virtually no communal holding. This would support the view that the sample consisted of particular parts of the areas, and that the figures for the area do not necessarily reflect those for the whole of that area. Where in the original text there seem to have been typographical errors which give incongruous results, the tables have been altered as indicated.

When we come to compare land holding in the two sources, as

shown by Tables 1.2 and 1.3, the patterns are very similar, and confirm in general the pattern already noted. In few areas does communal holding occupy less than 90% of area. The most important variation from the pattern noted earlier is the high proportion of communal holding shown for North west (Lake), West, and Belorussia. Each of these areas does have a lower proportion of communal holding than other areas, but, none the less, quite a high proportion.[1] One possible reason for this, the nature of the sample, has already been suggested. It is difficult to see how the varying patterns of holding existing in the Bashkir ASSR, Kirgiz ASSR, and Mountain Autonomous oblasts can be included under the Russian term 'obshchina', as they are in Tables 1.3 and 1.4, unless it is used in a very wide sense, and not the usual, narrowly defined technical one.

If we accept the probable limitations of these statistics, it is interesting to note variations in size of unit between areas. Table 1.5 shows how the size of commune in terms of area was smallest in the North west, West and Moscow Industrial areas, and was much larger in the South east. A similar pattern was observed in other forms of holding, but great significance should not be attached to the non-commune forms due to the small numbers involved. Even for the commune, great weight should not be put on the particular magnitudes. It is, however, noteworthy that the relative size of commune between areas does tend to reflect relative size of settlements between areas, although the size of commune and settlement rarely coincided.[2]

4 A REVIEW OF AREAS

North west and west[3]

These two areas are often grouped together by Soviet writers when discussing land holding. Although it would be desirable to separate

[1] Danilov, *Istoriya SSSR* (1958), no. 3 p. 100, seems to accept the figure of 65–75% communal holding in these areas when quoting these tables, and does not comment.
[2] See below, chapter 3(1).
[3] The north east area has been omitted as an area with very limited agriculture. North west area includes all or part of Leningrad, Pskov, Novgorod, Cherepovets and Murmansk guberniyas, with the Karelian A.R.
  Western area includes all or part of Smolensk, Bryansk, Mogilev, Vitebsk and Gomel guberniyas. Baranskii also includes Belorussia, but see below, p. 52, for this.

Table 1.5 [a] *Relative size of units of holding in sample in different areas, by land area.* (*Central Landworking area = 100*)

		Collective		Peasant farms		
	Commune	Commune	Artel	Only fields enclosed	Fully enclosed	State farm
North (excluding Far north)	30	110	80	50	110	10
North west	20	80	80	60	120	30
Belorussia	20	160	90	20	70	70
West	30	120	80	60	80	40
Moscow Industrial	20	90	50	40	90	30
Central Landworking	100	100	100	100	100	100
Volga-Kama	30	90	90	50	150	60
Urals	230	310	150	60	250	100
Bashkir ASSR	100	270	150	90	130	80
Volga (Lower Volga – no data)	300	270	220	100	360	150
Don and N. Caucasus	620	330	220	210	300	160
Mountain Autonomous oblasts	260	—	110	—	300	100
Ukrainian SSR	160	330	120	240	230	120
Crimean ASSR	110	350	90	—	870	200
Kirgiz ASSR (Orenburg guberniya)	300	150	390	210	390	290

N.B. Comparison can only be made vertically.

[a] Derived by the present writer from Table 1.4, and therefore subject to all the inaccuracies thereof.

the specific characteristics of each area, this is rather difficult in view of the general trend.

A variety of conditions encouraged land holding on the basis of the fully enclosed farm in the area. Historical–geographical factors were significant, as these were the areas bordering on the traditionally individual peasant lands of Latvia, Estonia, Lithuania, Poland and Finland. Natural physical conditions, with a mixture of forest and bog, with an extensive network of lakes and rivers, favoured live-stock rearing, rather than grain growing. Peasant economy was to a large extent centred on dairy production, and flax growing. The nearby town markets meant that agriculture was always more than subsistence farming in this area. Before the revolution, trade via the

Baltic was possible. Enclosed farms developed most strongly where market relations were strongest. Natural conditions meant that there were more than adequate sources of water, so that fully enclosed farms were possible.

It is difficult to establish an accurate picture of land holding in this area after the revolution. There is an apparent conflict between general statements suggesting that there was a preponderance of enclosed farms in these areas, and statistics showing non-communal holding to be confined to a more or less substantial minority of holdings.

General statements are in the vein that 'most of the peasantry in the West and North west guberniyas (Pskov, Novgorod, Petrograd, Smolensk, Vitebsk, Mogilev) are in fully enclosed farms',[1] or, 'in the North west krai the commune is fairly rare'.[2] The latter speaker commented further that, while it would be nonsensical to abolish communal holding in the central and south east areas, it would be reasonable to liquidate the commune entirely in the north west.

Such statistical evidence as is available suggests a rather different pattern. Pershin's researches into enclosed forms of holding showed that at the beginning of 1917, that is when the Stolypin reforms had reached their maximum cumulative effect, the percentage of households in enclosed farms was as shown in Table 1.6.[3]

Table 1.6

	Percentage
Petrograd guberniya	28·7
Pskov guberniya	17·6
Kovno	18·6
Vitebsk guberniya	28·7
Smolensk guberniya	15·9
Mogilev guberniya	14·6

While he does not give figures for the position after the revolution, it is only fair to add that he remarked that the move to enclosed holdings became 'almost uncontrollable' from 1920 onwards.[4]

[1] Oganovskii *Obshchina i zemel'noe tovarishchestvo* (Moscow, 1923), p. 9.
[2] Dubovskii, at discussion in the agrarian section of the Communist Academy. Reported in *Na agrarnom fronte* (1926), no. 10–11, p. 144.
[3] P. N. Pershin, *Uchastkovoe zemlepol'zovaniye v Rossi*, p. 9.   [4] *Ibid.* p. 37.

The commune : function and organisation

A substantial proportion of land held communally is likewise suggested by tables 1.2 and 1.3.[1] These figures are for 1922. According to the former, 68·9% of 'land' was held by rural societies, 10·1% was held by enclosed farms, and 20·1% by land organs in the Lake region (i.e. north west). According to the latter, 12% of land in the north west was held by enclosed farms, 25% was in the hands of land organs, and thus of uncertain use, and 57% was held communally. The Western area had a rather higher proportion of communal holding, 70%, with 18% in enclosed farms. Although there is some doubt about the reliability of these figures, it is worth noting that they give a fairly high proportion of communal holding for these areas, but do show these areas as having a lower proportion of communal holding than any other.

One reason for the apparent contradiction is that the situation changed considerably over time. In the immediate post-revolutionary years there was a fall in the proportion of enclosed farms. This was probably related to the activities of the Committees of Poor Peasants. We have seen already that this fall was not nearly so marked as in other areas, and in western guberniyas there was actually a rise.[2] From 1922 onwards there was nominally free choice of holding, but in the later twenties especially there was considerable administrative pressure against transfer from commune to enclosed farm. In Leningrad guberniya, communal holding rose from 79% to 80% between 1922 and 1928, with a fall to 75% in 1925. In Cherepovets guberniya there was a fall from 79% to 69% communal tenure between 1922 and 1925, with a rise to 71% by 1928.[3] (No indication whether percentage of households or area.) Kindeev noted that Leningrad guberniya land organs were only permitting applications for land use measures which were for improvement to the commune.[4] Elsewhere he noted similar pressures on enclosed forms of holding in Smolensk and Pskov guberniyas. The results he suggests for these areas are rather startling, and may well be exaggerated. For

1 See above, pp. 24, 25.
2 See above, p. 21.
3 Danilov, *Istoriya SSSR* (1958), no. 3, p. 122, quoting archive: Ts GAOR i SS f 4085, op 9, d 810, 1 287.
4 *Na agrarnom fronte* (1926), no. 10, p. 89. See also M. P. Kogtikova, 'O likvidatsii khuturov v SSSR 1935–41', *Istoriya SSSR* (1963), no. 4, pp. 120–7.

example, we have earlier noted 15·1% enclosed farms tenure in 1922 in Pskov guberniya.[1]

Table 1.7 [a]   *Percentage of land in various forms of holding*

	Fully enclosed farms	Farms with only fields enclosed	Commune
Pskov guberniya			
1923	84·5	—	—
1924	16·7	35·3	37·5
Smolensk guberniya			
1923	75·8	—	—
1924	25·4	8·8	38·2

[a] Kindeev, *Voprosy zemleustroistva* (based on NKRKI research) (Moscow, 1925), p. 50.

Kindeev was writing from a viewpoint which deplored the tendency of land organs to put pressure on those in enclosed farms. It is not possible to assess how far this process had gone by the eve of collectivisation. As late as 1929 there were expressions of concern at the proportion of fully enclosed farms in Smolensk guberniya. At the XVI Party Conference a delegate from the area regretted that, 'whereas before the revolution there were 16% of fully enclosed farms, now there are 53%'.[2] While the figures are open to question, it is obvious that this was a fluid time in the area as far as land holding was concerned.

While some of the confusion about holding in the area may well be a result of the changing pattern over time, it does not explain all of the contradictions. No complete explanation is possible, but a number of points suggest themselves.

The question of whether a given village or hamlet farmed as a commune or the inhabitants had their own individual enclosed farms is an oversimplified one. This is especially so in this area with very varied natural conditions. Livestock rearing played a major part in the economy of the area. Pasture and forest represented a large part of the land area. Thus it was quite legitimate to state that 'the tendency is to single peasant farming, especially for milk and meat,

[1] See above, p. 21.
[2] 'XVI-ya Konferentsiya KPSS', *Sten. Otchet*, p. 355.

as much drainage and tree felling would be needed for arable land'.[1] The same author could say in the next sentence 'arable land seems to be looked after by land societies'. The question is not one of a peasant farming his enclosed farm or being a commune member. He was probably both. If pastures were held in common, the animals were individually owned. Under such conditions there would be little need for communal organisation, except perhaps to hire a cowherd. In an area where animal husbandry was a major feature in the economy, the dividing line between enclosed and communal holding would be a difficult one to draw. Arable land was comparatively scarce and this would in all probability be held communally.

Closely related to this point is the question of units to which statistics relate. If one is considering percentage of households, the question 'either...or' is meaningless, as we have just seen. When such a question was put it would presumably be answered in terms of what was seen as the major part of the economy of the household. It is thus very likely that a comparatively small proportion of households would regard themselves as primarily attached to a commune. If the yardstick were percentage of land in these various forms of holding, one might expect a largely similar result, with perhaps a slightly higher proportion of communal holding. The statistics we have quoted give a very high proportion of communal holding, which leads one to suspect that they relate not to all agricultural land, but to arable land.

The pattern of these arable holdings was extremely confused. Not only did each household have its holdings in several places, but also each commune tended to a number of parcels of land. Interlocking of holdings between villages and hamlets was a very real problem. Physical conditions meant that settlements tended to be rather small, of 20–30 households, and their arable land would often be at a distance from the village, and mingled with land of another village. In Novgorod guberniya the average number of parcels of land belonging to a land society (commune) was 8–10, but reached 40–50 in places. This led to one form of the multi-settlement commune being a common phenomenon in the north

[1] *Sovetskoe zemleustroistvo i melioratsiya.* Perspektivny plan, ed. I. A. Teodorova (Trudy zemplana, Moscow, 1925), p. 53.

west.[1] There is hardly any information about the working of these institutions, and land use measures were directed towards concentrating the land of one hamlet in one place. The existence of these multi-settlement communes gives perhaps a further source of confusion about holding. It may be that there was no strongly developed communal feeling in individual hamlets. Although households may have held a large number of strips of arable land, redistribution was not purely an internal affair within one hamlet. The inter-hamlet communes were perhaps rather diffuse bodies from the standpoint of the individual peasant, and did not embody a local community spirit as was perhaps the case in other areas. The large communes probably concerned themselves with practical difficulties arising out of land distribution, and not with broader questions of local administration.

The characteristics of the households forming the commune in this area were those of the central industrial area, only more pronounced. Extreme interlocking of plots was a major problem. According to one source, in 1925 52·7% of households in the north west, and 81% in the north, had land in 41–100 places.[2] This was reflected in inter-village interlocking, and led to the multi-settlement commune. It would seem fair to say that the commune did not here become a focal point in rural administration. Thus there is a real sense in which communal holding did not predominate, although most statistical evidence suggests that only a minority of peasants, albeit a substantial one, were consolidated into enclosed farms. Strength is given to this view by events under German occupation. In the North Russia area centred on Pskov, 'Wirtschafts Inspektorat Nord', the population was given a choice of form of holding. In other areas the collective farms had been retained, under the name of commune (obshchina). In that area 165,000 households reverted to strip tenure, while 50,000 opted for enclosed farms.[3]

[1] Danilov, *Istoriya SSSR* (1958), no. 3, pp. 102–3. Quoting NKZ RSFSR, *Materialy po perspektivnomu planu razvitiya sel'skogo i lesnogo khozyaistva*, ch. 5, str. 6–7, and NKZ RSFSR, *Otchet NKZ XII Vserossiiskomu s'ezdu Sovetov za 1923–4* (Moscow, 1925), p. 349.

[2] Yakovlev, *K voprosu sotsialisticheskogo pereustroistva sel'skogo khozyaistva* (based on Narodnyi Kommissariat Raboche-Krest'yanskogo Inspektorata (NKRKI) research of 1925) (Moscow, 1928), p. 87.

[3] Alexander Dallin, *German rule in Russia, 1941–5* (New York, 1957), pp. 3, 350.

Thus, while communal holding probably accounted for a large part of the sown area, arable farming was not particularly important in this area. It is also probable that redistribution was not regularly carried out, and the stability of interlocking plots may have led some commentators to call this farming with only fields enclosed. While statistically most peasants were attached to a form of commune, this probably did not have the same implication as commune membership in other areas.

Central Industrial area[1]

Over most of this area, certain of the factors which favoured enclosed forms of holding in the north west and west operated. A fairly wooded area, and one where market relations between the town and surrounding countryside were well developed, it changed in character towards the south, where Tula and Ryazan had many of the characteristics of the grain-growing Central Black Earth region.

Over the area as a whole, communal holding predominated. In 1922, 88% of land was in the hands of 'rural societies' (sel'skie obshchestva), that is was communally held, 2% was held in farms with only fields enclosed, and 1·8% in fully enclosed farms.[2] It is not clear whether this refers to arable, or to all land. In Moscow guberniya in 1924, 81·4% of households were in 'pure, untouched communes'.[3]

There were quite strong pressures for change. In 1924, Moscow Worker–Peasant Inspectorate research in a sample survey claimed that 50% of commune members wanted to change to farms with only fields enclosed,[4] although by 1929 the great majority of households were still in communes.[5] Land use measures in the Central Industrial Area were largely concerned with improvement to the

[1] All or part of Moscow, Vladimir, Ivanovo-Voznesensk, Nizhnii Novgorod, Kostroma, Yaroslav, Tver and Kaluga, Tula, Ryazan and Tambov guberniyas.
[2] N. Nikitin in *Khozyaistvennye Raiony SSSR : TsPO. Sbornik statistik* (Moscow–Leningrad, 1927), p. 51.
[3] Moscow Guberniya Executive Committee research, quoted by Gurov, 'Predvaritel'nye itogi zemleustroistva', *Na agrarnom fronte* (1925), no. 10, p. 82.
[4] *Ibid.*
[5] *Moskva i Moskovskaya Oblast' 1926/7–1928/9*, Moskovskaya Oblast, Statisticheskii Otdel (1930). This handbook shows the vast bulk of peasants to be in land societies, pp. 244–7.

commune, but one fifth, by area, involved transfer of peasants from communes to farms with only fields enclosed by January 1928.[1] In no area to the south of this in European Russia did transfer to enclosed holdings occupy over one-twentieth of the work undertaken in land use measures.

It would seem that pressure to leave the commune for individual forms of holding was strongest in areas nearest to the towns. Thus, in Kostroma guberniya there was an average of 5·9% of households in enclosed farms throughout the guberniya as a whole, but in areas near to the towns this rose to 25–50%.[2] In Ivanovo-Voznesensk guberniya, it was noted that the demand for various land use measures varied between districts. In industrial areas from 1923 to 1926 the greatest demand was for transfer to farms with only fields enclosed, while in agricultural areas improvements to the commune formed the major part of the work.[3] It would seem that a nearby market, with fairly good communications, stimulated at least the more enterprising peasants to leave the commune to attempt to produce for the market. At the other end of the scale, individual forms of holding would have left members of a household more free to go and work in the town, and still retain a share of the land, and not have to consider the effect of their leaving on the family in the commune. There is some doubt about the position in Moscow guberniya. Danilov talks of 'a ring of enclosed farms round towns in Moscow guberniya'.[4] Moscow Guberniya Executive Committee research in 1924 was said to show that in agricultural volosts, 77% of households were in communes, but in volosts where industry predominated 88·7% of households were in communes.[5] To interpret this contradiction, one would need the original data. If 'industrial volost' included those where handicraft industry was on a large

[1] See below, Table 4.8, p. 188.
[2] Danilov, *Istoriya SSSR* (1958), no. 3, p. 109, quoting Ts GAOR i SS, f 478, op 59, d 559, ll 46–7.
[3] Ivanovo Voznesenskii Gubernskii RKI, *Zemleustroitel'naya pomoshch' krest'yanskomu naseleniyu* (Ivanovo-Voznesensk, 1927), p. 31. From 1923 to 1926, land use measures had been effected on 17·7% of sown area, 41·6% of this was improvement of communes, 35·1% transfer to farms with only fields enclosed, 19·1% to new settlements. Formation of collective and transfer to fully enclosed farms each accounted for just over 2% of work.
[4] Danilov, *Istoriya SSSR* (1958), no. 3, p. 110. Ts GAOR i SS, f 478, op 59, d 559, ll 46–7.   [5] Gurov, *Na agrarnom fronte* (1925), no. 10, p. 82.

The commune : function and organisation

scale, it could be that in such areas the attractions of improving agricultural techniques would be less than in other areas.

The main characteristics of the commune in this area were the fairly high number of strips per household, and the small size of these strips. A sample survey of households in Ivanovo-Voznesensk gave the figures shown in Table 1.8.[1]

Table 1.8

	Strips per household					
	4–7	8–13	14–20	21–30	31–40	40+
Percentage of all households	3	38	29	15	10	5

The strips were on average between 7 and 14 ft wide, and from 70 to 100 ft long.[2] In Ryazan guberniya it was said that 'there are places with up to 50 strips at a distance of 15–20 or even 25 versts (16–22, or even 28 km). The traditions of the old commune are too strong in our area, and in all the old Russian guberniyas.'[3]

Individual settlements (seleniya) tended to be fairly small in the area. In Ivanovo-Voznesensk the number of households per settlement (selenie) was as shown in Table 1.9.[4]

Table 1.9

Households per settlement	Percentage of settlements
Up to 20	57·8
21–50	34·1
51–100	6·6
100+	1·5

This does not *necessarily* mean communes. The average size of a commune in Moscow oblast was nearly 50 households.[5]

[1] Ivanovo Voznesenskii Gubernskii RKI, *Zemleustroite'naya pomoshch'*, p. 14.
[2] *Ibid.*
[3] 15-yi S'ezd KPSS, *Sten. Otchet*, p. 1059. Delegate Glinskii from Ryazan.
[4] Ivanovo Voznesenskii Gubernskii RKI, op. cit.
[5] *Moskva i Moskovskaya Oblast'*, pp. 244–7. In 1928 there were 7,100 land societies, and 350,000 households, and in 1929, 7,000 land societies and 330,000 households. For comparison of settlement and commune see below chapter 3, section (1).

37

These two factors combined to lead to interlocking of plots between one commune and another. An example of the land of four communes being intermingled in the hamlet of Gorodishche in Igor'ev-Pol'sk uezd was shown in a sketch map in a report on land holding in Ivanovo-Voznesensk guberniya.[1] Similar problems were met in Yaroslav, Vladimir, Kostroma, Tver, and northern Nizhnii Novgorod guberniyas,[2] but the further south one went, forest was less dense, and the problem consequently less severe. The conditions seem fit for multi-settlement communes, but there is no evidence of this.

Thus in this area the commune was the most common form of land holding. During the twenties, land use measures in the area concentrated on consolidating the land of each commune into one area, and, within the commune, reducing the number of strips per household. The inefficiency of small plots, and the proximity of town markets led a small, but significant proportion of commune members to leave to consolidate their land in a farm with only fields enclosed. Presumably fully enclosed farm was less favoured because of the existing pattern of settlement in small hamlets.

Central Black Earth area[3]

This was the most extensive area of communal holding. This area, and all those we will now deal with, are grain surplus areas, in contrast to those already described.[4] Natural conditions favoured grain-growing as the major agricultural activity. Market relations were less developed here than in the Ukraine and Volga areas, probably due to the less developed transport network. As late as 1929, 94·5% of land was in communal holding.[5] With less severe problems of shortage of land, the commune in this area was usually larger in population and area than further north. This led to the main problems of the commune being not only small size of plot,

[1] Ivanovo Voznesenskii Gubernskii, RKI, op. cit. p. 14.
[2] Danilov, *Istoriya SSSR* (1958), no. 3, p. 103.
[3] All, or most of Orlov, Kursk, Voronezh and Tambov guberniyas with southern uezds of Tula and Ryazan guberniyas.
[4] A useful map on grain deficiency and surplus areas, 1909–13, is found in Lyashchenko, *History of the national economy of Russia*, p. 537.
[5] P. N. Sharov, 'God velikogo pereloma v sel'skom khozyaistve Ts.Ch.O.', *Istoricheskie zapiski*, 51 (1955), p. 198.

but also the distance between the plots. There was far less interlocking of holdings between separate communes.

The most detailed information on land holding in the area comes from a sample of holding in Tambov guberniya; see Table 1.10. The last line of the table gives a misleading impression of the relative strength of the commune, as it counts each commune as one land user, although it may have had several hundred households, whereas the enclosed farms count each household as a separate land user. Thus a much larger percentage were commune members in terms of households. The difference in average area between 'large' and 'small' categories of commune suggests a considerable variation in size within the guberniya. According to this table, communes accounted for about 3·5 million desyatinas of land out of a total area of 3·7 million desyatinas. Thus 95% of all agricultural land in the guberniya was communal.

It is worth noting that the dividing line between a large and small commune should be set as high as 750 households. It has been said that in the Black Earth region as a whole, the commune consisted of up to 400–500 households.[1] The consequent difficulties were a frequent theme of writers on improvement of agriculture. Excessive time was spent carting and travelling between plots. A report by Worker–Peasant Inspectorate insisted there was a need to diversify the agriculture of the area, and that this aim could only be achieved by breaking up the large villages, and forming settlements of 20–30 households.[2] This happened to a limited extent with land released from state holdings in 1926, when 62% went directly to communes, but 23% to new settlements.[3]

Each household had a large number of strips. In Tambov guberniya there were up to 36 strips per household, in Kursk guberniya up to 40, and in Orlov guberniya as many as 60.[4] Where a household had a small allotment and was in a village with a large number of households, its strips tended to be so minute and distant that they

[1] Oganovskii, *Obshchina i zemel'noe tovarishchestvo* (Moscow, 1923), p. 8.
[2] Yakovlev (ed.), *K voprosu o pereustroistve sotsialisticheskogo sel'skogo khozyaistva* (Moscow, 1928), p. 89.
[3] N. K. Zem., *Otchet za 1925–6* (Moscow, 1926).
Danilov, *Istoriya SSSR* (1958), no. 3, p. 104, quoting Ts GAOR i SS, f 4085, op 9, d 195, l 3; d 525, l 136.

Table 1.10 [a] *Types of holding*

	Commune		Peasant farms		Collective				State land holdings		
	Size in households		Only fields enclosed	Fully enclosed	Commune	Artel	Society for collective working	State farm	Rented	Institutions	Reserves
	Large 750+	Small <750									
Units	1273	2442	143	344	17	159	162	128	1200	350	134
Area per unit, desyatinas	2092	307	21	19	139	115	104	739	—	—	—
Percentage of land users	19·7	37·9	2·2	5·3	0·3	2·5	2·5	1·9	18·6	5·4	2·1

[a] Tambovskaya guberniya, Statisticheskoe byuro i zemel'noe upravlenie, *Materialy po sovremennomu zemlepol'zovanii Tambovskoi gubernii* (Tambov, 1926), p. 5.

did not cultivate them at all. In Voronezh guberniya only 6% of households with less than six desyatinas did not cultivate their land in villages of up to 50 households, but this rose to 17·9% in villages between 101 and 250 households, and in the very largest villages of over 1,000 households, it was as high as 57·4% of households.[1] (One must allow for there being more involved in 'service' and light handicraft industry in a larger settlement.) This illustrates clearly that it was not only the most successful peasants who were hindered by the strip system. While there would be alternative employment possibilities in the larger villages, which would encourage the poorer peasant to leave a plot which he might have retained in a smaller village without such alternative opportunities, the pressures within the commune would seem to have squeezed the poorer peasant out of a living in the Black Earth and south east regions.

A more precise indication of the nature of the problem of distance between home and plots is given by the figures for North Voronezh guberniya (Table 1.11).

Table 1.11[a] *Percentage of communes having the boundary of their land over 5 km from the village centre*

Households per commune	Percentage of communes
Up to 50	3·2
50–100	10·8
101–300	40·8
300+	80·9

[a] N. K. Zem, RSFSR, *Materialy po perspektivnomu planu razvitiya sel'skogo i lesnogo khozyaistva* (Moscow, 1928), p. 153.

The commune was by far the most widespread form of land holding in the area. There seems to have been little demand to leave the commune. Land use measures were largely concerned with dividing large communes into smaller units, and by 1928, 17% of agricultural land was in the hands of communes which had been

[1] *Ibid.* p. 105, quoting Ts GAOR i SS, f 3983, d 45, l 271.

41

thus divided.[1] This must have gone some way to overcoming the problem of distance. Unfortunately we have no reports of how this division was undertaken in this, or any other, region.

Mid-Volga area[2]

Mainly a grain-growing area, with access to the market through the Volga network, this area was one of extensive communal holding. Although we have no figures for the proportion of communal holding in the area, figures describing aspects of land society holdings assume this form predominates. While enclosed forms of holding had gained a substantial foothold under the encouragement of the Stolypin reforms, Pershin remarked that, after the revolution, 'the movement against enclosed farms was especially strong in the Volga guberniyas and in some of the Southern guberniyas, i.e. in areas where the commune was most alive and enclosed farms...had at times been formed under compulsion'.[3]

The commune in the area tended to be of medium size. In Samara guberniya, the largest in the area, there seems to have been considerable change over time. Immediately after the revolution, 44% of communes had over 300 households, according to one sample,[4] but by 1927, 15% of households had formed new, smaller communes with an average membership of 54 households.[5]

The Mid-Volga krai contained eight oblasts and the size of a commune varied considerably between them at the beginning of 1930, as shown in Table 1.12.

There was also a considerable variation in size of commune within each oblast (see Table 1.13).

The figures suggest a rather smaller commune than those mentioned earlier for Samara guberniya. It is doubtful whether land use measures alone would be an adequate explanation for the proportion of societies with over 300 households being only 3·6% by 1 January 1930. Neither can the influence of collectivisation, which

[1] See Table 4.9, p. 189.
[2] Penza, Ulyanov and Samara guberniyas with parts of Nizhegorod guberniya, Tatar republic, and Chuvash republic.
[3] Pershin, *Uchastkovoe zemlepol'zovaniye v Rossi*, p. 9.
[4] Zemleustroistvo Samarskoi Gubernii *1927–8* (Samara, 1928), p. 1.
[5] *Ibid.* but from a different sample.

Table 1.12 [a] *Size of land society, Mid-Volga krai, 1st January 1930*

Oblast	Centres of population	Land Societies	Households	Population (thousands)	Households of Nat. Mins. (thousands)	Land Socs. per centre of population	Household per Land Society	Population per Land Society	Population per centre of population
Mordva	1,793	2,337	246,018	1,348	105	1·3	105	577	752
Kuznets	477	754	104,891	542	48	1·6	139	719	1,136
Penza	1,910	2,606	218,727	1,136	9	1·4	84	436	595
Syzran	815	1,314	108,811	534	17	1·6	83	406	655
Ulyanov	1,286	1,857	167,780	822	36	1·4	90	443	639
Buguruslan	1,892	2,398	139,715	727	68	1·3	58	303	384
Samara	2,156	2,857	185,015	915	26	1·3	65	320	424
Orenburg	2,198	2,451	159,612	793	23	1·1	65	324	361
Mid-Volga krai	12,527	16,574	1,330,568	6,817	331	1·3	80	400	545

The last four columns have been derived from the preceding ones.

[a] *Zemlepol'zovanie i zemleustroistvo srednevolzhskogo kraya* (Samara, 1930), p. 28.

Table 1.13[a] Distribution of Land Societies according to number of households

Oblast	Under 20	20–50	50–100	1–200	2–300	3–500	500–1,000	1,000+	Total
Mordva	421	491	514	491	187	163	35	35	2,337
Percentage	18	21	22	21	8	7	1·5	1·5	100
Kuznets	180	110	115	167	82	75	25	—	754
Percentage	24	14·6	15·3	22·1	10·8	9·9	3·3	—	100
Penza	550	756	657	442	112	70	16	3	2,606
Percentage	21·1	29·0	25·2	17·0	4·3	2·7	0·6	0·1	100
Syzran	358	315	250	212	86	59	30	4	1,314
Percentage	27·2	24·0	19·0	16·1	6·6	4·5	2·3	0·3	100
Ulyanov	323	463	435	360	156	89	29	2	1,857
Percentage	17·4	24·9	23·4	19·4	8·4	4·8	1·6	0·1	100
Buguruslan	990	730	305	237	80	41	12	3	2,398
Percentage	41·3	30·5	12·7	9·9	3·3	1·7	0·5	0·1	100
Samara	871	961	524	273	125	73	26	4	285
Percentage	30·5	33·6	18·3	9·6	4·4	2·6	0·9	0·1	100
Orenburg	712	861	467	221	98	67	19	6	2,451
Percentage	29·0	35·1	19·1	9·0	4·0	2·7	0·8	0·3	100
Mid-Volga krai	4,495	4,687	3,267	2,403	926	637	192	57	16,574
Percentage	26·6	28·3	19·7	14·5	5·6	3·8	1·2	0·3	100

[a] *Zemlepol'zovanie i zemleus troistvo srednevolzhskogo kraya* (Samara, 1930), p. 29.

The commune: function and organisation

had not affected the area too greatly at that date. The earlier figure was from a fairly small sample, and this must be the reason for the discrepancy.

Thus there was a very wide range in size between the largest and the smallest commune in the Mid-Volga krai. Over one quarter had less than 20 households, while there were a few with over one thousand households. There was a considerable variation in size between areas but, interestingly, ratio of numbers of land societies to centres of population was fairly constant between 1.1 and 1.6:1. The average size of commune in the Buguruslan oblast was less than half the 139 households in the Kuznets oblast. There was a considerable variation within each oblast. The average size of commune throughout the krai was 80 households, and three quarters had less than 100 households. We have already mentioned the economic implications of size, and will discuss the effects on the commune as an institution later.

This size of commune meant in this area that distance between house and plot tended to be considerable. In 1928 in Samara guberniya the authorities concerned with land use measures expressed concern at the problem, and gave the figures shown in Table 1.14.[1]

Table 1.14 *Percentage of households having their plots at a given distance from the house*

	Up to 3 km	3–5 km	5–7 km	7–10 km	10+ km
Percentage of an unspecified sample	7·3	17·2	17·8	23·2	34·5

The position seems to have been roughly similar in 1925, when 12% of settlements (selenii) had land at under 3·3 km, and 33% at 11+ km. At that time a 'significant number' had land as far away as 40–50 km.[2]

A commune with over 500 households would obviously be a very different institution from one with under 50. What is significant for

---

[1] *Zemlepol'zovanse i zemleus troistvo srednevolzhskogo kraya* (Samara 1930).
[2] Yakovlev, *K voprosu* (Moscow, 1928), p. 86. Sample of 329 settlements, conducted in 1925.

the moment is that these great variations existed not only within the krai, but within each oblast. This underlines the dangers of talking about anything so diffuse as the Russian Commune. Even generalisations about communes in particular areas must remain full of pitfalls.

Urals area[1]

Before describing what is known of the Urals oblast itself, we see that in what is now the Udmurt Republic the commune was the main form of land holding. This is noteworthy, as in the previous section the statistics likewise implied that the national minorities in the Mid-Volga krai used the communal form of holding. In the annual statistical report for what was then the Vot oblast, we find the figures given in Table 1.15 based on 3,254 out of the 115,800 households of the oblast. The method of sampling is unstated.[2]

Table 1.15

Households	Without arable land	Fully enclosed farms	No. of plots	Farms with only fields enclosed	No. of plots	Strip tenure no. of households	No. of plots
3,254	86	4	6	14	65	3,150	126,044

Thus 96% of this sample of households held land in communal tenure. There must have been a considerable problem with interlocking of plots, as each communal household seems from this to have had over 40 plots on average. There is no indication of the size of each commune.

In the Urals oblast a rather curious pattern seems to have evolved. Whilst each household did not have a great number of strips, there was considerable interlocking of the land of settlements. While there were extensive areas of forest, agriculture was fairly mixed, with wheat production and some livestock raising, and small production for markets near towns.

[1] Include here a brief reference to holding in the Vyatka-Vetluga Area for the sake of convenience.
[2] Votskaya oblast', *Statisticheskii ezhegodnik za 1927* (Izhevsk, 1928).

Table 1.16 shows the percentage of households with a given number of plots in the Cis-Ural and Central Urals area.[1]

Table 1.16

Okrug	Number of settlements[a] investigated	1 plot	2–10	11–20	21–50	50+		Maximum number of plots
Kungursk	430	3	59·8	14·2	16·7	6·3	100	228
Perm	570	23·2	48·9	12·1	8·0	7·8	100	363
Sarapul	160	33·1	43·8	15·6	6·9	0·6	100	201
Sverdlovsk	318	1·9	20·1	46·2	21·4	10·4	100	197
Shadrin	394	0·3	17·0	25·9	44·9	11·9	100	268
Whole area	1872	10·9	39·4	21·6	20·0	8·1	100	

[a] My italics.

This table serves to underline once more the considerable differences that existed within a given area. The overall characteristic is that nearly three quarters of households had twenty or less plots, and nearly half had ten or less. 63·6% of holdings were more than 8 km from the settlement.

By contrast with the relative compactness of individual holdings, the communes of which they were members seem to have had their land spread over quite a wide area. One investigation showed that 90% of settlements had their land in several places, 20% in 20–50 places. In Shadrin okrug the land use of 36 settlements was in 1,044 holdings. Under these conditions it is hardly surprising that there were problems of distance. An investigation into 1,872 settlements showed that 27·7% had land at 8–10 km from the centres, 36% at over 11 km, and in one a part of its land was as far as 73 km.[2]

Danilov has suggested that the data available show that where interlocking is at its worst, the problem of distance is least severe. This would appear to be likely, but the data he uses on the Urals do not bear this out. While he notes that Shadrin okrug had the highest weight of societies with 11+ km between plots, the handbook just quoted shows this okrug to have the highest, not as he

[1] Ural'skoe zemel'noe upravlenie, *Zemlepol'zovanie i perspektivy zemleustroistva na Urale* (Sverdlovsk, 1926), p. 14.   [2] Yakovlev, *K voprosu*, p. 86.

claims the lowest fragmentation, with 44·9% of households having 21–50 plots.[1] It may be that this okrug had a rather exceptional pattern of land use. On a national scale, his proposition is manifestly true, but this particular example does not support the general hypothesis.

There was strong pressure from the administration in this area on the enclosed forms of agriculture and long before the central government discouraged those forms, the Oblast party committee had decreed that it was not permissible to set up enclosed farms as a part of a general redistribution, except where natural conditions excluded other forms.[2]

Lower Volga area[3]

One of the most important factors in this area was the lack of water, which meant a high concentration of population in large settlements. 60% of the population were in settlements (seleniya) of over 300 households, spread ribbon-like along the river.[4] The characteristic problem of the commune in this area was distance between plots and house. Danilov gave a concrete example of such a situation. The village (selo) of Sredne Akhtubinsk had a land area of 200,000 hectares, which reached in an elongated area up to 117 km from the village. This 'huge commune' had a population of 27,000.[5] In Stalingrad guberniya, he noted, 82% of communes had an average distance from settlement to plot of over 10 km, and 56% a distance of over 20 km.[6]

What this meant in terms of communal organisation is not clear. Obviously redistribution of such large tracts of land would have been a vast undertaking. Without local maps of land holding, it is hard to get any inkling of what the commune meant in such an area. Kirpichev noted that 'in Black Earth and Steppe guberniyas, the

---

[1] Danilov, *Istoriya SSSR* (1958), no. 3, p. 106. He also quotes *Zemlepol'zovanie i perspektivy zemleustroistva na Urale*, ch. 15.
[2] Gurov, *Na agrarnom fronte* (1925), no. 10, p. 80.
[3] Stalingrad, Saratov, and Astrakhan guberniyas.
[4] Baranskii, *Ekonomicheskaya geografiya SSSR* (Gosizdat, 1926), p. 110.
[5] Danilov, *Istoriya SSSR* (1958), no. 3, p. 107, quoting N. K. Zem, *Otchet za 1924/5*, pp. 12–13.
[6] Danilov, *ibid.*, quoting Ts GAOR i SS, f 3983, op 1, d 34, ll 157, 213; f 4085, op 9, d 1, l 25; d 526, ll 6–7. Also N. K. Zem, *Materialy po perspektivnomu planu*, ch. 5, pp. 13, 14, 15.

North Caucasus, and Siberia, where a settlement could number up to 10,000 households...general meetings of citizens are called by districts of villages'.[1] Presumably in some communes, particular areas of land came to be the concern of particular groups of families within one commune. While individual points of settlement were large, there were communes which comprised a number of settlements. In Stalingrad guberniya there were complex communes of up to 50 settlements (seleniya), which redistributed land on the basis of all the settlements.[2] It is possible that redistribution was needed much less frequently in this Lower Volga Area than in the Central Black Earth region, as there was not such pressure on land, and that such unwieldy units from the point of view of redistribution remained so because of the infrequency of calls for redistribution. None the less, 80%, by area, of land use measures up to 1928 was concerned with division of large communes, which was the largest proportion of this kind of work of any area in the country.[3] The number of strips per household was comparatively few, although we have no precise indication.

We have no figures which show precisely what proportion of households held their land in communal holding. The extensive grain-producing characteristic of the area with developed market relations, and also a large-scale animal husbandry, suggest an area favourable to enclosed farms. However, it appears that enclosed households never formed anything other than a substantial minority of households. Pershin shows there to have been 16·4% in Saratov guberniya in 1917. This proportion fell very sharply after the revolution.[4]

Where enclosed farming was followed here, it was of the kind with only fields enclosed. Houses tended to be congregated near the few sources of water, and the hollows of river valleys afforded shelter from the plains. Under such conditions the enclosed holding of a household tended to be at a considerable distance from the home. In

[1] Kirpichev *Prava skhoda i sel'soveta*, (Moscow-Leningrad, 1928), pp. 35-6.
[2] Danilov, *Istoriya SSSR* (1958), no. 3, p. 102, quoting Narodnyi Kommissariat Zemledeliya RSFSR, *Materialy po perspektivnomu planu razvitiya sel'skogo i lesnogo khozyaistva 1928/9-1932/3*, Chast' 5 (Moscow, 1928), pp. 6-9, 11, 14.
[3] See below, Table 4.8, p. 188.
[4] Pershin, *Uchastkovoe zemiepot'zovaniye v Rossi*, p. 9.

some areas in summer time families temporarily moved to their holding for the season.[1] This was one of the few areas in Russia where over 10% of households were in enclosed farms in early 1917. One may note here that it is harder to distinguish between the farm with only fields enclosed and commune than between the fully-enclosed farm and commune, and this may lead to confusion in the statistics. A commune which did not redistribute could be loosely looked on as a group of individual farmers, especially in an area with comparatively few plots per household in the commune. This is further supported by Pershin, who noted that 'farms with only fields enclosed, to the extent of three quarters of their numbers, preserve some communal holdings, to the extent of 1/7 of their land. Pasture usually remained in common use.'[2] Although the lines between enclosed and communal forms may have been thus blurred, it does seem that the commune in the area was able to exert considerable pressure on individual peasants to return after 1917. Such pressure was not anything like so effective in the north west and west, the other areas with enclosed forms of holding in Russia.

North Caucasus[3]

This was a very rich agricultural area, with well-established production not only of wheat, but also fruit and meat for the market. The extent of communal holding in the area is hard to determine with any precision, but in 1925 it was suggested that 'the main task of land use measures in the krai is to get rid of, or to improve the commune'.[4] When land was freed from state holdings in 1926, 57% went to communes, a smaller proportion than in other areas, 5% to collectives and 38% to forming new collectives.[5]

We have some slightly more detailed information on the Kuban. Although this was a Cossack area, with rather special traditions of tenure, it seems that the commune predominated there. It may be, as Wesson suggests, that the old Cossack commune was not necessarily a land organisation, but rather an organisation for mutual help

[1] Pershin, *Uchastkovoe zemlepol'zovaniie v Rossii*, p. 22.   [2] Ibid. p. 17.
[3] This administrative unit is more convenient for our purposes than the Gosplan areas in this region.
[4] *Zemleustroitel'* (1925), no. 4, p. 54.
[5] N. K. Zem, *Otchet za 1925–6*, p. 49.

in defence, although the Russian word obshchina is used.[1] A statistical handbook for the Kuban okrug for 1924–6 said that of land in agricultural use 66·8% was in communal tenure, 1·2% in the hands of collectives, and 1·6% used by improvement partnerships (meliorativnye tovarishchestva). As no indication was given of other forms it may be that the figure for communes should have read 96·8%.[2] This suspicion is strengthened by figures for 1927, when 70·9% of land was held by 'large' (100 + household) communes, 26·2% by 'small' (less than 100 households) communes, 2% by collectives and 0·9% by enclosed households.[3]

It is likely that communes in the krai as a whole were large. A significant proportion of *settlements* had over 1,000 households: 9% in the Kuban okrug, 6·8% in the Armavir okrug, 6·9% in the Don okrug.[4] It would seem that this was an area where land use measures proved quite fruitful in improving the commune. By 1928 16% of land was farmed by societies which had been divided into smaller units, 21·9% of land had been converted to broad strips – the highest proportion in the whole of the RSFSR.[5]

Other areas

While our study is confined to European Russia, it may be of interest to note characteristics of land holding in three other major areas of the USSR.

The *Ukraine* was an area with large-scale capitalist agriculture before the revolution, especially in the sugar beet areas. The Stolypin reforms had a greater impact here than in other areas on peasant agriculture. After the revolution, communal holding developed but little. None the less communal tenure did exist in Southern Ukraine.[6] In view of this it is interesting that membership of a 'land society' was compulsory under the Ukrainian Land Code.

[1] Wesson, *Soviet communes* (Rutgers University Press, New Brunswick, 1963), p. 49.
[2] Kubanskii Statisticheskii Otdel, *Kubanskii statisticheskii sbornik za 1924–6*, Tom 1 (Krasnodar, 1928), p. 86.
[3] Cherny, 'Zemleustroistvo v Kubana', *Na agrarnom fronte* (1927), no. 11–12, p. 170.
[4] Danilov, *Istoriya SSSR* (1958), no. 3, p. 107, quoting Ts GAOR i, SS, f 3983, op 1, d 45, l 213, and *Otchet 'NKZ RSFSR za 1924/5*, p. 122.
[5] See Table 4.9, p. 189.
[6] P. Popov, 'Voprosy zemleustroistva na Ukraine', *Na agrarnom fronte* (1925), no. 5–6, pp. 52 ff.

In Russia, where there was no such compulsion, the word had become synonymous with commune. It is not clear what the functions of such a body were in the Ukraine.[1]

In certain areas of *Siberia*, communal holding predominated. While land area was vast, cleared arable land was more scarce. Baranskii noted that the development of land use was so rapid, that redistributional tenure was established within one or two decades after colonisation.[2] Thus, when in 1926 state land holdings were distributed, 70% went to land societies (communes).[3] The only Siberian area for which detailed statistics are available is Irkutsk okrug in 1927. Then 98·5% of households in the area farmed communally. The average size of commune was 76 households.[4] Over so vast an area, it would be unwise to generalise. In some parts, communes consisted of 10–15 households.[5] The part played by forestry and trapping would vary between areas of colonial settlement. None the less, communal tenure of arable land was a quite strongly developed institution.

In *Belorussia* enclosed farms predominated, and these increased as land from commercial estates became available after the revolution.[6] There was no communal holding in the area.

CONCLUSION

Table 1.17 draws together certain features associated with communal holding in the areas reviewed. There is a gradual progression from north west, and west, to the south east. A combination of historical and physical conditions made the commune relatively weak in the north west and west. The commune, as we define it, was an institution based on arable farming, and in these areas the natural condi-

---

[1] Popov, *loc. cit.*, touches on this question, noting that they varied between unions 'for the sake of the law', and communes.

[2] Baranskii, *Economicheskaya geografiya SSSR*, p. 184.

[3] N. K. Zem, *Otchet za 1925–6*, p. 49.

[4] *Zemlepol'zovanie i sel'skoe khozyaistvo Irkutskogo okruga v tsifrakh* (Irkutsk, 1928), p. 29.

[5] Yeltovskii raion was such a one, according to a delegate from the area to Ts SSSR: 4-yi sozyv, 4-ya sessiya, Dec. 1928. *Sten. Otchet*, Bulletin 15, p. 2.

[6] Baranskii *Economicheskaya geografiya SSSR*, p. 64.

tions were not suitable for anything but the smallest scale grain growing. However, there was production of industrial crops for the market. The north of the Central Industrial Region shared some of these characteristics, but towards the south wheat was grown. In all other areas of European Russia, commune holding predominated. In grain areas where production for the market was possible, due to proximity to towns, or good transport resources, there was more pressure on the commune, as individual peasants found it profitable to have their own holdings. This had not reached major proportions in these areas in the 1920s, after the retreat from Stolypin after the revolution.

Communes varied in their characteristics according to the local geographical, historical, and economic conditions. They did not necessarily coincide with settlement patterns.[1] Availability of water resources, and availability of good accessblie arable land were major factors in determining whether the commune's member had a large number of strips of minute size, as in the more northerly regions, or strips of adequate size at a great distance from their home, as in the south east. The communes themselves varied greatly in size, although no precise comparison is possible. In those areas where communes' land was intermingled, relationships would have been different from those where a commune had its land consolidated in one area. The multi-settlement commune was common in several areas, but little is known of its working.

In this chapter, we have established that the commune was the most usual form of holding over most of European Russia. Where possible, we have suggested what proportion of households or of area were involved in communal holding in particular areas. Certain crude differences have been established between communes in particular areas, but these have been enough only to suggest that in the following chapters, our discussion of 'the commune' is open to many pitfalls, as there must have been considerable local variations. Unfortunately there will be too little evidence to establish what effect these differences in holding pattern, stemming from a variety of economic, agricultural, and geographical pressures had on the commune as an institution. We are driven to recall the words of a

[1] See below, chapter 3, (1).

Land holding in European Russia in the 1920s

Table 1.17

	Main[a] crops	Role of animal husbandry	Transport	Market relations
North west	Flax, potatoes, oats, barley, rye	Dairy	River, road	Developed
West	Flax, potatoes, oats, barley, rye	Dairy	River, road	Developed
Central Industrial	As above, plus market gardening and some wheat, rye	Not major	River, road	Developed
Central Black Earth	Rye, wheat potatoes, oats, barley	Not major	Poorly developed	Not well developed
Urals	Oats, rye, wheat, flax	Not major	Poorly developed	Not well developed
Mid-Volga	Wheat	Not major	River, road, fair	Developed
Lower Volga	Wheat, rye	Not major	River, road, fair	Well developed
North Caucasus	Wheat, fruit	Meat, dairy	Sea, river	Well developed

[a] This largely reflects natural conditions – soil, temperature, rainfall, etc.

contemporary Soviet writer investigating similar problems:

The Land Code at present in force allows any form of working holding, including individual, artel, or communal. It would be extremely important to know how the present-day agricultural population uses its land, what forms are developing, what forms declining, which are the dominant forms in each area. Unfortunately there are no such materials at our command, and we must decline to describe the present land tenure of our people, even in a purely quantitative way.[1]

[1] S. P. Shvetsov, *Ekonomicheskaya geografiya sel'skogo khozyaistva SSSR* (Leningrad, 1925), p. 50.

The commune : function and organisation

Proportion of communal holding	Size of commune households	Size of settlement population	Strips per household	Other characteristics of commune
b	?	70	40+	Probable infrequent redistribution. Interlocking between communes
b	?	140		Probable infrequent redistribution. Interlocking between communes
80·6% of households	50	190	8–20	
95% of area	4–500	430	36–60	Instances of frequent redistribution noted
High	?	210	2–20	Instances of frequent redistribution noted
High	300+	500	—	
High	?	460	Small number	Multi-settlement communes
High	Large	470		

b See text, p. 32–3.

2

FUNCTION AND ORGANISATION

I FUNCTION OF THE COMMUNE

a *Introductory*

The Russian commune performed a number of functions, but what gave it its peculiar characteristics was that it was in the first place an institution for regulating the holding of land. The concept of property in land is not one which can be readily transferred to Russian conditions at this time. None the less, it would be safe to say that while the individual peasant would look upon the land he was using as indisputably 'his' by right as a peasant, he would acknowledge that he derived his use of that particular piece of land at that particular time from the commune of which he was a member. The basic function of the commune was to regulate holding within a given area. This was done by adjusting the holdings of the households which made up the commune according to fluctuation in size of household, and allocating each household a roughly proportionate share of different qualities of land.

It would be fallacious to interpret this in terms of some kind of primitive communism. A more realistic approach would be to view the commune as an institution which probably grew in most areas to reconcile conflict over peasant land holding. The equalising tendency was in part a result of the individualism of individual peasant households, each striving for the best land, not of any utopian striving for equality. We know most about the commune after 1861, when it became the instrument for repayment of redemption dues, and of taxes. In certain areas, the problem was not to prevent the most enterprising or powerful households from grabbing the land, but to force households to pay their dues on land for which they had no use. Again, the commune must, in this sense and at this period at least, be seen as growing out of conflict, rather than any more idealistic motives.

While redistribution of land, and the associated regulation of crop rotation, was the primary function of the commune, certain secondary functions grew from this, and came to have at least equal if not greater importance in continuing the life of the commune when, for example, the pressure of land shortage had gone after the revolution. The commune performed the function of a local gathering for deciding general questions of local importance. This was given a stimulus by making the commune the local tax and dues allocating and collecting institution after 1861. While these collecting functions were no longer performed by the commune after the revolution, its position as a unit of local administration had become so firmly established that it continued performing these broader functions of local administration.

There may thus be said to be three main functions which the commune performed. It redistributed land between constituent households, and, secondly, involved itself in deciding other agricultural questions, such as rotation. These will be dealt with here, as will the organisational shape which these gave to the commune. The third function, of local administration in a more general sense, is closely bound up in our period with the development of the rural soviet, and will be dealt with in the following chapter.

b *Redistribution*

With the movement of peasants back into the communes immediately after the revolution, the Bolsheviks were faced with a *fait accompli* as far as the countryside was concerned. They bowed to the inevitability of this development in the Decree on Land, and in the Russian Land Law of 1918. Both gave freedom of form of holding provided the holder of the land worked on it. They hinted that collective and co-operative forms should be encouraged. None the less, the Decree on Land assumed that the commune would be the normal form of land holding. Both decrees emphasised the need for some form of equality of holding. Ideally the Soviets' land departments were to control all distribution of requisitioned landlords' land, but this was never accomplished. The seizure of landlords' land was a more elemental movement than the weakly organised soviets could ever hope to control.[1]

---

[1] 'Dekret o zemle', 8 Nov. 1917. *Izvestiya*, *Pravda*, 18 Nov., and 'Osnovnoi zakon o sotsializatsii zemli', 19 Feb., 1918 (27 Jan.).

The commune: function and organisation

There were attempts to control the commune by legislation. It had performed a useful function in a time of revolution as communal pressures probably led to the relatively equitable distribution of seized land. From the Bolshevik point of view it brought with it a number of less desirable features. The obverse side of the coin was the hindrance to agricultural improvement implicit in equalising redistribution. If land was to be held in some sense equally, the commune usually allowed for small adjustments to be made regularly, and for periodic complete redistribution. Before the revolution there had been attempts to curb redistribution by legislation.[1] It is far from clear just how frequently redistribution was carried out in the years before the revolution, but it was a serious enough problem after the revolution for a series of laws to be passed which attempted to limit redistribution.

In July 1919, the People's Commissariat of Agriculture attempted to limit redistribution to cases where land use measures were being implemented. Further redistribution would then only be allowed on petition to the Volost Land Department. It would only be granted if there were patent injustice in the existing distribution, if households were going to leave, or if the commune were to transfer to multi-course rotation. No definite minimum time limit between the redistributions was recommended, and Uezd Land Departments were to work out detailed rules suited to local conditions. Periods between redistribution were to be such that 'a land-user, receiving land after a given redistribution, may utilise as fully as possible these expenditures of labour, fertiliser and other improvements made during his holding of land'.[2]

The following year, a distinction was made between full redistribution and partial redistribution which only concerned the land of a minority of commune members. Full redistribution was only to take place after at least three rotations. Earlier redistribution of all the commune land could only be undertaken under similar conditions to those laid down the previous year. Partial redistribution was allowed earlier if the rural soviet wished to increase the holding of a

[1] According to 'polozheniye o sel'skom sostoyanii', repartition was to be fixed for a period of 12 years. *Svod zakonov rossiiskoi imperii* (1910), Tom 9.
[2] 'On repartition in rural societies, villages, and other agricultural unions', 1 July 1919. SU 1919, no. 36, art. 362.

given household, take spare land from a household, or deprive a household which did not use fertiliser on its land. Such close supervision of the commune by the rural soviet was an early, and completely ineffective, attempt to bring the commune under close rural soviet control which was soon abandoned.[1]

Apparently the situation had not improved the following year. The preamble to a decision of the Central Executive Committee in March 1921, ran: 'regardless of the publication of the decree on redistribution of 30 April, forbidding frequent and premature redistribution...redistribution has not ceased'.[2] This went on to underline points in the decree, and call for speedier elimination of the worst features of communal holding. The 'Law on Land for Own Use' of May 1922[3] looked to the 1920 law as the basis for redistribution, but was soon superseded by the RSFSR Land Code.

Up to the time of collectivisation in 1929, the legal position with regard to redistribution was governed by the 1922 Land Code. This also allowed redistribution only after three rotations had run their course. Only if an improved lay-out were decided upon would earlier redistribution be allowed.[4] If in the period between redistributions there were requests for small readjustments of land between households, the commune could allow them provided no complaint was made to the Land Commission. If a household did object, the adjustment could only be made at the beginning of a rotation.[5] There was no attempt to involve the rural soviet in the internal affairs of the commune.

The procedure for redistribution laid down by the Land Code (1922) was as follows. The commune had to set out rules for equalising redistribution in its Land Statute. This was to state which communal lands were subject to redistribution, how the share of each household should be determined, and at what intervals redistribution should be undertaken. At the time of redistribution, a declaration on redistribution would be passed by a majority of

---

[1] Decree of SNK RSFSR, 30 April 1920 'On redistribution of land'. SU 1920, no. 35, art. 170, revoked 1 February 1923 as a result of Land Code.
[2] Published in *Izvestiya*, 23 March 1921. Quoted in *Sbornik dokumentov po zemel'nomu zakonodatel'stvu SSSR i RSFSR 1917–1954* (Gosyurizdat, Moscow, 1954), p. 88.
[3] SU 1922, no. 36, art. 426.
[4] 'Zemel'ny Kodeks RSFSR', 30 October 1922, arts. 121–2. SU no. 68, art. 201.
[5] *Ibid*. arts. 123–4, 93, note.

members, which would show how many 'redistribution units' were to be allotted to each household. This would come into force on registration with the volost executive committee. The redistribution had to be on the same basis for all households. If farm buildings had been erected on the land, or orchards or vineyards planted, the land was not to be redistributed, but the commune was to take this into account when distributing other holdings to this household. If the occupier had carried out some improvement to the land, he was to keep it, or, if this were impossible, be recompensed.

Some small amendments were subsequently made. From 1926 onwards a minority of members could demand redistribution where there had been no repartition since 1917, and there was marked inequality in holding.[1] The idea of this was presumably to attempt to counter entrenched rich peasant interests, and to use the commune to contain the growth of the rich peasant. No further change in the law on redistribution was made before the communes were overtaken by collectivisation. The 1928 'General Foundations of Land Holding' of the USSR left the framing of rules on redistribution to Union Republics.

The Land Code came closer to reality than most Soviet laws on the countryside, since it was an attempt to clarify the existing situation, rather than to prescribe goals. How and when redistribution was actually carried out must have varied greatly over the country. There is very little evidence on which to try and build a picture of the actual situation.

It would seem that complete redistribution upon seizure of the landlords' land (chernyi peredel) had been comparatively rare.[2] None the less, Danilov notes that from 1917 to 1922, 66% of villages underwent redistribution, 34% did not.[3] Whether redistribution was regular is hard to establish. Danilov quoted evidence from Kostroma, Penza, Tambov, and Orlov guberniyas, Ural oblast and North Caucasus krai, which suggests there was annual redistribution everywhere in these areas. In Voronezh guberniya, of 479

[1] SU 1926, no. 8, art. 58, amended SU 1927, no. 115, art. 569.
[2] Cf. Kochetovskaya, *Natsionalizatsiya zemli v SSSR* (Moscow, 1952), p. 123.
[3] Danilov, *Istoriya SSSR* (1958), no. 3, p. 91, quoting Ts SU enquiry in 29 guberniyas, samples of 1,000 villages with population of 172,000.

communes investigated, only 81 redistributed every 9 years according to the legal minimum, 202 redistributed after 6 years, 122 after 3 years and 74 redistributed annually.[1]

Delegates to the Congress of Peasant Members of Central Executive Committee commented on the position in their areas. Only of Siberia was it said that redistribution did not occur less than every 9 years. Most speakers noted that although general redistribution was not a frequent occurrence, continual minor adjustments made holding unsettled. A Black Earth delegate thought that minor adjustments were very necessary in areas with a shortage of land, where death and marriage could be compensated for as they happened. There was considerable opposition to allowing adjustments. A delegate from Ivanovo-Voznesensk guberniya claimed that experience in his own, and other central guberniyas such as Moscow, Tula and Ryazan, had shown this led to low standards. He remarked that 'today Siderov occupies this piece of land, but devil only knows where he'll be tomorrow'. Apparently the situation in Ulyanov was similar. In Voronezh minor adjustments took place annually in many villages, and in some of them, it was said, peasants stopped sowing and ploughing because they could be faced with a virgin field the following month. Delegates from Pskov and North Caucasus spoke in similar vein. In Kursk guberniya there was a compromise of full redistribution every 12 years, with adjustments every 3 or 4 years, which was said to work well. In winding up the debate, Milyutin emphasised the desirability of infrequent redistribution, and expressed the hope that frequent minor readjustments would be a thing of the past.[2]

The only area for which we have any detailed information on repartition is four uezds of Yaroslav guberniya, centred on the town of Rybinsk.[3] By the time of the research in 1925, it would seem that redistribution had taken place in approximately half the *settlements*. The detailed results are shown in Table 2.1. Voronev noted that the October revolution stimulated redistribution. Red Army men and workers leaving the towns wanted land 'in their own

[1] Danilov, loc. cit. p. 101, quoting Ts GAOR i SS, f 4085, op 9, d 526, l 158.
[2] Reported in *Na agrarnom fronte* (1926), no. 11-12, pp. 127 ff.
[3] Voronev, 'Agrarnye ocherki Rybinskogo Kraya', *Na agrarnom fronte* (1926), no. 1, p. 167.

Table 2.1 *Percentage of areas (un-defined) with a given proportion of settle-ments which had redistributed their land,* *1917–25*

In all settlements	22
75% and over settlements	25
Not in all settlements	32
Settlements undertook little redistribution	6
No redistribution	15
Total	100

commune'. Sometimes they were given a piece of a fellow-villager's land, or of landlords' land; and in other cases a general redistri-bution was undertaken. Such general redistributions reached their peak in the early years of the N.E.P. The percentage of cases of general redistribution of arable land noted in the research, happen-ing in a given year, was as shown in Table 2.2.

Table 2.2

	Percentage
1918	8
1919	13
1920	12
1921	14
1922	15
1923	16
1924	14
1925	8
Total	100

The percentage of general redistributions started to fall as com-munes began to redistribute parts of their land with increasing frequency. He suggested that redistribution was most strongly opposed by the wealthier peasants who had a vested interest in the status quo.

While much is made of the loss of time to peasants incurred because of excessive interlocking of plots, and distance between plots, another time-consuming element must have been the actual

Function and organisation

debates on redistribution. In Rybinsk area it was common practice for meadows to be redistributed annually. The writer of the article quoted describes how he attended a meeting where redistribution of the meadows was discussed. The peasants would stride over the land, measuring, checking, and arguing over little pieces of ground.[1] A graphic description of the atmosphere of a village gathering in the same guberniya by another author shows the chaos which often reigned. A gathering had been called where the commune was to decide what form of holding it would adopt for the future. Not strictly speaking the usual redistribution meeting, but probably similar in atmosphere:

A villager told me...the original discussion was a row, a noise or a bazaar, just as everywhere else in the volost. One person yelled 'I want a farm with only fields enclosed', another 'broad strip commune'. 30 muzhiks, heads of households, decided for enclosed farms, 20 for commune with broad strip. But the next day, it was the other way round. On the third day they were for broad strips to a man. But since only 23 households could properly be accommodated on broad strips, the others would have to go into farms with only fields enclosed. No way out. Then everyone decides the 'other' 23 can go to broad strips, and they will go for farms with only fields enclosed, and tell the surveyor to 'put me down for a farm with only fields enclosed'. A new decision – everyone wants to go to farms with only fields enclosed. The surveyor goes off his head. Then – a complication. Not far away are state holdings. So someone asks – can we go in for fully enclosed farms?...and so they changed their minds over and over again.[2]

Admittedly the question there discussed was what kind of holding to adopt, but the author remarked that once it had all been settled a tremendous uproar was made about fair shares.

The actual method of allocation varied. Danilov has given a broad description.[3] The Land Code merely stated that redistribution units should be on the same basis for all members of the commune. Allocation by number of members of the household was probably most common. This sometimes included those away from the village,

---

[1] Voronev, loc. cit. p. 171.
[2] Leonid Grigoriev, *Ocherki sovremennoi derevni* (Moscow, 1925), p. 63.
[3] See above, p. 7.

63

in the Army, or at work, but most usually did not. In some areas the number of children was taken into account, as was those who were unable to work, so that an excessive allocation was not made. Some even retained the old revision soul. (Before the 1861 reforms, landowners were taxed according to number of serfs attached to them ('revision souls') and redistribution within the commune was often by number of revision souls in each household.) In areas where the more prosperous peasants had a strong grip, distribution was by number of cattle, or some other measure of capital. While isolated instances of these methods have been noted, it is not possible to form a general picture. In Rybinsk area the distribution of arable land was organised as shown in Table 2.3.[1]

Table 2.3

	Percentage
By 'eaters' of both sexes	62
Roughly adjusted for household structure	21
With precise allowances for children and 60+	11
By revision souls	6
	—
Total	100

Meadows were usually distributed in proportion to the arable allocation although allowance was occasionally made for number of cattle. The peasantry of that area seemed divided as to whether this had led to the equality of holding promised as an aim of the revolution. 26% answered this question 'fully', 48% thought 'not fully' and 26% thought 'not at all'.[2] On the whole negative and positive replies were roughly balanced. Linking this with the revolution may have been something of a red herring in obtaining replies.

We have before lamented the lack of statistics allowing us to compare particular areas, but it would seem that the practice of redistribution varied greatly. It was probably commonest in the 'old' Russian central areas, but its frequency in the North Caucasus has also been remarked. There is a distinction between complete

[1] Voronev, *Na agrarnom fronte* (1926), no. 1, p. 168. [2] Ibid. p. 173.

redistribution of a commune, and adjustments to meet fluctuations in size of household from year to year. The latter appear to have been fairly common on an annual basis. The period between revolution and collectivisation was too brief for a stable pattern to emerge. The increase in the number of households suggests that adjustments would have been continually necessary, although splitting up of an individual household would not necessarily have involved a redistribution for other members of the commune.

c   *Other agricultural functions*

The commune gathering discussed a variety of topics related to the local economy.

The 1922 Land Code summarised the essential matters to be discussed by the communal gathering.[1] The gathering could decide upon and change the method of holding (poryadok pol'zovaniya) of the various holdings of the commune. It was supposed to draw up a land statute for the commune. It seems unlikely that many communes would draw up such a document. A form for such a statute in the Simferopol region was quite a lengthy document, but no statutes of actual societies seem to have been published.[2] The commune gathering discussed applications to join, and to leave with an apportionment of land. It could discuss changing its method of holding, either by improving communal holding, or turning to non-redistributable forms. Thus the commune was essentially concerned with holding, rather than technique of production. Work was on the whole done on an individual basis and was thus not the concern of the commune, but of the household, although cutting of hay was in some areas done by the commune as a whole. There is some slight evidence that some arable land was in places cultivated communally. In Moscow oblast two thirds of land societies had such land (obshchestvennaya zapashka). It was mainly used by organisations – Mutual Aid Societies held 43%, Machine Societies 29%,

---

[1] Land Code, art. 51.
[2] The need for a commune to have a statute was in keeping with a law of 1922, by which all organisations except Trade Unions had to register with the local People's Commissariat for Internal Affairs Office. Besides general information on organisation, the law required details of members which included social position, war service from 1914 onwards, party status, and property position. SU 1922, no. 49, art. 623 'Instructions on registration of societies, unions and combinations'.

Improvement Societies 10%, and by the commune itself in the remaining 18% of cases. The area used by each organisation was only 5¾ acres, and only 1·2% of sown area in the oblast was thus used.[1] All land in general use, such as pasture, local woods and water sources and local roads were under the control of the commune.[2]

One important area of technique discussed was general rotation of crops. Unfortunately there is almost no evidence on the nature of the rotations, or on how they were decided upon.

There was considerable pressure on the communes in the later twenties to concern themselves with matters of technique, and to become disseminators of agricultural knowledge. We shall see later how the commune came under increasing government pressure. Although the function of the communal gathering had always been to discuss largely parochial matters, it had inevitably been sensitive to the pressure of events in the wider world. The 'traditional' functions of the gathering were always performed within limits set by the government, and certainly for over half a century it had always been called upon to conduct the relations between peasant and government. Thus, while much may be made of the 'unchanging' nature of the Russian commune, outside events – most spectacularly the 1861 Reforms, the Stolypin reforms and the revolution – had their influence on what was possible for the commune. While the commune had greater freedom than ever when it came to exercising land-holding functions after the revolution, the Soviet government was attempting to limit its administrative functions. But even in its agricultural functions, the tensions between centre and commune were evident. These were nothing new in the Soviet period, and had always existed. The central government's interpretation of the commune's function was that it could be of use in a time of change and experimentation. Seen largely as an archaic institution, it was also recognised as the established method of agricultural organisation, and for a time government efforts were bent towards rationalisation, and encouraging the commune to perform wider functions in improving techniques among its members, taking part in marketing

[1] Moskovskaya Oblast, *Moskva i Moskovskaya Oblast'*, table 106.
[2] Land Code, arts. 51, 63.

by signing contracts, and even discussing collectivisation. It became clear that the commune could not be used as an instrument for change in this way; by its nature it was probably viewed by the peasants themselves as a means of perpetuating the relatively desirable position they had gained after the revolution.

2   ORGANISATION OF THE COMMUNE

a   *Membership and attendance*

Before the revolution, the commune was held to be a union of households. The communal gathering was not open to all villagers, but to the heads of the households forming the commune. The rigidly patriarchal family structure was being eroded before the revolution, and the 'decline of the household' had long been a theme of writers on the Russian countryside. While in many senses the revolution did not hit the countryside until 1929, it would seem that the freedom of choice of land holding and availability of more land after the revolution helped the younger members of a household to break away with land of their own. 'Decline of the household' was largely a matter of the family being less authoritarian. It did not mean decline in an economic sense. While the number of households increased, land available had also increased, so that the average size of holding rose from 1916 to 1927 from 25·2 to 33·1 acres.[1] The Land Code allowed partition of households, but instructed Guberniya Executive Committees to establish minimum size of holding to prevent excessive fragmentation. This would be enforced compulsorily with non-redistributable forms of holding, but a commune was left with the option of making a 'declaration of non-fragmentation', which could also be made voluntarily by households within the commune.[2]

While the Land Code retained the concept of the commune being a union of households, it counted as members all persons regardless of age or sex who were members of these households, and those over

[1] Cf. Danilov, *Istoriya SSSR* (1958), no. 3, pp. 94 ff. On fragmentation of household, see also Luzky, *Voprosy Istorii* (1956), pp. 59–71, and Sharapov, *Voprosy Istorii* (1957), no. 3, pp. 113–19.
[2] Land Code, arts. 85–7.

18 had full rights, which included attendance at the commune gathering, provided they worked the land.[1] This obviously reflected the views of the government on democratic control. Women and younger men were to be allowed a formal voice in the commune's affairs for the first time. This presented a further threat of erosion to the patriarchal family structure.

All the writers on the period agree that in fact tradition died hard, and that attendance at the commune gathering remained on the basis of households.[2] The legal position was that a quorum consisted of the heads, or representatives of not less than half the households, exactly the same as in Imperial legislation.[3] If a question of changing method of holding were under discussion, this was increased to two thirds, and at least half the members.[4] Thus the law used, on the whole, representatives of households as the criterion for attendance. This was different from the qualification for admission to the gathering, and for working the land, and tempered the legislator's aims with a concession to the existing local concept of the commune.

It seems that attendance rarely came up to this standard. Rezunov noted that attendance at the gathering was usually on the basis of households, and quoted Worker–Peasant Inspectorate research in 25 settlements in various areas. In 11 of these under 20% of members attended, in 12 attendance varied from 25–30% of members. The highest were 40–50% attendance.[5] In some areas it was the general rule for the head of a household to attend, or his eldest son, but for all members of the household to attend if a question of special relevance to their own holding was to be discussed.[6] Where

[1] Land Code, arts. 47–52. Draft for the Land Code had made membership of a 'land society' a condition for holding land. (All-Russian Central Executive Committee, 9th convocation, 4th session.)
[2] E.g. Kiselev, *Soveshchanie po voprosam sovetskogo stroitel'stva pri Prezidiume TsIKa*, p. 31, delivering report on commission on vik and rural soviet; Karp, *Izvestiya*, 15 December 1927, no. 287; Luzhin, *Organizatsiya sel'sovetov* (Moscow, 1930), p. 67; Kozhikov, *Na agrarnom fronte* (May 1928), no. 5, p. 64; Kirillov, 'Sel'sovet i skhod', in Yakovlev and Khatdevich, *VIK i sel'sovet* (Moscow, 1925).
[3] Land Code, art. 53; *Svod zakonov rossiiskoi imperii* (1910), Tom 9. 'Osoboe Prilozhenie', art. 63.
[4] Land Code, art. 53.
[5] M. Rezunov, *Selskie sovety i zemel'nye obshchestva* (Moscow, 1928), p. 42.
[6] Karp, *Izvestiya*, 15 December, 1927, no. 287. He notes this in Ulyanov, Penza and Tver guberniyas.

matters which did not concern the village directly were for discussion, attendance was very low. Statements that around 10% of villagers attended a commune would be consistent with at least half the heads of households attending.[1] Thus it would be wrong to deduce that low attendance at the gathering was necessarily a sign of weakness of the commune. The feeling of the peasantry about the commune would be indicated rather by the proportion of heads of households attending. Thus it was probably true that, as several writers suggest, women and young people stayed away, but this was probably in part because they did not look upon it as their business to attend. It would be interesting to know what proportion of the heads of newly formed households attended.

With the growth of rural soviets, co-operatives, and a rudimentary Party and Komsomol organisation, it may well have been that the young would turn to them, as offering more scope than the communal gathering. The complaint was often voiced that only the old attended the gathering. This, of course, was consistent with old heads of households attending. A letter from a peasant in Novgorod guberniya suggested that 'few people attend except the old, the young can't see any sense in it...there's a lot of noise at the meeting, but not much sense'.[2] It may well be that the young had always had this view of the gathering, but that only after the revolution were there other means of expression. If the Russian household was as authoritarian and patriarchal as pre-revolutionary writers suggested, the younger members would have had little opportunity to voice their opinions on the running of the household, let alone of the commune. Fragmentation of households may have given younger members of the commune an opportunity to voice their opinions, especially those who had been away to war, but the gathering remained a forum for heads of households. This would not be surprising if purely agricultural matters were discussed, as the head of a household could reasonably represent the views of his household on changes in his holding, as the household remained the basis of holding. When the commune discussed affairs of general local

[1] 'Soveshchanie pri prezidiume TsIK SSSR po voprosam sovetskogo stroitel'stva', *Materialy komissii po ukrepleniyu raboty sel'sovetov i vikov* (Moscow, 1925). Notes 'very low' attendance of 8–10% which could be thus interpreted (pp. 51–3).
[2] Kirpichev, *Prava skhoda i sel'soveta* (Moscow–Leningrad, 1928), p. 14.

significance, it may be thought there was some ground for the commune gathering being considered less than democratic, as one household with its age and sex differences would not be so likely to be of one mind. In a sense, representation by heads of households could be justified if the gathering was one of 'managers' of economic units to discuss technical problems. Where it dealt with wider issues there was a conflict with the new Soviet concept of democracy.

Women rarely attended the gathering even though it was legally possible for them to do so after 1922. Central Executive Committee research in 1925 showed that 2–3% of those attending certain gatherings were women.[1] Worker–Peasant Inspectorate came to the conclusion after research in 1926–7 that 'women play very little part in the commune gathering'.[2] There is no suggestion who those women were who went to the gathering, but they would probably be widows. Despite the efforts of propagandists, the situation changed little in the twenties. In 1930, Luzhin gave evidence for five unnamed guberniyas in an area where many men went away to work in the towns. 16% of people attending the gathering there were women. He noted that in purely agricultural areas, the proportion was much lower. Thus in Buzuluksk okrug (now in Chkalov oblast) in early 1928, no more than 7–8% of those attending the gathering were women.[3]

To say that women did not attend the gathering is not to suggest that they did not have a powerful influence in the commune. The traditional view of the Russian peasant's wife is of a woman firmly under the authority of her husband, who reinforced this with occasional beatings, and of a woman who could take little independent action outside the household. While husbands may have been strongly authoritarian, this is not to say that women could not have a considerable influence in the village.[4] Novels about the countryside in the twenties are largely set in non-communal areas, but they suggest that the women of a village were a strongly conservative

[1] T. I. Kruglov, *Osnovnye zadachi vika i sel'soveta* (Moscow, 1925).
[2] Quoted by Rezunov, *Sel'skie sovety i zemel'nye obshchestva*, p. 41.
[3] Luzhin, *Organizatsiya sel'sovetov*, p. 70.
[4] In a different context, Frankenberg in *Village on the Border* (Cohen and West, London, 1957), shows how women exerted powerful influence on village affairs without being represented on any of the formal committees of a Welsh border village.

element. There were probably considerable variations from area to area. The attempts by the Bolsheviks to organise 'women's peasant delegate meetings' possibly reflect not only an attempt to organise an under-privileged group to support the government, but also a realisation that women had influence over their menfolk.[1]

It is dangerous to quote a Ukrainian example to demonstrate a Russian situation, but the situation of women was similar there, and is well shown by Ivan Stadnyuk in his novel on the collectivisation period *People are not Angels*:[2]

The women of Kokhanivka are very stubborn. It seems that if they were given the power, they would certainly compel their husbands to do everything, even deliver their children. Every one of them is capable of persuading her husband at mid-day that it is mid-night: the man would believe it and go to sleep on the spot.

It was no wonder that, in spite of many unanimous decisions to organise a Society for Collective Working of the Land in the spring, every peasant went out to plough his fields instead of giving up his fields to the Society. This was because the men forgot to ask their wives' permission before voting in favour of the Society. And though later on communist youth went from house to house trying to make the men see sense, by then it was too late.

Sholokhov likewise portrayed his women as having real influence over their men, and plotting their manoeuvres by the village pump. Female opposition to collectivisation was not confined to the pages of novels. Letters from the 'twenty-five thousanders' sent out to the country from towns in 1929–30 show strong resistance from the women folk of the villages to which they went.[3] Thus, while women had no formal voice in the commune, and did not take advantage of their new rights of participation in the gathering after 1922 (if indeed they knew anything about them), their influence on communal affairs was probably considerable.

While these attempts were being made to widen the membership

---

1 Letters from factory workers in Tambov guberniya suggested they met most resistance to collectivisation from women. A typical comment was 'women's meetings would not agree in any way to collectives'. (Document 35, *Materialy po istorii SSSR* (Akademiya Nauk, Moscow, 1955), Tom 1.)
2 English translation by Spalding and Antonenko (Mono Press, London, 1963). Published in Neva, Leningrad, December 1962, p. 54.
3 Cf. *Materialy po istorii SSSR*, 1, 1955. Letters from Tambov region.

basis of the commune, suggestions were frequently made that there should be restriction on a 'class' basis. It was often argued that the gathering could do little more than endorse what the most influential peasants in the commune wanted. This was especially disturbing from a Soviet point of view, as the influence of the gathering was not confined to agricultural matters. We shall see later how this caused the very existence of the commune to be questioned. An attempt to counter kulak influence on local affairs via the gathering was made in 1927 by legally clarifying the distinction between the 'general meeting of citizens', which only people with soviet voting rights could attend, which was to be under the control of the local soviet, and the 'land society gathering', which was to continue on the basis of the Land Code. Whilst the decree made clear the legislators' dilemma, it was a dead letter.[1]

That there is nowhere to be found an example of a peasant being barred from a commune gathering on account of his wealth may suggest not so much that the kulak was all-powerful and able to force his will on other peasants, but rather that the feeling of local peasant solidarity was fairly strong at this time.

From a legal point of view, the kulak was in any case still free to wield influence on agricultural matters and obstruct change in the village, as his power in the commune, as a 'land society' was left undiminished. The XV Party Congress was very much concerned with differentiation in the countryside, and called on the Central Committee to take measures to ensure that persons without electoral rights be barred from voting at the land society meeting.[2] In winding up the debate on agriculture, Molotov remarked 'up to now, once we have enlivened a soviet, the kulak has dug in at the land society'.[3] Legislation on this was not forthcoming until the end of 1928, when those excluded from soviet voting rights were excluded from voting rights in the land society, and barred from holding office in the land society (commune), although they could still be members.[4] While this finished the anomaly in law of the rich peasant being

---

[1] 'Ob obshchikh sobraniyakh grazhdan (skhodakh)', SU 1927, no. 51, art. 33. Ts IK 14 March 1927. See below, p. 109.
[2] XV-yi S'ezd KPSS. Resolution 'O rabote v derevne', part IV, art. 8 V.
[3] *Sten. Otchet*, p. 1086.
[4] 'Obshchie nachala zemlepol'zovaniya i zemleustroistva', SZ 1928, no. 69, art. 642.

allowed to hold office in the commune while being excluded from the rural soviet, it is unlikely that it had any practical effect. Typical local comments were that 'at gatherings there are representatives of households regardless of inclusion in voting lists – nobody bothers about it' (Novgorod guberniya),[1] and 'Kulaks are excluded from voting at only one meeting in the year – rural soviet elections' (Ulyanov guberniya).[2]

Preoccupation with the 'class' basis of membership of the commune led also to pressure from the centre to widen membership to include rural labourers (batraks). Sukhanov had advocated admitting blacksmiths, teachers, and labourers on the ground that the rural community would come to form the lowest unit of government.[3] Such an extreme position was not essential to advocate commune membership for these groups. The problem was aired at the Conference of Peasant Members of the Central Executive Committee in 1926.[4] A delegate from Kursk was for the shepherd being allowed to vote at the gathering. In the nature of his work, he had no chance to have land of his own, being away in the fields throughout summer. He was none the less a vital member of rural society, and to exclude him from voting at the gathering was wrong. A delegate fron Ivanovo-Voznesensk was chary of the idea. It made sense for the landless labourer to vote, but he wondered what would happen in villages of the Central Industrial Region where perhaps 10 people worked on the land, and 80 in factories. Another delegate suggested a compromise. It would be rare for a blacksmith not to have at least a garden plot. Therefore it would be logical to allow him and others in a similar position to vote at the gathering on questions of communal amenities, and on pastureland topics if he had cattle, but to be barred from voting on questions of land holding and its distribution. The conference voted in favour of agricultural labourers, blacksmiths and similar rural workers being allowed to vote at commune gatherings. This view was endorsed by Central Executive Committee in the December 1928 debate, where Milyutin

---

[1] Kozhikov, *Na agrarnom fronte* (1928), no. 5, section 6.
[2] Karp in *Izvestiya*, 15 December 1927, no. 287.
[3] 'Obshchina v sovetskom agrarnom zakonodatelstve', *Na agrarnom fronte* (1926), no. 11–12, pp. 98–109.
[4] Reported in Ibid. pp. 127 ff.

emphasised that this would bring rural soviet and commune on a similar basis for membership. The resulting decree allowed membership to 'people who are not members of peasant households, but who partake with their own labour in the agriculture of a given land society, or of member households, or who serve them, if these people have soviet voting rights (agricultural labourers, shepherds, blacksmiths, etc.)'.[1] It is not clear whether this included the village intelligentsia. Milyutin had brought up the question, but felt that some degree of participation in production should be a qualification.[2] The aim was to transform the commune towards collective farming by 'improving' the class structure of the commune.[3] In the event, mass collectivisation came too soon for the law to have any effect.

Joining and leaving the commune by peasants with land was at the discretion of the commune gathering.[4] Where a household or individual applying for membership had no land, he could only be admitted with the commune's agreement. If the commune had spare land, the applicant could be admitted by order of the land organs.[5] In 1930 this requirement was altered to meet the spirit of the times. A commune could be forced to give up land which was unused or badly cultivated. If removal of such land from the society to collective or state farms were impracticable, the raion land organs could force the commune to receive into its membership 'citizens needing land'.[6] (An indication that the commune may have continued well into 1930 is that a minor modification to this was confirmed as late as December 1930.)[7]

If the commune changed to a different form of holding, those who

[1] 'Obshchie nachala zemlepol'zovaniya i zemleustroistva', art. 486.
[2] TsIK SSSR, 4-yi sozyv, 4-ya sessiya. December 1928. *Sten. Otchet*, Bulletin 12, pp. 73–7.
[3] Karp, *Izvestiya*, 15 December 1927.
[4] Land Code, 1922, art. 51b. This section is based on Land Code arts. 51, 91, 17, 19, 60, 61, 137–40.
[5] Although the Land Code originally made no qualifications about who could hold land, provided they worked it themselves, an amendment to article 9 in May 1925 (SU 1925, no. 29, art. 206) forbade former landlords and large-scale landowners to hold land in a guberniya where they formerly held land. A fuller decree (SZ 1925, no. 21, art. 136), claimed there was a tendency for old landlord–peasant relations to remain, and counterrevolutionary tendencies to breed where a landlord held land in his former area.
[6] SU 1930, no. 1, art. 1.
[7] SU 1930, no. 50, art. 596. See below, p. 237.

disagreed with the change could leave and be given their share of commune land in one place. In the case of a member leaving his household and commune for more than two crop rotations he was on his return given spare land, or, if there were none, given equal standing with other members of the commune at the next redistribution. If he were away for less than two rotations, his share of land remained with his household. Likewise his household would retain his share if he were called away for military service, or elected to soviet or other social responsibilities.

A member could be expelled temporarily by the commune if he left land untended without good cause, or rented out his plot illegally. Such expulsion was for a maximum of one crop rotation. Cases of bad husbandry could be punished similarly by decision of the commune, or on the initiative of the land organs. In 1928–9 the Peoples Commissariat of Agriculture ordered krai and oblast land boards to encourage rural soviets to exercise strict supervision over decisions of the land societies on this question (of reducing sown area). Apparently such cases were widespread.[1]

Withdrawal from the existing form of holding by a household, or group of households with their share of land was possible at any time with the agreement of the gathering. Withdrawal with land was possible without the agreement of the gathering at a time of general redistribution. If there was no general redistribution withdrawal with land was allowed if demanded by no less than one fifth of the households in the commune, and no less than 50 households in a commune of over 250 households. This was the same proportion as under the Stolypin reforms. Separation of any number of households with the agreement of the gathering was possible if the commune had vacated isolated land, and if a general redistribution would not be needed as a result. After 1928, with the increased emphasis on collective farming, it was possible for a group of households to leave with land at any time if they wished to form a collective farm.[2]

Households leaving the commune to hold their land in enclosed farms did not always sever all links with the commune. Of 6,804

---

[1] Danilov, *Istoriya SSSR* (1958), no. 3, p. 126, quotes this circular from Ts GAOR i SS, f 5201, op 6, d 76, l 12.　　[2] Decree of Ts IK 30 April 1928. SU no. 50, art. 378.

such households in October 1925, 2·6% claimed to be members of a 'land society', and still counted themselves members of the commune from which they had withdrawn 'their' land.[1] This gives substance to the point made earlier when discussing the north west,[2] that a peasant household was not either a member or not a member of the commune, but that peasants either participated or did not participate in the commune for certain functions. Where a household did not participate in the major functions, and was less involved in communal affairs, it would not completely cease to be a member.

Legislation on conditions of leaving the commune has varied with the government's view of the desirability of communal holding. The Stolypin reform had eased the conditions, yet there was a flow back into the commune after the revolution which was not reversed to any large extent by the restitution of the 'Stolypin' conditions as far as freedom to leave the commune without consent of all the commune was concerned.[3]

b   *Frequency of meeting*

There was no legal definition of how often the commune gathering should meet, and there is little evidence to show how often gatherings were in fact held. Such evidence as there is was concerned to use this as an indicator of the rivalry between rural soviet and commune. It was noted that there was a great diversity of frequency.[4] There are cases reported of one or more per week.[5] Several writers point out the greater frequency of commune gatherings compared with rural soviet gatherings over a given period. The legal requirement for the rural soviet was not less than once every 2 weeks.[6] Kozhikov noted the greater frequency of commune gatherings in Vologda, Vladimir, Urals and North Caucasus, and cited two examples in Tambov guberniya. There Peresipinsk rural soviet and its sections met

[1] Danilov, *Istoniya SSSR* (1958), no. 3, p. 97. Ts GAOR i SS, f 478, op 59, d 26, ll 19–20.   [2] See above, p. 33.
[3] On the actual numbers transferring to non-redistributable forms of holding, see p. 189.
[4] 'Soveshchanie pri prezidiume Ts IK SSSR po voprosam sovetskogo stroitel'stva', *Materialy komissii po ukrepleniyu raboty sel'sovetov i vikov* (Moscow, 1925), p. 52.
[5] Kirillov, 'Sel'sovet i skhod'. He notes in Ruzdelinsk raion, 71 per annum; in Ivanovo Voznesensk guberniya, 'one a week' in 1924.
[6] 'Polozhenie o sel'sovetakh', 16 October 1924, art. 17.

eight times, and discussed 17 questions, while the commune gathering met 71 times and discussed 200 questions.[1] Rezunov gave similar evidence for Tula guberniya. In 22 raions, there were 5,166 rural soviet plenums, while there were 19,242 commune gatherings.[2] Such figures could be rather misleading in themselves as indications of relative strength, as in most areas there were several communes to one rural soviet.[3] Where a commune covered a large area, it seems gatherings of part of the commune were called as well as general commune gatherings. This was the case in North Caucasus where both individual hamlets, and the 'stanitsa' as a whole, held meetings.[4] We have no evidence of how these related to each other. If gatherings were as frequent as once a week, it is doubtful whether there would have been a quorum of members, especially at busy times of the agricultural year. In any case, the distinction between a gathering proper, and a group of peasants meeting informally after work, was probably not a very clear one. The frequency of meeting is in part explained by the commune not having a well developed system of delegation to its officers. The delegated powers of the elder or executive of the commune were nothing like so great as those of the rural soviet chairman and secretary, whose function was rather different

c *Officers of the commune*

Before the revolution the gathering elected its elder (starosta) to act as chairman at the gathering, and represent the commune in its dealings with outside bodies. According to law, his functions were to call and dismiss the gathering, and maintain order; put to the gathering all matters concerning the needs of the commune; implement decisions of the gathering, and orders from the volost about land use of the commune members; see to the integrity of boundary marks; supervise maintenance of roads; supervise payment of taxes, and act as collector where appropriate; compel peasants to fulfill agreements between each other; inform the volost

1 Kozhikov, 'Zemel'noe obshchestvo i sel'skii sovet', *Na agrarnom fronte* (May 1928), no. 5, p. 64.
2 Rezunov, *Sel'skie sovety i zemel'nye obshchestva*, p. 33.
3 See below, p. 88.
4 Kirillov, 'Sel'sovet i skhod', likewise Kirpichev, *Prava skoda i sel'soveta*.

elder (starshina) of any reason why he should not issue permit to reside in, or leave the commune; supervision, in manner decided by the gathering, of the commune's finances, and of communal grain reserves; take measures for the maintenance of law and order, and fulfill all legal demands of higher authorities.[1] He was elected from heads of households for a maximum of three years. A head of household could not refuse election unless over 60 years old, or if he had any other excuse the gathering found reasonable.[2] While in form the elder was at the apex of a patriarchal system, in fact the elder seems to have exerted no special authority among his fellows beyond that of keeping a semblance of order, and the unpopular task of seeing to tax collection. The position was usually one that no one wanted to fill, and only those with a large household would have the time to fill. It was said that the man who agreed to take on the position was drunk at the time.[3] The position was probably not the means by which the more prosperous peasantry could enforce their will.

The function which the elected officer performed after the revolution probably did not change greatly. However, the law did make some changes. Under the Land Code, the commune gathering was to elect officials to carry out day-to-day administration. They were to be known as 'agents for land affairs' (upolnomochennye po zemel'nym delam).[4] It is interesting that no mention was made in the Code of the office of elder. It may be that the new term was used to emphasise the break with the old, as the gathering was now more democratically organised. The Code also mentioned that the gathering would have a chairman and secretary.[5] No mention was made of the duties of any of these officers. Provision was made that where the commune and rural soviet coincided in area, the executive work of the commune could be undertaken by the rural soviet.[6] (We shall see in the following chapter that this rarely happened.) From 1928 on, it was legally possible for a commune to entrust its executive work to the rural soviet if it wished, regardless of boundaries.[7]

[1] *Svod zakonov rossiiskoi imperii*, tom 9, pp. 74–9.   [2] Ibid. pp. 188–9.
[3] Cf. Hubbard, *The economics of Soviet agriculture* (Macmillan, London, 1939), introduction.
[4] Article 50. This should not be confused with the office of sel'skii ispolnitel', whose function was to enforce law and order.   [5] Art. 56.
[6] Art. 50, note.   [7] 'Obshchie nachala zemlepol'zovaniya' already quoted, art. 50.

A little more light is thrown on what the agents were in law supposed to do by a draft 'Statute of a Land Society' published in 1924 in Simferopol.[1] This is not necessarily a reflection of the actual situation, but the interpretation placed on the Land Code by the local authority. The statute goes into the functions of agents in much more detail than the Local Code. They were to be elected by the gathering, and paid by the commune (the elder had been unpaid). The chairman of the gathering could not be an agent, but the statute has little to say on what function the chairman and secretary of the gathering were to perform. The agents were to lead the affairs of the society, and act on its behalf without the need for special authority in its relations with its own members, and with outside people and institutions. They were to take a leading role in spreading agricultural knowledge, maintain close contact with organisations dedicated to improving land use, and help strengthen agricultural co-operatives. In this way, they were seen as a means of influencing the commune to change. They would thus act as agents in urging the commune to change in a way no outsider could hope to do.

The internal duties of the agents were given in some detail. They were to be responsible for drafting projects and rules about holding of land, to set them before the gathering, and register their decisions with the appropriate authority. They were responsible for looking after the commune's undistributed land and property. They were to see that the land which had been redistributed was being properly cultivated. The forests, roads and waters near the commune were to be looked after by them in co-operation with the appropriate authorities. They were to look after the finances. In short, where the statute of the society required action, the agents were to carry it out.

There was to be a 'Council of Agents' (Sovet Upolnomochennykh), consisting of three full and two candidate members, elected by the commune gathering. Their term of office was one year. Perhaps an indication of the official view of their function was that they were to be removed from office on the instigation of the Raion Land

[1] A collection of documents published without a title in Simferopol, 1924. They included: (1) 'Uchreditel'nyi prigovor zemel'nogo obshchestva'; (2) 'Spisok chlenov zemel'nogo obshchestva'; (3) 'Ustav zemel'nogo obshchestva', art. 22–35, 30–40, 51 quoted here; (4) 'Prigovor zemel'nogo obshchestva'.

The commune: function and organisation

Department, or of the commune gathering with the permission of the Raion Land Department.

There are references to agents at work in particular areas. The views of the work these officers performed varied. At the one extreme, they were seen as a reincarnation of the elder. The movement to strengthen rural soviets meant these bodies were at an increasing distance from individual hamlets or communes. The power of the agent could be correspondingly great. Kirillov noted that 'the agents are nearest to the peasant, and are defenders of peasant interests, but the rural soviet is a distant institution set up to fulfil state obligations'. He equated this with 'the old system of elders'.[1] He noted they acted on the initiative of the gathering, and disregarded the rural soviet. An émigré writer said that in Ivanovo-Voznesensk guberniya, these officials were called elders, and were usually not rural soviet members.[2]

In some instances agents did keep the rural soviet informed of what the commune had decided. The legal position was confused because of the artificiality of the Law on Village Meetings. After 1927 they were artificially divided, in theory, into land society gathering and general meeting of citizens, the former having no obligation to report to the rural soviet, the latter very much under its control. In many areas the agents of the commune made their reports to the rural soviets, which were passive recipients of information about what had been done.[3] There is some suggestion in places that they went as delegates from the commune to the rural soviet.[4] A bone of contention in at least one area (Kostroma guberniya) was that they were better paid than the rural soviet chairman.[5] Paying the elder was not a practice of the commune before the revolution. On the whole it seems difficult to differentiate in fact between elder and agent. There were variations. In one village in North Caucasus, agents were elected for certain specific tasks.[6] The responsibility for organising self-taxation to meet local needs was placed on the agents

[1] Kirillov, 'Sel'sovet i skhod', p. 54.
[2] Timashev, *Sovremennye zapiski* (Paris, 1928), XXXIV, 453.
[3] Kozhikov, *Na agrarnom fronte* (1928).
[4] *Materialy komissii po ukrepleniyu raboty sel'sovetov i vikov. Soveshchanie po voprosam sovetskogo stroitel'stva pri TsIK* (1925), p. 56.
[5] Timashev, *Sovremennye zapiski*, p. 495.
[6] Kirillov, 'Sel'sovet i skhod', p. 53.

Function and organisation

by a decree of North Caucasus Krai Executive Committee in 1926.[1] There are no more precise indications whether the position of the agent differed from that of the elder.

There is some confusion in the literature on the countryside, as rural soviets, where they encompassed several settlements, could appoint agents (upolnomochennye) from the Soviet to the settlements.[2] This was obviously a rather different official from the agent of the commune, but a confusion is apparent in some writers which probably reflects a rather tangled local situation. It was suggested by some that the same person should carry out both offices. Where this did happen, it seems that the desired result of stronger rural soviet control over the commune was not achieved, but rather the reverse.[3] The idea that the agent of the commune could be an instrument for the rural soviet to control the commune gained currency in the later twenties. Luzhin gave an example of what, to his regret, was one of the few rural soviets conducting its business 'properly' in this respect (his view had no basis in the law of this time). Novosel'skii rural soviet in Ryazan okrug 'agreed on measures for the gathering beforehand with the land society agent'.[4]

It appears that in only one area did the land societies hand over their executive powers to the rural soviets, as empowered by the Land Code, to any large extent. This was the Volga German Republic, where the office of land society agent was abolished. What this meant in terms of local distribution of authority is not clear. However, this was an area where communal holding was not very common, which suggests that a land society was not a very powerful institution where it did not have the economic basis of communal land holding.[5]

We have seen that the 1928 'General Foundations of Land Holding and Land Use Measures' did give the commune the possibility of entrusting its executive affairs to a rural soviet even where the two did not coincide in area.[6] Milyutin, in introducing a

[1] Kruglov, 'Derevenskie obshchestvennye kapitaly', *Izvestiya*, 30 October 1926.
[2] 'Polozheniye o sel'sovetakh', 16 October 1924, art. 14, note 2. SU 1924, no. 82, art. 827. Cf. also SU 1927, no. 44, art. 284, whereby settlements of 50–100 inhabitants had a rural soviet member appointed as agent of rural soviet to the settlement.
[3] M. Ustinov, 'Zemel'noe obshchestvo i sel'sovet', *Izvestiya*, 22 August 1929.
[4] Luzhin, *Organizatsiya sel'sovetov*, p. 64.
[5] Rezunov, *Sel'skie sovety i zemel'nye obshchestva*, p. 59.   [6] See above, p. 78.

discussion on the project for this law, suggested this would be a useful means of control by the rural soviet. He thought this would work by the commune electing as its agents members of the rural soviet, who would be given authority to look after the commune's affairs.[1] He strenuously denied that this meant replacing the management of the commune by that of the rural soviet. To do so, he claimed, would be to make a similar mistake to that of replacing the management of collective farms by the rural soviet. They would remain distinct bodies. None the less, it would seem that there is only a very fine, if not negligible, distinction between abolishing the office of agent, and having them as an integral part of the rural soviet.

Who became agent of a commune is an impossible question to answer. It is doubtful if the richer peasants took on this function. More likely it would be less prosperous peasants who were unlikely to step out of line with the wishes of the economically more influential peasants. This was interpreted by some Soviet commentators as presenting a threat to the Soviets along class lines. In fact, as we shall see, the threat to the rural soviet did not come specifically from the richer peasants, although this latter group no doubt played a leading role.[2] How far the agents exerted any great degree of initiative is not clear. If they were, as the elder was in all probability, content to reflect the will of the commune gathering, their power would derive from the pressures within the commune. The soviet view was that they should perform a more positive role in linking the commune with institutions outside, and in exerting pressure for improved methods in agriculture. The frequency of communal meetings suggests they had no great room for exercising discretion, but that in their dealings with outside bodies they were able to reflect the not inconsiderable power which the commune exercised as an institution, for reasons we will examine in the following chapter.

Our conclusions must remain tentative. We have noted the confusion in the literature between the office of agent of the commune and agent of the rural soviet. Later there was a further official, the

[1] Ts IK SSSR, 4-yi sozyv, April 1928. *Sten. Otchet*, p. 761.
[2] See below, p. 162ff.

'agricultural agent'. He was appointed by the rural soviet explicitly to secure improved cultivation in the commune and hasten collectivisation.[1] The Russian village did not have a tradition of a powerful formal organisation. It could be that this changed as a result of the pressure of the rural soviets – their formal organisation would perhaps need to be confronted by a rather more formalised organisation of the gathering. Probably the arrangements were as numerous as there were villages in Russia. These offices worked at the nodal point in relations between commune and rural soviet, old and new, but little is known of how they came to be elected, who was elected, how they worked, or what influence they had within the commune. We now turn to examining in more detail the nature of the confrontation between the commune and the rural soviet.

[1] See below, p. 198.

PART II

THE COMMUNE
AND SOVIET SOCIETY

3

THE COMMUNE AND THE SOVIET
NETWORK

The confused relationship between the rural soviet and the commune expresses in a microcosm one of the central dilemmas of the Bolshevik government: its relationship to the peasantry. The revolution had given a new burst of life to peasant organs of self-government. In this local sense, the peasantry had become increasingly politically active. The government was uncertain how far to concede to peasant economic demands. It tried to use the rural soviets as a means of gaining peasant support for, or at least interest in, its policies. Nominally the rural soviet was to interest itself in most matters of local administration. In fact it was usually weak and ineffective. Throughout the twenties the government wrestled with the problem of whether to allow the commune its head, or oust it by securing its submission to, or replacement by the rural soviet. For much of our period, the government's decisions on the question did not greatly affect the local situation. This lack of central influence over the local situation was one, albeit a minor one, of the pressures which led to enforced collectivisation. The decision of the government to confront the peasantry, rather than continue in stratagems to win their support, meant the end of the commune with the setting up of a completely new form of agricultural organisation. The economic and political decisions meant a complete change in the organisational setting in which the conflict of interests of peasant and government was played out.

I RURAL SOVIET, SETTLEMENT AND COMMUNE: SIZE

We have already noted that the areas of rural soviet and commune rarely coincided. It is difficult to make any precise comparison of size for lack of accurate numbers of communes both in particular areas and in the RSFSR as a whole.

The most likely estimate for the number of communes in the

mid-twenties in the RSFSR is around 319,000.[1] On the basis of this, Milyutin concluded that there were four land societies to one rural soviet.[2] It seems likely that he was confusing statistics for USSR and RSFSR, as there were 70,000 rural soviets in the USSR and 53,000 in the RSFSR in 1926.[3] There would then be six land societies to each rural soviet. Even on these assumptions, this figure is not quite accurate, as one would need to deduct the number of rural soviets in areas of non-communal land holding. This would only make a slight difference. Some confirmation that such a comparison is of the right order of magnitude is provided by a statement in 1927 that 'there are on average 3–5 land societies to each rural soviet'.[4]

More exact comparison is difficult, as the situation was changing over time. In the interests of efficiency the number of rural soviets was being reduced. It is difficult to establish the number of rural soviets before 1923. One suggestion was that they coincided in area with the rural societies, the lowest pre-revolutionary administrative unit, of which there were said to be 88,992 in 1915. However, its proponent, Zaitsev, gave no really good grounds for making this assumption, merely stating that 'being unable to estimate the number of rural soviets formed in settlements without rural societies, we will take the latter as the initial figure and reckon that the number of rural soviets in the first years of soviet power was equal to the number of rural societies'.[5] Rural societies usually covered a rather larger area than the commune and rural settlement. They were never a particularly thriving institution, and it would be surprising if the early rural soviets coincided in area with them. It would seem more likely that in the early days of rural soviets they coincided sometimes with the commune, as Kiselev has suggested,[6] and sometimes with the settlement. There was probably considerable variation from area to area, according to conditions under which the rural soviet was formed.

---

[1] See above, p. 11.   [2] See above, p. 11.
[3] Ts SU SSSR, *Mestnye btudzhety za 1926–7* (Moscow, 1929), pp. 8–10.
[4] Quoted in *Khozyaistvo i upravlenie* (1927), no. 11–12. Figures to support the statement are not given.
[5] P. Zaitsev, *Printsipy i praktika organizatsii sel'sovetov. Sovetskoe stroitel'stvo, Sbornik no.* 50 (Moscow, 1926), p. 146.
[6] Speech to XIV All-Russian Congress of Soviets, Kiselev.

The commune and the soviet network

From 1922 to 1924 there was a movement to concentrate rural soviets. In 1923 there were 80,000 in the RSFSR.[1] From 1926 onwards the number remained fairly steady, and by January 1929 there were 55,340 rural soviets in the RSFSR.[2] At the same time that the number of rural soviets was falling the number of communes was rising. One feature of land use measures was breaking up large communes, but it is not possible to estimate the number of 'new' communes. The effect of these policies was to divorce the commune from the rural soviet geographically to an ever increasing extent, at a time when the aim was to increase administrative control by the rural soviet.

The relationship between commune and settlement is a difficult one to establish. The rural settlement was an administrative unit whose identity was not always easy to clarify. In practice it was taken to be any separately identifiable group of houses and building. Statistics on this basis were of very variable quality from area to area.[3] The difference between an urban and a rural settlement was held to be that an urban settlement had over 1,000 population, with less than 25% of its inhabitants engaged in agriculture.[4] The rural settlement was thus likely to have been what was regarded locally as the village. While this may have in many areas have corresponded to the commune, this was by no means always so. A settlement was a unit of habitation, whereas the commune was a unit of land holding. The settlement could be a part of a complex land holding unit, the multi-settlement commune. Also inhabitants of a single settlement could be members of two or more different communes, often as a result of historical conditions with holdings having been on the territory of two or more landlords. These different conditions lead to confusion in the use of the word. Reference could be made to a settlement in the purely administrative sense of a unit of population, but a rather broader use is possible, referring to the settlement as the group of buildings plus the land and other holdings attached

[1] A. Lepeshkin, *Mestnye organy vlasti sovetskogo gosudarstva 1921–36* (Moscow, 1959), p. 59.
[2] See below, Table 3.3, p. 92.
[3] See S. A. Kovalev, *Sel'skoe rasselenie* (Moscow State University, Moscow, 1963), p. 10.
[4] Narodnyi Komissariat Vnutrennykh Del SSSR (NKVD), *Administrativno-territorial'-noe delenie SSSR* (Moscow, 1929), introduction.

The commune and soviet society

to them. This, however, is not strictly speaking a unit of land holding, as the inhabitants could all be part of a larger unit (commune),
or be members of different units. On occasion, the word settlement
is used in a loose way to describe a unit of land holding, and the
interchangeable use of 'land society' and 'settlement' may well have
been a local usage. (For example, in the figures for the Urals quoted
below, settlement and land societies are equated.) At other times,
one suspects a real confusion existed in the mind of those using the
terms. Thus a speaker at the Central Executive Committee remarked
that 'in the North and Central guberniyas there are 27–35 settlements per rural soviet' in a context which suggested he meant land
societies per rural soviet.[1]

Local variations are so considerable that to give overall statistics
for the RSFSR has little real meaning. One may just note the position, shown in Table 3.1:

Table 3.1

Mid-twenties communes	Rural settlements 1 January 1929	Rural soviets 1 January 1929
319,000	476,641	55,340

We have some indications for particular areas summarised in Table
3.2.

Too much weight should not be placed on a break down into such
large areas, as large variations could well be disguised by our
averages. Thus, with the North Caucasus krai, one source stated that
in 1927 there were 30–35 land societies per rural soviet,[2] while
another suggested that the North Caucasus was one of the few
places where the boundaries of land society and rural soviet coincided.[3] The only area for which we have a more detailed break
down is the Mid-Volga krai. Although the size of commune in the
area varied from 58 to 139 households according to district, the

[1] Levenets, Ts IK SSSR, 4-yi sozyv, 4-ya sessiya. Dec. 1928. *Sten. Otchet, Bull.* 17, p. 13.
[2] Verlinskii and Viktorov in *Khozyaistvo i upravlenie*, 11–12, 1927.
[3] Karp, *Izvestiya*, 15 December 1929, no. 287.

Table 3.2

	Communes	Rural settlements	Rural soviets	Rural settlements per Commune	Rural settlements per Rural soviet	Communes per rural soviet
Moscow guberniya[a] 1929	7,000	9,400	2,900	1·3	3·3	2·4
Tambov guberniya[b] 1925	3,715	5,100	736	1·3	7	5
Mid-Volga krai[c] 1 January 1930	16,574	11,355	3,542	0·7	3·2	4·7
North Caucasus krai[d]	15,358	14,385	1,994	1	7·8	7·7

[a] Assuming land societies = communes. Source for number of land societies is statistical handbook for the guberniya, quoted above, p. 35. Source for rural settlements and rural soviets: NKVD, *Administrativno-territorial'noe delenie SSSR* (1929), with a proportionate reduction from the latter to allow for Lenin uezd, which was not included in the land society figures.

[b] For figure for communes, see above, p. 40. For rural settlements and rural soviets, table in Luzhin, *Ot volosti k raionu* (Moscow, 1928), p. 103.

[c] For figure for communes, see above, p. 43. For rural settlements and rural soviets, NKVD *Administrativno-territorial'noe delenie SSSR* (1930), table XII. The local handbook quoted gives 12,527 rural settlements, which leads to 0·8 settlements per commune and 3·5 rural settlements per rural soviet.

[d] For figure for communes, see Danilov, *Istoriya SSSR* (1958), no. 3, p. 123. For rural settlements and rural soviets, NKVD, *Administrativno-territorial'noe delenie SSSR* (1929).

ratio of commune to rural settlement did not vary to such a large extent, being 1.1–1.6 per rural settlement.[1]

The only safe general conclusion on the relationship between communes and other units is that in most areas there were several communes to each rural soviet. There was such a wide variety of cases of relationship between rural settlement and commune that any general statement would be meaningless.

The relationship between rural soviet and rural settlement in 1929 is shown in Table 3.3 and in the maps (2–4) derived from it.

Rural soviets were largest in terms of population in the north and south east. In the north, this was because they linked a large number of small settlements, whereas in the south east there were a small number of large settlements to each rural soviet.

Size of rural settlement, in terms of population, rises from the

[1] See above, p. 43.

Table 3.3 *Rural soviets, Rural centres of population: their size and relationship, 1 January 1929*
Figures in cols. (1) (2) (3) from *Administrativno-territorial'noe delenie SSSR*, NKVD 1929. Cols. (4) (5) (6) derived therefrom.

	Rural soviets	Rural centres of population	Rural population 1926 (in thousands)	Population per rural soviet	Population per rural centre of population	Centres of population per rural soviet
USSR	72,163	599,475	123,556	1,700	200	8
RSFSR	55,340	476,641	85,233	1,500	180	9
Belorussian SSR	1,419	38,060	4,170	2,900	110	27
Ukrainian SSR	10,621	54,999	24,372	2,300	440	5
North krai	981	23,720	2,150	2,200	90	24
Archangel guberniya	260	3,026	340	1,300	100	12
Vologda guberniya	445	10,544	963	2,200	90	23
Komi Autonomous Republic	36	1,323	202	5,600	150	37
North Dvina guberniya	240	8,827	645	2,700	70	37
Leningrad-Karelia raion	2,666	62,737	4,459	1,700	70	24
Leningrad oblast (excluding city)	2,475	59,884	4,225	1,700	70	24
Karelian ASSR	191	2,853	237	1,200	80	15
Western oblast	3,379	35,754	4,894	1,400	140	11
Bryansk guberniya	1,109	8,431	1,755	1,600	210	8
Kaluga guberniya	923	8,382	1,041	1,100	120	9
Smolensk guberniya	1,347	18,941	2,099	1,600	110	14
Central Industrial oblast	6,259	40,741	7,181	1,100	170	7
Moscow guberniya (excluding city)	3,180	10,373	1,957	600	190	3
Ryazan guberniya	1,402	5,342	2,021	1,400	380	4
Tver guberniya	810	19,899	1,964	2,400	100	25
Tula guberniya	867	5,177	1,238	1,400	240	6
Central Black Earth oblast	4,821	24,107	10,306	2,100	430	5

Nizhnii Novgorod oblast	2,812	37,881	5,614	2,000	150	13
Vyatka guberniya	1,275	20,907	2,100	1,600	100	16
Nizhgorod guberniya	993	10,241	2,369	2,400	230	10
Vot AR	349	4,163	680	2,000	160	12
Mari AR	195	2,678	2,464	1,300	90	14
Ivanovo Voznesensk oblast	3,172	32,809	3,749	1,200	110	10
Vladimir guberniya	1,544	4,800	1,081	700	230	3
Ivanovo Voznesensk guberniya	655	7,503	869	1,300	120	11
Kostroma guberniya	405	8,163	707	1,500	90	17
Yaroslavl' guberniya	508	12,343	1,092	2,100	90	24
Urals oblast	3,144	26,439	5,637	1,800	210	8
Mid-Volga krai	7,691	18,895	9,476	1,200	500	2
Mid-Volga oblast	4,233	11,327	6,301	1,500	550	3
Tatar ASSR	2,835	5,079	2,325	800	450	2
Chuvash ASSR	623	2,489	850	1,200	300	4
Lower Volga krai	2,844	9,778	4,477	1,500	460	3
8 Okrugy	2,532	7,814	3,816	1,500	490	3
Kalmyk autonomous oblast	30	619	150	5,000	240	20
Volga German ASSR	282	845	511	1,800	600	3
Crimean ASSR	404	2,665	398	1,000	150	6
North Caucasus krai	1,994	14,835	6,902	3,500	470	7

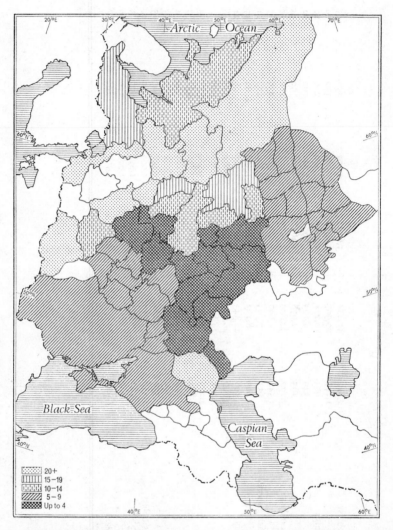

Map 2. Rural settlements per rural soviet, 1 January 1929. SOURCE: Table 3.3.

Boundaries on Maps 2–4 differ from those shown on Map 1 to allow for changes in administrative areas by 1929.

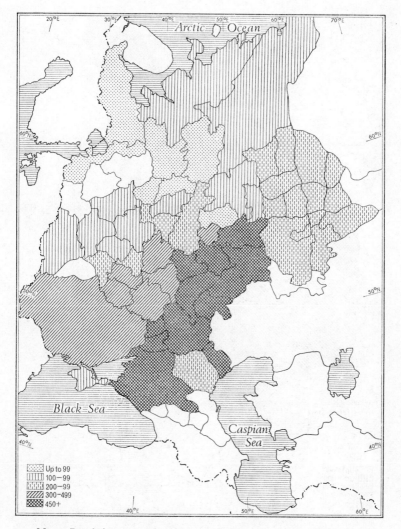

Map 3. Population per rural settlement, 1 January 1929. SOURCE: Table 3.3.

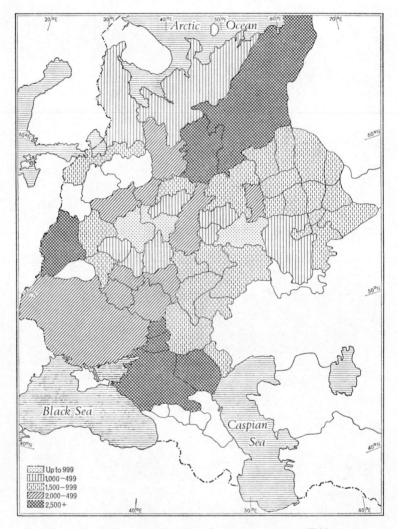

Map 4. Population per rural soviet, 1 January 1929. SOURCE: Table 3.3.

north west, with small settlements in marsh and forest, through the Central Black Earth regions, to the largest settlements in the south east. Our knowledge of rural soviets is not extensive enough for any attempt at suggesting whether rural soviets were stronger where they had a large or small number of settlements, and, in any case, this would probably not have been the critical variable. Likewise, it is very tempting to relate these patterns to the land holding pattern, and make certain general statements, but it is best to refrain, as any general statement conceals too many local variables about which we do not have sufficient information.

2   THE LEGAL POSITION IN 1924

The system of rural soviets was, by its nature, a threat to the system of peasant self-government embodied in the communes. While the threat was not clearly apparent in the chaos of the years immediately following the revolution, the position began to crystallise in the early years of N.E.P. In view of the numbers of peasants leaving the commune in the pre-war years, one must be wary of describing the commune as the established, traditional form of local self-government. None the less in many areas the commune did emerge after the revolution as the most significant local organ of government. This position was strengthened with the crumbling of the less orthodox peasant soviets which sprang up after the revolution. Professor Taniuchi has traced the emergence of this pattern in the early post-revolutionary years.[1]

The dual functions of the commune, agricultural organisation and local self-government, meant that there were two major ways in which the newly established network of rural soviets potentially encroached on its preserves.

The commune had acted as the lowest organ of government in pre-revolutionary times. Its concerns were, it is true, very minor and restricted. It acted as intermediary between the peasant household and the government, and was entrusted with administering its own internal affairs. Thus the commune gathering had a variety of tasks

---

[1] Unpublished manuscript, in English, of a book in Japanese. See also, for the later period, his monograph *The village gathering in Russia in the mid-twenties*, Soviet and Eastern European Monograph No. 1. Centre for Russian and East European Studies (University of Birmingham, 1968).

to perform. It was responsible for passport matters, and could control movement to and from the village. It discussed social needs, the improvement of local amenities, and the question of literacy. It appointed guardians for orphaned children. It would organise savings banks, and discuss liability for military service. The elder supervised maintenance of roads and bridges. He was responsible for keeping law and order, and could pass sentence on petty offenders. Most important of all, the commune apportioned all taxes.[1]

While the gathering was an organ of local self-government in the sense of administering affairs within its own boundaries, its competence was very restricted. It had neither legal authority to discuss, nor power to change, the overall framework within which it worked. The guberniya and uezd authorities, who confirmed its decisions, could use the meeting as a sounding board for peasant feelings through the reports of the local officials (zemskii nachal'nik and mirnyi posrednik), but there was no official machinery for presenting directly the views of the commune on national issues, or issues which affected it closely. The democracy of the commune consisted in administering decisions taken at higher levels, and working out local arrangements within the given framework. The volost gathering had no greater powers than the commune gathering. It elected representatives to the zemstvo until 1890, after which one candidate was selected by the governor.

The rural soviets were entrusted with most of these administrative functions formerly performed by the commune. In practice the position of the rural soviets in relation to higher organs of government may have worked out little differently from that of the commune. In theory, the position was quite different. The gathering was at the foot of a chain of command, while the rural soviet was intended to involve the peasantry in the wider affairs of government. While in practice the machinery did not involve the peasantry in decision-making at the higher levels, at least the rural soviet was

[1] *Svod zakonov rossiiskoi imperii*, tom 9, kniga I, st. 62–4, 74. This section refers to the rural society (sel'skoe obshchestvo) rather than the commune, but in practice the distinction was often very blurred and this section gives redistribution of land as a rural society function. For a detailed discussion of this point in pre-revolutionary Russia cf. G. T. Robinson, *Rural Russia under the old régime*, ch. v.

integrated into a nation-wide system of government, rather than being a purely parochial affair. The Tsarist system assumed that the peasant had no interest in affairs of state beyond the boundaries of the village, and may not have been far wrong in this. The Soviet system tried to involve the peasantry in the changes taking place in society. The dilemma of the soviets was that the more closely they tried to involve the peasantry in the central, town-centred, policies, the less were they able to attract the peasant. The peasantry expressed their demands by economic pressure, as it was apparent that the soviets were not an effective means of expressing their demands. Indeed, it is unlikely that they would have expected a government organ to act in their interests. Their expectations from the gathering were for purely internal demands, as it was largely a one-way channel of communication as far as peasant–government relations were concerned.

The Soviet government was always quite clear in wanting these functions of local administration transferred from the communes to the rural soviets. In reality this proved difficult, but there was comparatively little dispute at the centre that these were properly the functions of the rural soviet, either in its own right, or acting as agent for the volost or raion. An attempt at compromise was made, we will see, by trying to turn the gathering into a meeting of electors to which the rural soviet reported, but this proved abortive.[1]

The second area in which the rural soviet encroached on the work of the commune was in the administration of agriculture. Here ambiguity was greater and the room for debate wider. The rural soviet was from the first entrusted with encouraging improvement in agricultural technique, yet at the same time the commune was left intact to organise its use of the land. The question of commune independence became increasingly important in the later twenties as the debate on the proper organisation of a socialist agriculture came to a head.

The basis of the government's policy on the commune and rural soviet had been crystallised in two laws, enacted in the early years of N.E.P. The Land Code of 1922 was largely a reflection of the exist-

[1] See below, p. 109.

ing position in the countryside, and owed much to pre-revolutionary legislation. The Law on Rural Soviets of 1924 laid down the functions of these bodies in a fuller and more systematic manner than hitherto, marking the start of the policy of 'revitalising the soviets'. Comparison of the two laws shows that they reflect the dilemma of the government in tackling rural soviet–commune relationships.

Early legislation had attempted to place the commune under the control of the rural soviet. The Russian Land Law of January 1918 entrusted the land department of local and central soviets with the equitable apportionment of the land among the working agricultural peasantry.[1] This obviously had far-reaching implications for the redistributing functions which lay at the heart of the commune. The seizure of land by the peasantry was in fact conducted without any such guidance from above, and the strengthening of the commune may well have been a result of the break down of the forces of law and order. We have seen already[2] that an attempt was made in 1919 to make commune decisions on redistribution subject to control by the volost land department. The following year something approaching the merging of the commune into the rural soviet seems to have been envisaged. While the 'rural society'[3] and rural soviet were mentioned as separate bodies, it was the rural soviet which would present the request of the commune to redistribute land to the volost. The volost would grant this if the rural soviet gave grounds for wishing holdings to be reallocated. Moreover, requests for permission to undertake full redistribution were to be brought by the rural soviet 'on a declaration made by 2/3 of rural society members having soviet electoral rights'.[4] The decree thus assumed that the rural soviet would come near to taking over all the administrative work of the commune, that the commune was answerable to soviet authority in its redistribution, and that only qualified voters could partici-

[1] Art. 11.
[2] See above, p. 58.
[3] The Russian term here is sel'skoe obshchestvo. It is not entirely clear whether this was the old unit, which was larger than the commune or, as in the case of zemel'noe obshchestvo, a synonym for commune. The sense suggests it meant obshchina. See Glossary.
[4] Decree SNK. RSFSR, 30 April 1920, 'O peredelakh zemli'. SU 1920, no. 35, art. 170.

pate in its decisions. None of these assumptions were upheld in the 1922 Land Code. The 1919 law was an attempt to bring some element of stability into the chaotic state of land holding, but such direct government action proved unrealistic for many reasons. It was not until the rural soviets were considerably stronger, in 1928, that such an attempt at direct control over the commune by the rural soviet was made again. In the intervening years, a clear distinction was made between the functions of 'land society' and rural soviet; the assumption (an unrealistic one, as it transpired) being that the land holding and local administrative function of the commune could be split off one from the other.

The Land Code gave peasants very broad rights to organise and cultivate the land in the manner they chose. It reflected the spirit of N.E.P. in giving the peasantry a wide element of freedom in ordering their own affairs.[1] In keeping with this, the commune, or land society as it was to be known, was made responsible to the government only in the most general terms for its stewardship of the land which was, in theory, granted to it by the state for its use.[2] The code dealt only with the land functions of the commune, which laid the basis for the legal fiction of general local administration being undertaken by the rural soviet, and land affairs being in the hands of the commune under a new name.

The earlier attempts at control of the commune by the rural soviet were abandoned. Under the Land Code, the land society was to have no dealings at all with the rural soviet, save in the exceptional case where the two coincided in area. Then the rural soviet could act as the executive of the land society. In general, the rural soviets were too weak to exercise even the general supervision required by the Land Code, and these duties were laid on the volost executive committee. This body was to ensure that the land society implemented the law correctly. However, the land society was not obliged to notify the higher authorities of its decisions, except on specified matters. Decisions on redistribution of the societies' land had to be

---

[1] 'Zemel'ny Kodeks RSFSR, 30 October 1922', SU RSFSR, 1922, no. 68, art. 901. Cf. diagram 1.
[2] While the term 'land society' covered all forms of land holding, and the commune was, strictly speaking, 'land society with communal land holding', the terms land society and commune came to be interchangeable. Cf. Glossary.

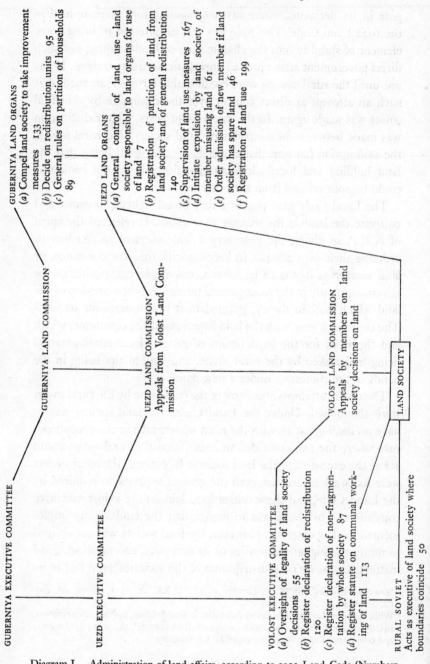

Diagram I. Administration of land affairs, according to 1922 Land Code (Numbers refer to articles of the Land Code)

registered with the volost executive committee, which could reject the request if it infringed the rules on redistribution. Other matters which had to be registered were declarations by the society as a whole that its member households would not fragment, and decisions to cultivate land by communal labour.

Matters which affected the shape of the society more radically were to be registered with the uezd land organs, to whom the society was responsible, as were all land-users, for their use of land. Land holding was to be registered at the uezd level. Partition of land from the society had to be registered with them. The uezd level organ did have certain compulsory powers. They could order the expulsion of a member misusing land, and the admission of a new member, if the society had spare land. The uezd could not compel a society to undertake land use measures; this could only be decided by guberniya land organs. General policy was also to be laid down at guberniya level, such as the units of redistribution which societies should use, and general rules for partition of households were also to be decided at that level. While placing even these general functions at a higher level may have meant they were to be undertaken by a more competent body, the distance of even the volost from the commune, and the immense pressure of work on these bodies, probably ensured that the commune did not undergo even the modest degree of control outlined in the Land Code.

While the commune did not, as a body, have any relationship with the rural soviets under the Land Code, member households did have to apply to the rural soviet for permission to engage in certain activities which related to the land. Where a household wished to change its head, the household was to ask permission from the rural soviet to petition the volost executive committee. Why this should not have been arranged via the commune is not clear – it may have thought that, as the commune gathering before the revolution consisted of heads of households, it would be loth to agree to any change in the headship of a household. Equally it is not clear on what grounds such a petition would be brought. Presumably it would be after a family quarrel where the eldest member of the household was considered to be intractable, or of unsound mind. The household was also to petition the rural soviet directly for permission

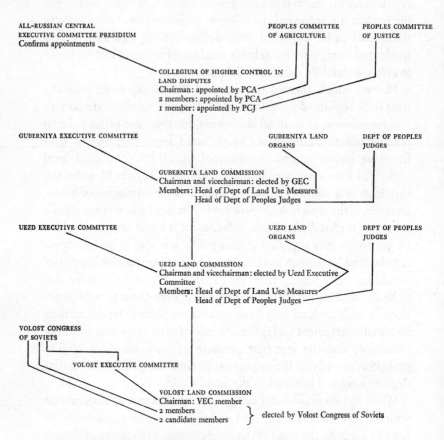

Diagram II. Land Commissions, as set out by 1922 Land Code.

Competence:

Guberniya LC (1) Disputes between institutions at state and guberniya level.
(2) Appeals from Uezd Land Commission.

Uezd LC (1) Disputes on inter-volost land use measures.
(2) Disputes in land use measures involving state or collective farms.
(3) Disputes in right to land where one sale is state or social organ.
(4) Appeals from Volost Land Commission.

Volost LC (1) Disputes in inter-village and intra-village land use measures.
(2) Disputes in right to land of individuals, households and land societies.

to rent out land.[1] If a household split up its land holding, this was to be registered by the household directly with the volost executive committee, rather than via the commune.

Where there was internal dissension in the commune on land matters, appeal was to be to the volost land commission.[2] Land commissions were appellate bodies, organised at guberniya and uezd level under the land organs, and at volost level under the volost executive committee. In the higher levels they consisted of a chairman and vice-chairman elected by the corresponding soviet executive committee, plus the Head of the Department of Land Use Measures of the Ministry of Agriculture, and the Head of the Department of People's Judges. At volost level the Chairman was a volost executive committee member, and four members (two full, two candidate) were elected by the Volost Congress of Soviets.

Under the Land Code, the volost land commission heard appeals from members on land society decisions on the following matters:

(a) Minor readjustment of holdings by the society (skidki i nakidki).

(b) On division of land, where a new, non-redistributing form of holding was decided upon by the society.

(c) Appeal on suspension from using land for illegal renting, non-use, or mis-use of land.

(d) Disputes over land use measures.

(e) Disputes over separation of land from the society by a member, and over redistribution.

Little is known of the actual working of these bodies, and whether disputes between peasants and the commune of which they were members were taken to a soviet-oriented body. It would seem unlikely on the face of it.

Thus the Land Code placed the commune in a fairly loose relationship with the volost centre, and allowed it to be independent of the rural soviet as far as land affairs were concerned. There was probably an average of around 40 communes in each volost in the

[1] This was when it was renting less than half its area. If more, it applied to the volost executive committee.

[2] Abolished by decree of VTsIK SNK, 10 October 1930 (SU no. 51, art. 623). Superseded by appeal to courts, where individual peasants in dispute.

early twenties, with the number rising with creation of raiony, so that supervision could never have been very firm.[1] The shortage of trained personnel at volost level was acute. In thought and distance the uezd was proportionately further distant from local reality. The need for a wide measure of latitude was recognised in the Code itself, which provided that the rights and duties of land users and societies were established not only by the law, but also, when it did not conflict with the law 'by local custom'.[2]

The rural soviet was given very broad responsibilities under the 1924 statute which, ideally, shaped the pattern of rural soviet work in the middle and late twenties. It was to 'discuss and work out all questions concerning the life and economy of the countryside'.[3] The preamble suggested that the function of the rural soviet was to be a transmission belt for the values and technical skills of the higher, urban-based soviet institutions:

The rural soviet, being the organ of power within the limits of its territory, has as its main tasks – raising peasant economy, the struggle with ignorance, darkness, illness and other backwardness of country life, the defence of the rights of the working population on the basis of the union between workers and peasantry, the most precise and full implementation of the laws of the Worker–Peasant Government, having as its main aim the improvement of the life of the workers, and general introduction of the peasantry to the government of the state...

The decree went on to list nearly all those functions of local government undertaken by the commune before the revolution, such as keeping local roads, bridges and canals in good order, and the administration of taxation. What was potentially more threatening to the commune, even as constituted in soviet terms as a land society, was the extent to which the rural soviet was to involve itself in agriculture.

[1] On the assumption of 8,566 volosts in RSFSR in 1924 (*Administrativno-territorial'noe delenie SSSR* (1929), Introd.) and 320,000 land societies. In 1928 there were 2,791 volosts and 986 raions. For later period, see p. 131, note 5, below.
[2] Land Code, art. 8.
[3] 'Polozhenie o sel'sovetakh', 16 October 1924. SU no. 82, art. 827, section 1.

The extent of proposed rural soviet involvement in agriculture can be seen from the following list of duties of rural soviets in this sphere:[1]

(*a*) Taking measures to introduce improved methods of agricultural production (machine working, multi-course rotation, abolition of border strips, early first ploughing, etc.), and hearing reports from agricultural institutions.

(*b*) Helping the organisation and development of collective farming...

(*c*) Organisation of machine hire, services, veterinary and winnowing stations.

(*d*) Helping agronomic, land use measures, melioration, forestry and veterinary personnel.

(*e*) Leading work for organisation of a local seed fund.

(*f*) Taking preventive measures against spread of livestock diseases.

If the rural soviet were to carry out these obligations, it would obviously infringe the rights of the land society as laid down in the Land Code. In those areas where some attempt was made to follow the position as laid down by the government, a genuine dilemma was presented to the rural soviet. In most areas rural soviets were in no position to attempt to fulfil these ambitious aims, having no funds of their own, and meagre staff. None the less Kursk guberniya land board (upravlenie) did find the problem sufficiently real in their area to ask for clarification from the People's Commissariat of Agriculture. The reply noted that there was no problem where the rural soviet and land society coincided in area, as the rural soviet was to be the executive of the land society, but continued: 'the land society is not, in general, under rural soviet control, as, according to art. 55 of the Land Code, supervision of the correct implementation by land societies of the law is imposed on the volost executive committee. Thus demands on the part of a rural soviet, or groups of rural soviets, for reports, money etc. infringe the Land Code, and this demand cannot be based on the decree on rural soviets'.[2]

---

[1] 'Polozhenie o sel'sovetakh', 1924, section 8.
[2] 'Razyasnenie narkomzem RSFSR k Kurskomu gubernskomu zemel'nomu uprav-

The 1924 decree caused further confusion by recommending as one of the means by which the peasantry was to be involved in soviet government the holding of 'general meetings of citizens', to be known as gatherings (skhody). The decree ignored the existence of the land society and its gathering. It was not very explicit about the composition and function of the general meeting of citizens. On the one hand, the rural soviet was responsible to the volost executive committee, and called the meeting 'to get the peasantry to take part in the government of their affairs'. On the other hand, the rural soviet was to 'execute all legal decisions of the general meeting of citizens' and to present to higher levels where necessary 'all decisions of the general meeting, its wishes and petitions'. While this was presumably an attempt to channel the commune gathering to soviet ends, it appears to have been inept, not only because of the recognition of the land society in other spheres, but also because the area of the commune and rural soviet rarely coincided. The situation was probably further confused by the existence of election meetings as a further soviet institution. There was no qualification that only those with electoral rights attend the general meeting.[1] The election meetings elected rural soviet delegates. The soviet itself elected its own officials, but the general meeting of citizens was able to petition the volost executive committee for their removal.

The legal anomalies were tackled in 1927. One of the dangers of the situation, as seen from the centre, was that the rich peasant, 'kulak', could quite legally exercise a powerful influence over the rural soviet. There was no restriction on those excluded from soviet electoral rights holding office in the commune, and taking a leading part in the gathering. As there was no clear distinction between a gathering of the commune, and a gathering called by the rural soviet, this was seen as a lever which could be used by the kulak in subverting rural soviet work. The law on village gatherings of 1927 approached the problem in a legalistic manner, which did not attempt to deal with the underlying social and economic problems.

leniyu', 17 August 1926, 33/170/142/303/11, quoted by Verlinsky and Viktorov in *Khozyaistvo i upravlenie* (December 1927), 11–12.
[1] The confusion was even more marked in the 1918 Constitution of the RSFSR, which noted that 'in rural localities, wherever possible, questions of administration will be settled directly by the general assembly of electors of the village concerned'. Art. 57, note. *Izvestiya*, 19 July 1918.

The commune and the soviet network

It decreed that there would be two gatherings. That of the 'land society' would remain as in the 1922 Land Code, while the 'gathering (general meeting of citizens)' was to be a separate meeting, organised very largely on the lines suggested by the 1924 Decree on Rural Soviets. Only villagers with electoral rights would be allowed to attend the latter meeting.[1] It is clear that such an administrative solution to the problems of government in the countryside was doomed to failure, as it merely tried to alleviate the symptoms, rather than tackle the causes of the weakness of soviet power at local level. In reality the measure did not even have any effect on the symptoms.[2]

This law was a dead letter from the moment of publication.[3] It tried to solve three main problems – lack of peasant support for rural soviets, duality of function of local gathering, and the increasing remoteness of the rural soviet from the population under regionalisation. Commentators agreed that it was implemented almost nowhere. 'In practice, up to now [May 1928], in the overwhelming majority of villages in the RSFSR, the land society gathering is not differentiated from the village gathering.'[4] 'Division of the gathering would be very difficult – to get the same people together for two gatherings is a break with custom and seems pointless. Almost all materials show there is no difference in fact.'[5]

---

[1] Decree of VTsIK. 14 March 1927, 'On general meetings of citizens (gatherings)'. SURSFSR, 1927, no. 51, art. 333. This decree is still in force. See p. 214, footnote 1.

[2] In broad outline, the provisions of the decree were as follows: The 'general meeting of citizens' was to be very much under rural soviet control. It was to be called either by the rural soviet, or its agents, or at the request of one fifth of the electorate of a given settlement (selenie). Emphasis throughout the decree was on rural soviet initiative. Thus 'the rural soviet puts forward speakers on questions which are to be brought before the gathering by the soviet, which also works out projects for the corresponding decrees to be made by the gathering'. The individual villager's right to put proposals for decrees to the gathering is also guaranteed, but in a footnote to the clause just quoted. Gatherings would be held in the settlements in the area of the rural soviet. A united gathering could be held on questions touching several settlements.

[3] The idea seems to have been revived during the collectivisation campaign. See below, p. 203.

[4] Rezunov, Sel'sovet i zemel'noe obshchestvo (Moscow, 1928), p. 24.

[5] Kozhikov, 'Zemel'noe obshchestvo i sel'skii sovet', Na agrarnom fronte (May 1928), no. 5, p. 64.

3 THE ACTUAL SITUATION

We have seen that there were some anomalies in the law on the relationship between rural soviet and commune. When we come to study the actual situation, we see how far removed the law was from practice. It is, however, not possible to give a systematic picture of the situation. It would be particularly valuable if we could relate the variations in commune–rural soviet relationships to the study of the commune by area in Chapter 1. The sources are not adequate to do this. We have already noted the difficulties of studying the commune. There are similar problems with rural soviets. As Danilov has noted, there has been very little serious soviet work on the question of the peasantry in the soviets.[1] While much was written in propagandist vein on the problems of enlivening the soviets, on re-election campaigns, on sections, and so on, there is little that shows awareness of the actual problems at local level.

The case least often described was where the rural soviet had considerable influence over the commune. There is some difficulty in interpreting the situation due to the two senses in which the word 'gathering' could be used. However, as the distinction was a purely legalistic one, it seems likely that the gathering in the village would be looked upon as one institution which usually met on the initiative of its own officers, but was occasionally summoned by the rural soviet. Thus, even in areas where the commune was virtually independent of the rural soviet, there were instances of the gathering being summoned by the rural soviet to apportion self-taxation, to announce decisions on taxes, and other directives from the volost and uezd. One Siberian peasant, on being summoned to a gathering called by the rural soviet is said to have remarked: 'some tax or other again'.[2]

Research by Worker–Peasant Inspectorate early in 1927 suggested on the face of it that most of the questions discussed at the gathering were introduced on the initiative of a soviet body.[3] This showed that questions discussed at the gathering fell into the categories shown in Table 3.4. In half of the cases, questions were discussed on the initi-

[1] Danilov, 'K itogam izucheniya istorii sovetskogo krest'yanstva i kolkhoznogo stroitel'-stva SSSR', *Voprosy istorii* (1960), no. 8.
[2] Kirillov, 'Sel'sovet i skhod', in Yakovlev and Khataevich, *VIK i sel'sovet* (Moscow, 1925), p. 54.
[3] Quoted by Rezunov, *Sel'sovet i zemel'noe obschestvo*, p. 27.

Table 3.4

	Percentage
Land and agricultural	39
Finance and tax	16
Administrative	15
Cultural	9
Public services	8
Other	13

ative of the rural soviet, 17% of the volost executive committee, 11% of 'other institutions' with 22% at the instigation of individuals. This finding is at variance with most other sources. Without the original source, which is inaccessible, it is difficult to interpret the findings. The sample may have been of these few areas where a gathering was held independently of the commune. It could be that the rural soviets in the area (unspecified) covered by the research were little more than executives of the commune.

Usually cases of rural soviets leading the commune are given as exceptions. Thus Kirillov, after noting that in the Stavropol okrug of the North Caucasus the commune gathering was the most influential local organ, mentions that there were rural soviets where the gathering was merely a stamp of rural soviet decisions.[1] The Commission on Strengthening Work of Rural Soviets and Volost Executive Committees, reporting to the Conference on Questions of Soviet Construction in 1925, came to the conclusion that 'leadership by rural soviets in work of the gathering is altogether weak, and absent altogether in some villages'. There were a few exceptional cases, such as Chadayevsk rural soviet in Saratov guberniya, where, instead of a gathering, the rural soviet called an expanded rural soviet session.[2] In presenting the report, Kiselev remarked that where there was a degree of rural soviet leadership, speeches so often ended with 'give money', or 'give bread' that the peasants lost interest in the gathering.[3]

[1] Kirillov, 'Sel'sovet i skhod', p. 54.
[2] 'Soveshchanie pri prezidiume Ts IK SSSR po voprosam sovetskogo stroitel'stva'; *Materialy komissii po ukrepleniyu raboty sel'sovetov i vikov* (Moscow, 1925), pp. 51–3.
[3] Kiselev, Speech in 'Soveshchanie po voprosam sovetskogo stroitel'stva, Aprel' 1925', *Otchet* (Moscow, 1925), p. 31.

In some areas instructions were issued on the proper relationship between commune and rural soviet. These tended to take a far less liberal attitude towards the commune than was allowed for in central decisions. In 1926, Urals oblast executive committee instructed rural soviets that 'among questions the presidium of the rural soviet prepares for the plenum...are examination of the decisions of the gathering and of the land society from the point of view of expediency and legality'.[1] This was clearly contrary to central policy.[2]

Leningrad guberniya executive committee issued instructions on the 'general meeting of citizens' gathering before the central decree tried to resolve the problem in 1927. This gathering was to be under strong rural soviet influence, being called by the soviet, with a member of the soviet in the chair. It largely followed the 1924 decree on rural soviets. It went further in trying to grapple with the problem of relationships with the commune, but only at the expense of further contradiction. In deciding land questions, the appropriate articles of the Land Code were to be observed. This evaded both the question of attendance and rural soviet control over the commune's land functions. Attendance at the gathering was to be compulsory, and people who called a gathering without rural soviet permission were to be called to account. The gathering was seen largely as a means of informing and educating, despite a proviso that it could 'define its wishes and put them to higher organs via the rural soviet'.[3] It is worth noting that this was not one of the strongest areas for communal holding.[4]

In the Crimean ASSR draft statues,[5] the land society was more directly responsible to the raion land department than in the Land Code. The raion land department could put questions to the land society gathering, and even put a motion for removal of office-bearers in the land society from their positions. The statute ignored the rural soviet, presumably because of that body's weakness.

Rezunov, in the most thorough work on the whole field of rural

[1] *Sbornik rukovodyashchikh materialov dlya sel'sovetov*, Troitskii okrispolkom (Troitsk, 1929). [2] See above, p. 101.
[3] Instruktsiya sel'sovetam i vikam 'O sozyve i reshenii voprosov na osg (skhod)'. Confirmed by presidium of Leningrad g.i.k. January 1925. Published as a pamphlet.
[4] See above, p. 28ff.
[5] See above, p. 79. Scheme shown in diagrammatic form on p. 113.

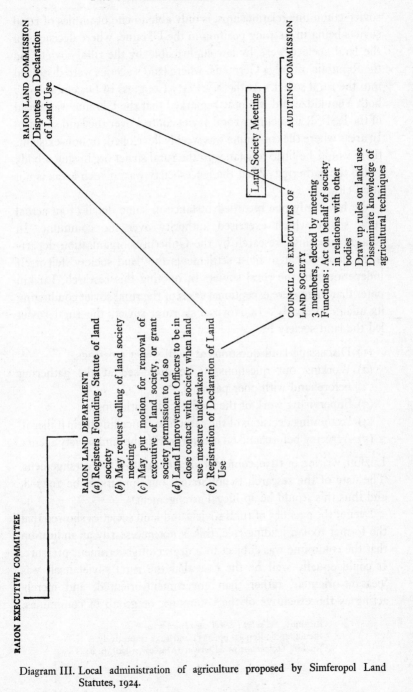

Diagram III. Local administration of agriculture proposed by Simferopol Land Statutes, 1924.

soviet–commune relationships, is only able to cite examples of rural soviets being in a strong position in the Ukraine, where decisions of the land society were by law confirmable by the rural soviet, and the Republic of Volga Germans, where land societies were dissolved into the rural soviet.[1] At the XV Party Congress in December 1927 both Yenukidze and Molotov remarked that the Ukraine was ahead of the RSFSR in securing rural soviet control over the land society.[2] In areas where the commune was weakly developed, or non-existent, there would be little resistance to the rural soviet organising a body called the gathering. What the land society was in such areas is not at all clear.

We have only one recorded instance in some detail of an actual rural soviet which exercised authority over the commune. In Ryazan guberniya, research by the Guberniya organisation department showed that in most settlements the 'land society' felt itself independent of the rural soviet. In quoting this research, Luzhin notes that there were exceptional cases of the rural soviet conducting its affairs 'properly'. In Novosel'sk rural soviet, the rural soviet led the land society by

(1) Discussing land questions at rural soviet meetings.
(2) Working out questions to be discussed at the gathering beforehand with poor peasants.
(3) Supervising work of the land society gathering.
(4) Examining decisions of the gathering, cancelling them if illegal.
(5) Agreeing beforehand on measures with the land society agents.

Luzhin, writing in 1930, commented favourably on this arrangement. The date of the research is not stated, but appears to be 1927–8, and thus this would be an illegal arrangement.[3]

Even if the agendas of rural soviets and land societies showed that the former took a leading role, this is not necessarily an indication that the commune was subject to a degree of government pressure. It could equally well be the case that the rural soviet itself was 'peasant-oriented' rather than government-oriented, and merely acting as the executive of the commune, or group of communes.

[1] Rezunov, *Sel'sovet i zemel'noe obshchestvo.*
[2] Stenographic Report, pp. 1111 and 1231 respectively.
[3] Luzhin, *Organizatsiya sel'sovetov* (Moscow, 1930), p. 64.

The commune and the soviet network

The legal policy of separate 'general meeting of citizens' gatherings was implemented in very few areas.

In a few areas, it seems that rural soviets called village meetings, which were not directly related to commune gatherings. A report on 'Lower Soviet Apparatus' by Worker–Peasant Inspectorate in 1925 was based on a sample of 44 rural soviets in an unspecified area. At these 'rural meetings' (sel'skie sobraniya) a member of the rural soviet presided, in other cases the chairman was elected by those present. An average of 29 (3–102) of those meetings were called each year by each rural soviet (without knowledge of number of settlements to each rural soviet, it is impossible to say how many meetings would be held in any one place per year). Questions discussed are listed in Table 3.5.[1]

Table 3.5

	Percentage
Agriculture	26·2
Politics	15·2
Organisation	13·4
Finance and tax	12·4
Other	8·4
Reports	8·3
Cultural	6·6
Mutual aid	5·4
Public services	2·8
Co-operatives	0·9
Health	0·2
Insurance	0·2
Total	100

There is no indication whether these rural soviets were in areas of strong communal holding. If they were, it would be evidence to support the view that the rural soviets in some areas did try to take the initiative in acquainting peasants with soviet policy. Indeed the calling of a separate meeting could have been an attempt to break away from entrenched interests at the commune gathering. As there is no information on support for these meetings, or details of where

---

[1] I. Murugov and A. Kolesnikov, *Apparat nizovykh sovetskikh organov, po materialam obsledovaniya NK RKI RSFSR, 1925 g.* (Moscow–Leningrad, 1926), pp. 112–13.

115

they were held or who attended them, it is difficult to come to any firm conclusion. A broader investigation at the same time rejected the idea that such meetings were at all widespread, remarking that 'land societies, on the basis of our materials, have not been formed, and in most cases land society and gathering are one and the same'.[1] There is some local legislation, but it was largely ineffective.[2] There is just the occasional reference which quite clearly suggests there were separate meetings. In a commentary on the 1927 law on 'general meetings of citizens', the legislative provision is described in considerable detail, but there is only once a hint that something approaching the position envisaged by the law existed. A letter is quoted from a Cossack village in Don okrug, where a peasant complained that 'in our village we have four masters: the land society, the general meeting of the five hamlets, the rural soviet, and the mutual aid society'.[3] Probably the commonest situation was that, no matter whether the rural soviet were strong or weak, a meeting would be held, probably based on commune membership, at which a representative of the rural soviet would announce tax assessments, and mention other matters of central concern.

The most common position was a complicated interlocking of function, with the rural soviet more or less subservient to the commune. In the extreme case, rural soviets came to regard themselves as responsible to the commune for their work, and sent their decisions to the commune gathering for confirmation.[4] Where the commune was fully developed, it was independent, having no need of the rural soviet, and did not even give executive function to the rural soviet. In some areas, the right to organise unions of communes

---

[1] *Materialy komissii po ukrepleniyu raboty sel'sovetov i vikov; Soveshchanie po voprosam sovetskogo stroitel'stva* (Moscow, 1925), p. 56.

[2] Tver guberniya executive committee amplified the law on 'general meeting of citizens' gatherings by listing topics for discussions as follows: (*a*) Organisation of public services, fire protection, repair and construction of roads and bridges, street cleaning, etc. (*b*) Finance and tax; insurance; savings bank; taxes. (*c*) Trade and co-operation – consumer, agricultural, industrial and credit. (*d*) Post. (*e*) Education. (*f*) Labour. (*g*) Insurance. (*h*) Self-taxation. (*i*) Other cultural, social and economic questions. Having given these details, Rezunov (*Sel'sovet i zemel'noe obshchestvo*, p. 26) remarks that in most villages the distinction between commune and general meeting gatherings had not been made, because of the former's superior material position.

[3] Kirpichev, *Pravo skhoda i sel'soveta* (Moscow–Leningrad, 1928), p. 15.

[4] Rezunov, *Sel'sovet i zemel'noe obshchestvo*, p. 27, and Luzhin, *Organizatsiya sel'sovetov*, p. 64.

(multi-settlement communes?) strengthened them further.[1] As one writer has suggested, in many areas the rural soviet not merely remained in the background when faced by the land society, it fell into direct dependence.[2] In Valdai uezd of Novgorod guberniya, it was estimated that 10% of rural soviets in the area were completely under the control of the commune, and even implemented illegal decisions of the commune gathering. Of the remainder, over half were potentially dependent on the commune. In some rural soviets of Troitsk uezd in Leningrad guberniya, the commune gathering even confirmed the plan of work of the rural soviet. In Kanalinsk rural soviet of Stalingrad guberniya, the commune elected the rural soviet chairman.[3] A report of Worker–Peasant Inspectorate to the Soviet of People's Commissars of the RSFSR in March 1928 pointed out that 'there is a kind of dual power in the village, where land societies use their material superiority to subject the rural soviet, and have the decisive voice in both the economic and ad-ministrative life of the country'.[4]

In some areas there seems to have been such a confusion of function that it is not possible to suggest who was the leader. In the hamlet (derevnya) of Butovo, Volokolamsk uezd, Moscow guber-niya, 'typical' agenda are available.[5] The rural soviet concerned itself, quite properly, with matters such as appointment of village execu-tive, repairing roads, looking after the park. But it also ventured into purchasing a seeder, discussing former land-lord land, and pasture rights. The 'land society' agenda started with the question of helping people who lost possessions in a fire. It confirmed, quite illegally, the minutes of the rural soviet. It discussed insurance, as well as agricultural tax, carting firewood to the hospital, and drawing up lists of those using local woods. Although over half the questions discussed by the land society gathering were properly a matter for the rural soviet, there was also a meeting which the author calls a 'village gathering' (sel'skii skhod), which met twice in the second half of 1927 to discuss a report of the rural soviet and its auditing committee. It is difficult to comment on such material without

[1] Cf. Karp, *Izvestiya*, 15 December 1927, no. 287.
[2] Kozhikov, *Na agrarnom fronte* (1928), no. 5, p. 21.   [3] Ibid.
[4] Quoted by Kiselev, XIV All-Russian Congress of Soviets, May 1929. *Izvestiya*, 14 May 1929.   [5] Rezunov, *Sel'sovet i zemel'noe obshchestvo*, p. 28.

knowing something of the dynamics which lay behind the situation, especially how far the rural soviet was oriented towards the centre.

The commune would on occasion concern itself with religious matters. Little is known of the influence of the priest on the commune. This was probably not great in view of Orthodox belief. In some areas the commune would deal with secular arrangements for the church, and elected a night watchman, or made a tax for improvements to the church.[1] In one area, the commune decided to grant the request of a priest for hay, after it had been turned down by the volost executive committee.[2]

An example of the breadth of topics which could be tackled by the commune gathering is seen in a gathering in Sosnovsk volost, Tambov guberniya.[3] There matters discussed included liquidation of illiteracy, opening a reading room, repair of the school, organising classes of those over school age, benefits to the needy from public funds, construction and cleaning of wells, repair of roads, building a fire station, election to Peasant Mutual Aid Committee, punishment for allowing stock to stray. Certain subjects were discussed at the instigation of the volost executive committee, such as 'loan for industrialisation', collection for a fund called 'Our Answer to Chamberlain'. This confirms the view that the interest of the soviet organs in the commune were often largely financial. In this village, which was the largest of the volost, the rural soviet discussed reports from land society representatives, from consumer co-operative, from the school and the agronomist, and from the rural soviet sections, which hardly ever met. It seems that in many areas the rural soviet was able to keep its fingers on the pulse of the countryside, but little more. The commune continued to discuss all matters of importance within its boundaries. Research in Atyushchev volost, Ulyanov guberniya, showed that at 15 gatherings, 69 questions were discussed: two of these were to do with land use measures – the rest were about non-land matters such as schools, repair of roads, bridges and so on.[4]

[1] Rezunov, *Sel'sovet i zemel'noe obshchestvo*, p. 31.
[2] L. Grigoriev, *Ocherki sovremennoi derevni* (Moscow, 1925), p. 41.
[3] Kozhikov, *Na agrarnom fronte* (1928), no. 5, p. 65.
[4] Karp, *Izvestiya*, 15 December 1927, no. 287. Gives similar data for Kursk okrug, Tver, Smolensk and Penza guberniyas.

It would seem that the typical case was where the commune
dealt with matters legally the province of the rural soviet. Kiselev
bemoaned the lack of any exhaustive research into the subject, but
quoted the following situation as typical. On the territory of Evlashev-
skii rural soviet, Kuznets uezd, Saratov guberniya in 1927 there
were two communes. While the rural soviet discussed 75 questions,
the communes dealt with 175. The interlocking is shown by the
summary of questions given in Table 3.6.[1]

Table 3.6

	Rural soviet	Land society
Public works	9	13
Land use measures	20	27
Sowing campaign	4	1
Self-taxation	1	11
Administration tax	39	10
Other economic questions	2	26

In this village, as in many others, the rural soviet administered
and collected taxes, while the commune managed the affairs of
local importance. As one commentator remarked, 'the October
revolution changed much in the country, brought much new, but
passed the village gathering as if not noticing it'.[2] In fact the revolution had unwittingly given a stimulus to the commune in many
areas where its fortunes were declining under Stolypinism. The
reasons for the commune's strong influence continuing can be given
in general terms, but it is not possible to give precision to these
arguments by observing under what conditions, and in what areas,
the commune retained, or increased its influence, and under what
conditions and in which areas the rural soviet was strong or weak.
It is a tempting hypothesis that rural soviets would have stronger
support in the areas where communal holding was not well established, and from that to argue that those rural soviets would probably be less government-oriented, while in areas of traditionally

[1] Kiselev, Report to XIV All-Russian Congress of Soviets, reported in *Izvestiya*,
24 May 1929. Presumably the second column referred to one land society.
[2] Kirpichev, *Prava skhoda i sel'soveta* (Moscow–Leningrad, 1928), p. 14, quoting a
letter from a village in Orlov guberniya.

strong communal holding, the rural soviets would be either weak, and centre-oriented, drawing on dissident population, or mere executives of the commune. Within a single volost the picture would probably vary, with the picture complicated in rural soviets with a large number of settlements, where central influence waned the further from the soviet one travelled in some cases, while in others the rural soviet acted as a focus for co-ordinating local activity, and was not in any case centre-oriented.[1] What determined the peasantry to act in different ways in different places cannot be established. Probably the factors making for strength or weakness of the commune mentioned in the Introduction apply in reverse here. Certainly the economic factor appears to have been crucial. The communes in most areas had their own sources of income, while the rural soviets in the mid-twenties had to rely largely on grants from the volost. This was probably the most decisive factor in securing the commune's independence of the rural soviet, and will be discussed separately. While the reasons were complex, the overall picture was that 'there is in most cases the following division of labour – all necessary and useful things for the peasant are done on the initiative of the gathering, and done without the rural soviet by special executives elected by the gathering'.[2]

4 DISCUSSION

There were two main aspects of the debate on the position of the commune in Soviet society. Here we will be concerned with the debate on the position of the commune in local administration, its proper place within the system of local soviets. In the following chapter we will review the debate on communal holding as a possible form of agricultural organisation in a socialist society. The confused situation in commune–rural soviet relationships was first seen as an important problem in 1925 when the first serious attempts were made to strengthen the network of local soviets. As the economic pressure

[1] By decree SU 1927, no. 27, art. 284, in settlements of 50–100 inhabitants, a rural soviet member could be appointed agent (upolnomochennyi) of the rural soviet for contact with the settlement. An example of this in practice is provided in Akimov, *Novyi zakon o sel'sovetakh* (Moscow, 1930), p. 8.
[2] Kirillov, 'Sel'sovet i skhod', p. 54.

on the peasantry increased in the later twenties, so the problem of
the commune became increasingly acute, as it symbolised in institutional form the divorce of the peasantry from the government. A
peasant body, apart from the soviet network, and at times distorting
the work of the soviets, could not be integrated into the apparatus
of government at a time when the central government was becoming
increasingly preoccupied with the problems of industrialisation. The
prolonged discussion on a new land law for the USSR culminated
at the end of 1928 with the soviets being given control over the
commune, and the abandoning of ideas that the commune should
form a primary cell of local self-government. Such ideas could be
advocated in the early years of N.E.P. In the event, collectivisation
changed the terms in which the problem was discussed.

The impetus to discussion of the relationship between commune
and rural soviet came from the conference in January and April 1925
on Soviet Construction. This conference clarified in some detail the
main problems of local administration. In the January meeting a
number of speakers from various regions complained, as soviet
workers, about the strong influence of the gathering, and the weaknesses of the Soviet organs. One of the problems examined by the
Commission on the Rural Soviet and Volost Executive Committee
appointed at the January conference was the working of the gathering. In the debate in April, Kaganovich put forward the view that
'the gathering must be less haphazard, the rural soviet must lead
the gathering, and every peasant be made to look on the gathering as
a local organ of power, part of the worker State'.[1] The pressure to
bring the gathering under rural soviet control, typified in this
approach, was to gain ground. This approach led to the artificial
distinctions made by the 1927 decree on the General Meeting of
Citizens, which was based on the conclusions of the conference, and
the conference did not grapple with the questions of what a gathering was. None the less, it is useful as a source of information. The
most realistic point was made by Kiselev, chairman of the Commission on Rural Soviet and Volost Executive Committee, when he
asked for time for his commission to study the demarcation of
authority between mutual aid committee, land commission, land

[1] *Sten. Otchet*, p. 12.

societies, and local soviet organs. The study was never published, even if it was undertaken.

Before the leadership of the rural soviet could be established, there had to be improvement in the work of the soviet organs, and much of the discussion on the countryside at the time centred on means of improving the rural and volost soviets, rather than on their relationship with the commune. The commune in the mid-twenties remained in law under loose control of the volost executive committee. The general approach at this time was summed up by Kalinin in winding up the debate 'On Soviet Construction' at the Third All-Union Congress of Soviets in May 1925. He concluded his speech thus: 'The most democratic organ in our countryside is the village gathering. At present the decisive body in most cases in the country is not the rural soviet, but the gathering. We must approach replacement of the gathering by the soviet very cautiously. In any case, we must thoroughly consider this point before going on to decide the question of the gathering.[1]

The view that the rural soviet should come to have control over the commune, either directly or indirectly, gathered weight as the situation in the countryside became a little more clear to those concerned with policy at the centre. The Party took little interest in the commune until the XV Party Congress in December 1927.[2] While it is doubtful whether it is in any way useful to call this the 'congress of collectivisation', it was a congress in which especial attention was given to the situation in the countryside in the light of difficulties in grain procurement. Thus the means of increasing party and government influence in the countryside were of especial importance. In this context, Kossior remarked that 'along with the soviets, there are certain organisations, for example the land societies, to which we have given too little attention'.[3] Enukidze bewailed the impotence of the rural soviet before the land society, and suggested that dealing with the land was one of the basic objectives of the rural soviet.[4]

[1] M. I. Kalinin, *Voprosy sovetskogo stroitel'stva* (Gosizdat, Moscow, 1958), p. 252.
[2] The XIV Party conference and congress had discussed enlivening the soviets, but the land society and gathering were not mentioned in the resolutions on the subject.
[3] XV Syezd KPSS Stenograficheskii Otchet, p. 91.
[4] Ibid. p. 1111.

The commune and the soviet network

At this congress, the problem was seen as the kulak influencing rural soviets away from Soviet objectives. Molotov, in his report on agriculture, remarked that 'new poles of activity for the rural soviet open up by subordinating the land society to its leadership. Only then will "all power to the Soviets" be realised in the countryside. Up to now, once we have enlivened a soviet, the kulak has dug in the land society'.[1] We will later comment on the problem of peasant differentiation and the commune. Whatever solution to the problem may have been regarded as ideal, there were severe practical problems. In another speech, Molotov pointed the dilemma. 'In connection with rural soviet work, we speak a good deal about "enlivening the Soviets". In a good many districts (especially the East) we should speak of creating them.'[2]

There was some debate as to whether the need was to improve relations between rural soviet and commune to the former's advantage, or to achieve rural soviet domination. From Siberia, Zilin felt that the question was not one of 'improving relationships', but of subjecting the land society to the rural soviet, as the 'dual power' was one of the greatest hindrances to enlivening the Soviets.[3] Glinskii was more cautious; perhaps significantly he was from Ryazan. While urging that the rural soviet should squeeze out the land society function by function, he emphasised that this should not be done in an administrative way, but in a battle for the initiative – who would first concern itself with this or that measure, such as providing a bull for communal use.[4]

The note of caution carried the day. In his closing speech, Molotov admitted that the Ukraine had passed a decree that summer, but went on to add that submission of the land society to the rural soviet could not be brought about in one moment, by a single circular. He urged caution against the 'rush and directness advised by some comrades'. 'Remember', he concluded, 'it is not for nothing we have made no resolution about this in the last ten years.'[5] The decree was a relatively mild one, and was identical with the decision of the October Plenum. It charged the Central Committee of the Party with 'working out improved relations between rural soviet

[1] Ibid. p. 1085. [2] Ibid. p. 259. Report on work in rural districts.
[3] Ibid. p. 1143. [4] Ibid. p. 1130. [5] Ibid. p. 1231.

and land society, with a view to assuring the leading role of the soviets and exclusion from voting in the land society gathering of those disenfranchised in soviet elections'.

During 1928, discussion on the future of the gathering intensified. Work in improving the rural soviets was showing ever more clearly how fruitless this was likely to be as long as the land society remained independent of the rural soviet. Discussions on the appropriate form of socialist agriculture pointed to the need for a replacement for the 1922 Land Code. The debate on the projected 'General Foundations of Land Use and Land Use Measures' provided a focal point for discussions of the commune. Draft statutes had been prepared in 1925 by the Commission on Legislative Projects of the USSR Soviet of People's Commissars, and one by the RSFSR Soviet of People's Commissars. The latter was revised and set before the All-Union Central Executive Committee for discussion in 1928.

A strong advocate of placing the land society under direct control of the rural soviet was Kozhikov.[1] He sought to do away with the ambiguities of the legal position by ensuring general leadership by rural soviet. His practical proposals were such as to virtually emasculate the land society. The editors of *Na agrarnom fronte*, which printed his proposals, took the unusual step of adding a note that 'we do not agree with the author's suggestions for subjecting the land society's function to the rural soviet'.

In the Central Executive Committee debate itself, there were advocates of this extreme view. Buskakova pressed for the rural soviet to take over administration of the land society, so that the land society executives would be rural soviet members.[2] Shchur saw the difficulty if there were more than one land society in the area of the rural soviet, and suggested the soviet should then set up a commission to administer this.[3] Milyutin, summing up the debate, injected a note of realism. There were on average four land societies per rural soviet. To load a typical rural soviet with the affairs of four land societies would be to overburden it grossly. The rural soviet would then have to bother itself with a host of minor ques-

---

[1] Kozhikov, *Na agrarnom fronte* (1928), no. 5.
[2] Ts IK SSSR, 4-y sozyv, 4-aya sessiya. Dek. 1928. *Bulletin* 12, p. 21.
[3] Ibid. *Bulletin* 15, p. 38.

tions. To say the least, such a measure would be precipitate in view of the weakness of the rural soviets. He agreed that in the future the two could be united in some way. If that were done immediately, the danger of the rural soviet being a mere executive of the land society would be increased, not lessened. It is interesting that he did not make any objection in principle to the rural soviet perform-ing the economic function of running agriculture. However, he did make an analogy with collective farms, saying that no one pressed for management of the collective farm to be replaced by the rural soviet. (In fact the reverse often happened.) He concluded with a rather contrived point that to remove the element of self-manage-ment from a hamlet of, say, 20 households, would mean that its economy would thereby become *less* socialised. Thus he saw quite a wide scope for local initiative to be still channelled through the commune gathering, but under greater rural soviet control.[1]

This view was supported by Rezunov in his conclusions after the most comprehensive review of the land society to be published.[2] We will later mention the crucial financial position; here we note that he recommended that all rural soviets should have their own budget, and items be transferred from land society budgets to rural soviet budgets. In his view, the land society should remain separate from, but subservient to, the rural soviet. His most radical point, in looking to the future, was that rural soviet agricultural sections could be strengthened to replace land societies in many areas.

There was a minority view at the centre in favour of making the land society into the lowest organ of the soviet system. The most outspoken protagonist of this view was Sukhanov. We will consider his views more fully in the next chapter, but it is worth noting that he regarded the commune as '$\frac{3}{4}$ lowest Soviet state unit, $\frac{1}{4}$ voluntary association'.[3] Thus the commune would be not only a primary unit in socialist agriculture, but also in soviet government. This view, with its Poputist overtones, was not taken up seriously.

The 1928 General Law on Land Use and Land Use Measures dealt with the administrative side of the relationship between the

---

[1] Speeches at April meeting, *Sten. Otchet*, p. 761, and December, *Bulletin* 12, p. 22.
[2] Rezunov, *Sel'sovet i zemel'noe obshchestvo*.
[3] *Na agrarnom fronte* (1926), no. 11–12, pp. 98–109. See below, p. 177.

two bodies.[1] The XIV All-Russian Congress of Soviets tackled the financial aspect. This provided the last central discussion on the land society before mass collectivisation dissolved the land societies. The discussion pointed to the need to subordinate the land society to the rural soviet. Delegates from as far apart as Vladimir, Moscow, Nizhnii Novgorod, Urals and North Caucasus took up this theme. There was an element of despair in some of the comments. Despite the enlivening of the soviets, in his opening speech Kiselev quoted with approval a comment that 'our rural soviets are pygmies before the growing giant'.[2] Before looking at the action taken in the field of financial relationships, we will briefly survey the progress which had been made in attempting to establish the rural soviets as a viable alternative form of local administration.

5 MEASURES AIMED AT STRENGTHENING THE RURAL SOVIET

a *Rural soviet elections*

During our period peasants took an increasing part in rural soviet elections. Their share rose from 22·3% of rural electors (who were not necessarily peasants) in 1922[3] to 61% in 1929.[4] The course of the campaign for revitalisation of the soviets from 1924 to 1926 has been charted in detail by Professor Carr[5] and it is not our purpose here to follow this process further. The point is that peasants were being increasingly involved in the rural soviet at election times at least. No doubt this involvement was to some extent on paper only. The government regarded elections as a means of broadcasting what it was trying to do, and of attempting to involve the peasantry in this work. In this period, elections were not quite the device they later became for demonstrating mass support.

The reasons behind the figures of electoral turn-out of peasants were diffuse and varied from election to election, and cannot be considered in any detail here. It is perhaps relevant to our main theme to ask not so much why voting was below 50% for most of

[1] See below, p. 152.   [2] *Izvestiya*, 24 May 1929.
[3] Lepeshkin, *Mestnye organy vlasti sovetskogo gosudarstva* (Moscow, 1959), p. 58.
[4] Kiselev, *Izvestiya*, 10 May 1929.
[5] E. H. Carr, *Socialism in one country*, part II, pp. 304–72.

the period, but rather why it should have been as high as over 40%. A major reason for this was that while the soviets were responsible for taxation, there was a need for peasants to take an interest in which people were to administer the taxes and who was to interpret central government policy in general at the local level. Administrators rather than representatives were being elected. Peasants did become rural soviet representatives, and officials, but those in higher positions at raion level and above were often not peasants. A study of the motivation of peasant soviet members would be an interesting exercise. It would also be interesting to trace variations in the voting pattern between areas. A possible hypothesis is that where the commune was weak, the rural soviet was more active, and seen as a useful means of local organisation, but the present writer has not found evidence with which this could be tested. Overall, however, it seems that peasant voting at rural soviet elections was in part a response to outside pressure to exercise the vote, and in part an interest in securing the most congenial interpretation of central decisions at local level.

b *Rural soviet staff*

One of the perennial problems of the rural soviet was staffing. The rural soviet chairman was in a difficult position 'between two fires – government and people'.[1] It had always been difficult to fill the post of elder (starosta) in the commune. The problem of staffing the rural soviet was correspondingly greater. The government lay store on education, social group and Party membership, but saw weakness in all these areas in the rural soviet. Rural soviet chairmen and secretaries were nearly always peasants. This usually meant they were barely literate – 'a mass of laws come down to the chairman, but he usually finds it difficult to read them, let alone do anything about them'.[2]

The abilities needed for organising a rural soviet were not usually to be found among the poorer strata in the countryside even if they had been able to afford to do the work with its low pay.[3] The fullest

[1] Kirillov in Yakovlev and Khataevich, *VIK i sel'sovet*, p. 50.
[2] Fillipov, XIV All-Russian Congress of Soviets. Stenograph report.
[3] Average pay chairman, 24–30 rubles per month in 1929 reported at XIV All-Russian Congress of Soviets. Resultant decree raised scales somewhat, cf. SU, nos. 85–6, art. 841.

published investigation of peasant activity in social institutions showed that while the weight of the middle peasant category was roughly the same for the total of households investigated and households with rural soviet members, the poorer were under-represented and the richer over-represented in rural soviet membership.[1] In part, this reflected general policy before the 'wager on the strong' had been completely abandoned in economic policy.

The proportion of Party members in rural soviets rose. In 1922, 6·1% of delegates to rural soviets were Party members. In 1928-9, this was as high as 15%, with 37·7% of rural soviet chairmen being Party members.[2] While this is quite high for a predominantly peasant group, this over-estimates potential Party influence in rural soviets due to the poor quality, from a Party point of view, of peasant Party members.[3]

The criteria on the basis of which rural soviet chairmen were, in fact, elected were rather different from those noted. One rural soviet chairman remarked they were usually elected because they had a large family and could spare the time from work.[4] The rate of turnover was very high. Annual elections were designed to provide a 'school of government', but in many areas chairmen did not even last out a year.[5]

While the rural soviet was becoming an organ with officials who may have been capable of providing a local administration able to rival the commune, it was far from efficient. A number of points remain unclear. Holding office in the rural soviet, or even being a member, was said to be unpopular, none the less large numbers of peasants did participate. In 1927, there were 1,315,765 rural soviet delegates, the bulk of them peasants.[6] With annual elections and a high turnover of chairmen, it would seem that possibly a substantial minority of peasant households had a member in a rural soviet at

[1] *Sel'skoe khozyaistvo SSSR, 1925-8*, Ts SU 1929, pp. 134-5. Sample of 615,400 households.
[2] See Gurvich in Yakovlev and Khataevich, *VIK i sel'sovet*, pp. 42-9; Kiselev, *Izvestiya*, 10 May 1929, Enukidze, Speech at XV Party Congress, *Sten. Otchet*, p. 1104; Carson, *Electoral practices in the USSR* (N.Y., 1955), p. 39.   [3] See below, p. 132.
[4] A. A. Yakovlev, *Derevnya kak ona est'* (Kursk oblast, 1923), cf. Maynard's remark that a man would be elected to the rural soviet to spite him, *The Russian peasant*, p.176.
[5] Kiselev, Speech to XIV All-Russia Congress of Soviets, *Isvestiya*, 10 May 1929.
[6] Enukidze, speech at XV Party Congress. *Sten. Otchet.* p. 1104.

some stage in the twenties. Statistics on the social composition of rural soviets in areas where communes were strong and where they were weak would possibly be helpful here. A clue to the situation may be provided by the low age of rural soviet chairmen. In one sample in 1925, 58·5% were under 25.[1] While this may well be something of an exaggeration of the trend, it would seem that rural soviets attracted the younger members of the household. It may be that they saw little future in the perpetuation of the patriarchal household, especially after a wider experience fighting outside the village in the war.

c *Rural soviet sections*

One of the means of involving the rural soviet more closely in rural life, and vice versa, was supposed to be the 'section'. In 1918, all soviets had been charged with setting up specialised departments or commissariats.[2] Obviously, no rural soviet would have been capable of organising the dozen committees mentioned. The 1924 decree on rural soviets was, to some extent, more realistic, in that it merely mentioned 'the formation of commissions in necessary circumstances, giving various tasks to individual citizens and groups of citizens' as just one of the possible means of influencing peasants to take an active interest in government.[3]

While there was no lack of resolutions that sections should be encouraged, research in 1925 showed they were not widespread, and even when formed were often to cope with a specific once-for-all problem.[4] There was no strong drive to organise sections until the later twenties, partly because the rural soviets themselves were so weak. Once some progress had been made in enlivening the soviets, consideration could be given to involving wider groups in their activity. In 1927, a law was passed listing formally the duties of 'permanent commissions' as the sections were to be called. The proposed sphere of action of the agricultural commissions would

[1] Gurvich in *VIK i sel'sovet*, pp. 42–9.
[2] 'Instructions regarding the organisation of soviets', Collegium NKVD 9, January 1918. Cf. J. H. Meisl and F. S. Kozera, *Materials for the study of the USSR* (Ann Arbor, 1950). [3] 'Polozhenie o sel'sovetakh', 16 October 1924, art. 3 (ii).
[4] *Soveshchanie po voprosam sovetskogo stroitel'stva. Materialy kommissii po ukrepleniyu raboty sel'sovetov i vikov*, p. 49. Murugov and Kolesnikov, *Apparat nizovykh sovetskikh organov*, p. 110.

obviously have overlapped considerably with the commune.[1] The idea was obviously to try and supplant the commune in one area by having the commission as initiator of agricultural improvement.

While there were areas where the commissions did perform the functions expected of them, the overall impression is that in many areas they were just not formed, and in many others existed only on paper. It was claimed that in 1927, there were two million rural inhabitants involved, as well as one million rural soviet members.[2] While such impressive statistics were not uncommon, most reports on the quality of their work suggests they were purely formal organisations.[3] They were superseded in December 1929 by 'production conferences', another more or less 'paper' organisation.[4]

d Rural soviet functions: legal provision

From 1924 to 1929, the problem was not so much how to widen the functions of the rural soviets as to encourage them to use the quite wide powers available under the 1924 decree. While most rural soviets fulfilled their tax-collecting role, work related to agriculture was especially weak.[5] There were certain minor measures, but the functions in law of the rural soviet did not change until 1930, after the collectivisation campaign was under way.[6] In the event, the

[1] 21 March 1927, SU RSFSR, no. 39, art. 250.
[2] Enukidze at XV Party Congress. *Sten. otchet* p. 92.
[3] Cf. discussion on Kiselev's report at XIV All-Russia Congress of Soviets. Comments by delegates from Lower Volga krai and Central Black Earth oblast. A letter from Krasnoyarsk guberniya executive committee to all raion executive committees, and rural soviets, noted how few sections were organised. Cf. Krasnoyarskii okruzhnyi ispolnitel'nyi komitet, *Zadachi sel'sovetov v dele razvitiya i pereustroistva sel'skogo khozyaistva* (Krasnoyarsk, 1924).
[4] SU 1929, no. 87-8, art. 865. See below, p. 198.
[5] See, for example, Murugov and Kolesnikov, *Apparat nizovykh sovetskikh organov*, p. 85.
[6] In 1926, the rural soviet was recognised as a legal person. In 1927, a variety of administrative duties were transferred from raion or volost to enlarged rural soviets under decree of *SNK*, 23 July 1927 (published in *Izvestiya*, 24 July 1927), but this was not such an extensive measure as is suggested by Lepeshkin, *Mestnye organy vlasti sovetskogo gosudarstva*, pp. 172-3.
   The February 1930 Basic Statute on the Organisation of Rural Soviets (*SZ SSSR* (1930), no. 16, art. 172) made little organisational change, but emphasised the position of rural soviets as leaders of the collectivisation campaign, fighting 'distortions of the Party line'. See also *SZ SSSR* (1930), no. 7, art. 785, On new tasks for soviets in relation to widely developing collectivisation, and *SZ SSSR* (1930), no. 9, art. 106, On re-elections to soviets not doing their duty in collectivisation.

rural soviets were too weak to have an independent significant effect, and measures had to be taken to prevent them being swallowed up by collective farms.[1]

e *Volost and raion executive committees*

The volost executive committees suffered from many of the problems which beset the rural soviets, and were unable to give the leadership required. While they had a wide range of functions on paper,[2] in practice they were largely concerned with tax administration.[3] They were quite unable to exercise any sort of supervision over communes.[4] This is hardly surprising, as there were probably, on average, 60 communes in each volost in 1928 (and correspondingly more in each raion).[5] In some areas, they did receive minutes of the 'land society' but nothing like all decisions went into the minutes. This echoed the pre-revolutionary position where only the most important matters were inscribed in the village decisions book.[6]

The main approach to solving the problem of weak volosts was consolidation into raions. One main aim was to economise in the very limited number of suitable staff. The number of administrative units at this level was halved from 1924 to 1930. This led to an increased distance of the volost or raion soviet from the peasantry, both physically and mentally.[7] While a substantial proportion of volost executive committee members were described as peasants, these were often employees of peasant origin, rather than being actively involved in agriculture. Even this proportion was falling.

[1] On this, see Party Decree of 29 December 1929, Document 67 in *Kollektivizatsiya sel'skogo khozyaistva*. Cf. Larin's speech in 'Konferentsiya agrarnikov-marksistov', Otchet, p. 69; B. Kavraiskii, *Sel'sovet i kolkhoz* (Novosibirsk, 1930); Karp, *Izvestiya*, 15 December 1927; M. V. Kozhevnikov, *Zadachi sel'sovetov v svyazi so sploshnoi kollektivizatsii* (Simferopol', 1930); Lepeshkin, *Mestnye organy vlasti sovetskogo gosudarstva*, p. 235.

[2] 'Polozhenie o volostnykh s'ezdakh sovetov i volispolkomakh', *SU 1924*, no. 82, art. 826.

[3] See, for example, Murugov and Kolesnikov, *Apparat nizhovykh sovetskikh organov*, pp. 86–7; Ryklin article in *VIK i sel'sovet*, ed. Yakovlev; *Soveschanie po voprosam sovetskogo stroitel'stva pri prezidiume TsIKa Yanvar', 1925*, p. 68.

[4] See Rezunov, *Sel'sovet i zemel'noe obshchestvo*, p. 47.

[5] Assuming four communes to each rural soviet (see above, p. 88) and 15 rural soviets to each volost (see Luzhin, *Ot volosti k raionu*, p. 103).

[6] Kozhikov, *Na agrarnom fronte* (1928), no. 5.

[7] Murugov and Kolesnikov, *Apparat nizavykh sovetskikh organov*, have an interesting demonstration of distance, related to one day's travel by a peasant.

In the important position of chairman of the raion executive committee, less than half were even said to be of peasant origin in 1929.[1]

The increasing remoteness from the peasantry does not seem to
have been counterbalanced by a greater ability to give support to
the rural soviets. Neither were the raions successful in transmitting
government policy downward. The administrative structure reflected the deeper dilemma of the government's policy toward the
peasantry.

6 THE COMMUNE AND PARTY ORGANISATION

The specific question of the relationship between local Party
organisations and the commune cannot be divorced from the wider
problem of the situation of the Party in the countryside. While there
were central Party decisions on the need for communists to interest
themselves in the 'land societies',[2] there was little attempt at a local
level before 1929 for Party members to use the commune gathering
as a means of putting over Party policy. Rezunov remarked that
'very few details are known about Party influence in the gathering,
but there seems to be a tendency for Party workers to look on the
gathering as beneath their attention'.[3]

The weakness of rural cells when compared to town cells can
only partly be illustrated by quantitative illustrations. In September
1924 there was one rural cell to 800 peasants (including children)
and one rural cell to approximately six rural soviets. There were
8–12 members per cell, compared with over 40 per town cell.[4]
There were fluctuations between guberniyas in the number of
non-Party adult peasants to each Party peasant. One of the lowest
was about 281:1 in Leningrad guberniya; the highest, not surprisingly, was in the Central Black Earth area, with Tambov guberniya
weakest of all, with 926:1 in one published comparison of 15 guberniyas.[5]

The number of rural cell members increased, so that by 1929

[1] Lepeshkin, *Mestnye organy vlasti sovetskogo gosudarstva*, p. 231.
[2] Cf. above, p. 123.   [3] Rezunov, *Sel'sovet i zemel'noe obshchestvo*, p. 40.
[4] Khataevich, 'Partiya v derevne', *Na agrarnom fronte* (1925), no. 2, p. 103, gives
figures for numbers of rural party members. I give these figures assuming 120 million
peasant household members and 80,000 rural soviets.   [5] Ibid. p. 105.

there were almost twice as many rural cells and members as in 1924.[1] By then, there were 25 settlements, or three rural soviets per cell. With the introduction of 'face to the countryside', the Party's wariness in admitting peasant members, which went as far as a total ban in early 1924, had been relaxed. The difficulty which presented itself when recruiting rural soviet workers was even more acute where Party membership was concerned. On the one hand, Party peasants were required to be exemplary in their own agricultural methods; on the other hand, on ideological grounds the greatest effort had to be made to attract the poorest peasants. Studies showed that well-to-do peasants tended to be over-represented, and poor peasants and agricultural labourers under-represented although absolutely their number was not large.[2] It was this peasant group that was most heavily purged after the XVI Party Conference in April 1929. 17·6% of peasant members were purged as compared with 7·5% of worker members.[3] At the same time, there was a drive to recruit more agricultural labourers, which met with some success.

The proportion of Party members labelled as 'peasants' remained fairly stable. It was 23% in 1924[4] and 27% in early 1930.[5] While this was a heavy under-representation in a country with an overwhelmingly peasant population, this was a substantial proportion, given the aims of the Party. One of the major difficulties was that, of this number of 'peasants' in the Party, only a minority were actively engaged in agriculture. The rest were in fact full-time officials. It was estimated that in 1924, only a third of the members of rural cells were actively engaged in agriculture, including collective farms. There could hardly have been more than 15% of members of rural cells who were peasants working their land.[6]

The rural cells were weakened also by the educational level of their members. In 1927, a survey in a number of guberniyas showed 12·8%–23·3% of rural cell members to be illiterate. 71·5%–76·1%

[1] See Konyukhov, *KPSS v bor'be s khlebnymi zatrudneniyami v strane 1928-9 gg.* (Moscow, 1960).
[2] See *Sel'skoe khozyaistvo SSSR 1925-8 gg.* (Ts SU 1929), pp. 134-5. Also *Pravda*, 6 February 1929.
[3] *Partinoe stroitel'stvo* (1930), no. 12, p. 45.
[4] See Khataevich, *Na agrarnom fronte* (1925), no. 2.
[5] Cf. Kaganovich, *XVII S'ezd KPSS, Otchet*, p. 557.
[6] Khataevich, *Na agrarnom fronte* (1925), no. 2, p. 106.

had only primary education.[1] Party members were sent out from
the towns to try and improve rural cells, a process which reached a
peak at the time of collectivisation, but had begun in 1923.[2] By
1929, 29% of chairmen of rural cells were workers.[3] They found
themselves in a difficult position, often shunned by the local
inhabitants and local Party organisations.[4]

The problems outlined meant that the rural Party cell was far
from being the vanguard of the proletariat in the countryside. The
most detailed study of the problem, from which we have already
quoted, was published in 1925 by Khataevich.[5] He regarded the
problem of remoteness as crucial in most volosts where there were
only one or two cells. As it was rare for all the members of a cell to
be from the same settlement, they often had to travel 15 or more
kilometres in order to meet with other communists at the cell. Thus,
most peasant Party members worked alone and, whatever their
motives in joining, either identified themselves less with the Party
and more with their surroundings, or went to the opposite extreme
and became petty tyrants. He suggested that, rather than try to
send communists to as many villages as possible to become rural
soviet chairmen, certain villages should be selected for concentrated
effort. He criticised the content of rural cell work, noting that it was
rare for a cell to discuss agricultural problems, such as land use
measures, at all, but rather it became involved in a ceaseless round
of campaigns. He felt there was a need for men from the towns to
liven the cells up, but stressed that a man who knew the countryside
should always be sent. He felt that only one third of 4,500 town
workers sent out in 1923 had proved capable and valuable, overcoming their great initial difficulties.

The general picture of the difficulties of a rural Party cell is
confirmed in an excellent local study of rural cells in the Second

[1] I. Makarov, 'Ukreplenie sel'skoi partiinoi organizatsii v periode podgotovki massogo kolkhoznogo dvizheniya', *Voprosy istorii KPSS* (1962), no. 3, p. 114.
[2] Cf. Konyukhov, *KPSS v bor'be s khlebnymi zatrudeniyami v strane 1928–9*; Lepeshkin, *Mestnye organy vlasti sovetskogo gosudarstva*, pp. 196–7.
[3] Makarov, *Voprosy istorii KPSS*, p. 120.
[4] Cf. below, pp. 200ff.
[5] 'Partiya v derevne', *Na agrarnom fronte* (1925), no. 2; also 'Itogi vypolneniya post-anovleniya Oktyabr'skogo plenuma Ts K. RKP(b) o rabote v derevne', *ibid.*, no. 5–6.

Don okrug of Stalingrad guberniya.[1] The author sets the Party firmly in the perspective of local economic and geographical conditions. He enumerated a dozen quite specific tasks which he saw as necessary to help alleviate the most pressing problems in the agriculture of the area. He asked 'what did the Party do to lead agriculture from this cul de sac?' and concluded 'nothing'. He saw the main problem as the quality of rural cell members. Seventeen of 533 members and candidates in the okrug were completely illiterate, and 394 'politically illiterate'. He thought that the cultural level of the members was below that of most of the villagers. In contrast to the national position, it seems that the Party members were largely drawn from the smallest peasants. 'The Party cells could not show off anything, as their members usually had the worst managed plots.' On further investigating the position, he found that all peasants with more than two horses had been expelled, which was at that time against Party policy. He put forward a number of plans for ways of influencing the wider peasantry, but underlined his conclusion that the Party members were, as things stood, a disincentive to others to join. A further factor accounting for the situation in the area was probably that most inhabitants were Cossacks; he admitted that on the whole there was a state of 'armed neutrality' between communities and the bulk of the peasantry in the okrug.

While means of making closer links between Party and peasantry were being discussed, the discouraging results at local level suggested that this was not an attainable end.[2] The economic climate came to favour those who put forward a much more forthright line for workers in the countryside. Organisationally, this was reflected in the founding of Departments for Work in the Countryside in all Party organisations down to okrug level,[3] and, later, the creation of raion Party conferences and committees.[4] The tasks of the cells

[1] M. Latsis, 'Sostoyanie sel'skogo khozyaistva vo vtorom Donokruge i zadachi sel'-yacheek v dele vosstanovleniya sel'skogo khozyaistva', *Na agrarnom fronte* (1925), no. 4, pp. 78 ff.
[2] Cf. *Pravda*, 8 February 1928; reports from localities appeared in *Pravda* throughout February and March.
[3] Decision of Central Committee, 15 May 1928, in *Kollektivizatsiya sel'skogo khozyaistva*, p. 50.
[4] Decree of Ts K KPSS 'O sel'skikh partorganizatsiyakh', 1 July 1929. *Kollektivizatsiya sel'skogo khozyaistva*, p. 186.

became more narrowly focused – firstly, getting grain and, later, in 1929, forming collectives. This led to problems with Party peasants who refused to join collectives. The new, more clearly defined tasks called for the measures we have already outlined in an attempt to convert the rural cells into forceful implementers of Party policy. The new atmosphere is reflected in a statement in a recent history that 'In North Caucasus all Party works sent to the country were given the right to annul all decisions of local Party and soviet organs, which contradicted the directives of the Central Committee and Krai Committee in the field of grain delivery, and were themselves to give orders which were compulsory for all local organs'.[1]

The commune as an institution seems to have been virtually disregarded by rural Party workers until the late twenties. There was no question of Party workers using the gathering to promote better techniques in agriculture. However, with the grain delivery campaigns, it seems that the Party began to make use of the commune gathering in some areas. There is a somewhat hazy area of what were referred to by Party workers as 'peasant meetings'. Apparently, in Tula guberniya during the grain delivery campaign, 'there were individual and group discussions with peasants, poor peasant meetings and general peasant gatherings'. Thus, one Party cell recorded that it had addressed 35 village gatherings.[2] In another raion, at the time of the spring sowing campaign, a 'month of involving peasants in the gathering' was instituted.[3] Purges of the Party were also put to a gathering for discussion.[4] It was noted in the North Caucasus, and Lower and Mid-Volga regions that the Party cells 'saw to the regular calling of general meetings of citizens.[5] The gathering was also used as a platform for Party activists to argue the advantages of collectivisation, as we will see later.[6] Apart from these very specific ways, the gathering was not used in any more subtle manner in the earlier attempts to bring the peasantry closer to the Party. With the structure of the rural Party cells as it was, the isolation of their members from the general peasant community and the lack of peasant members to convey the feel

[1] Konyukhov, *KPSS v bor'be s khlebnymi zatrudneniyami v strane 1928–9*, p. 122.
[2] Podchufarov, *Tul'skie kommunisty v periode podgotovki massovogo kolkhoznogo dvizheniya, 1924–9*, pp. 23 and 84.   [3] Ibid. p. 107.   [4] Ibid. p. 65.
[5] Makarov, *Voprosy istorii* (1962), no. 3, p. 118.   [6] See below, pp. 200 ff.

of their area to the cell, it was probably inevitable that rural cells concentrated their rather feeble efforts on the rural soviets until they were jolted into both action and disorganisation by the demands of central government.

7 FINANCE IN THE COMMUNE AND RURAL SOVIET

One of the focal points in the disparity of influence between commune and rural soviet was the source of finance. While the rural soviet was given a wide range of topics to discuss in law, the budgetary arrangements were far from adequate to support any decisions taken, even if the rural soviet had been capable of implementing them on all other grounds. The rural soviet, under the 1924 decree on rural soviets, did not have an independent budget, but sent estimates of income and expenditure for inclusion in the volost budget.[1] Only in exceptional circumstances would large rural soviets be allowed to have an independent budget. This hamstrung any attempts at local initiative, and was further hindered by the weakness of volost budgets, which had only been established in 1924–5.[2] The position was not substantially changed by the 1926 regulations on local finance.[3]

The effect of this was to reduce most rural soviets to financial impotence. Sums granted by the volost executive committees were barely sufficient to pay the meagre salaries of rural soviet staff, and occasionally included sums for specific projects. The communes, by contrast, were able to find the finance to implement decisions which they made. Their financial arrangements were nowhere legally defined, and studies have only been fairly sketchy.

The income of communes was derived from a variety of sources. They included communally held land, gardens, fisheries and other holdings, communal enterprises and undertakings such as mills, creameries, smithies, equipment hiring stations, and insemination

---

[1] 'Polozhenie o sel'sovetakh', cf. above, p. 107. As revised by SU no. 31, art. 221, 1925.

[2] Decree of Ts IK 19 November 1923, quoted by Lepeshkin, *Mestnye organy vlasti sovetskogo gosudarstva 1921–36*, p. 186.

[3] 'Polozhenie o mestnykh finansakh RSFSR'. VTsIK SNK, 19 November 1926, SU 1926, no. 92, art. 668.

points.[1] The elusive 'Model Statute of a Land Society' of 5 January 1926 apparently included the following sources of income: membership fees, state and co-operative loans and grants, rent from land, forest and communal enterprises.[2] A major source of income was self-taxation, as we will shortly see.

The varying relationships between commune and rural soviet often reflected the financial position in a particular area. In many areas the rural soviet was reduced to financial dependence on the commune. Rezunov argues very strongly that rural soviets were in most cases dependent financially on the land society. His conclusion after taking examples from a wide area was that 'thanks to the fact that the rural soviet has no strong material base, it is obliged to put many questions which involve expenditure to the gathering for discussion'.[3] He quoted as an example a delegate at the XV Guberniya Congress of Soviets of Saratov guberniya who complained that 'it is said here that rural soviets are dragged at the tail of the general meeting. This is the reason. They do not feel themselves materially well supplied, and this explains their instability. On every question – repair of a school, hiring a watchman, and so on – every day they have to have a talk with the general meeting, every day they have to ask for money.'[4] It is no coincidence that at the same time a writer in *Izvestiya* was complaining about the inadequacy of volost budgets, let alone those of rural soviets. He remarked that the budgets of many rural soviets were made up almost entirely from self-taxation.[5]

A major handicap for the rural soviet was that it could not effectively enforce any tax for local needs. Since 1924 it was legal for sums to be raised by 'self-taxation for the satisfaction of local social needs'.[6] Such sums could only be exacted from those voting for that expenditure at the gathering (or equivalent meeting – self-taxation was permitted to other organisations). The rural soviet and volost executive committee themselves were forbidden to raise money by this means. The gathering could raise self-taxation 'for

[1] Decree on changes to decree on local finances, 7 October 1929, SU no. 77, art. 751, listed these sources of income to be transferred from land society to rural soviet.
[2] *Khozyaistvo i Upravlenie* (1927), no. 12.
[3] Rezunov, *Sel'sovet i zemel'noe obshchestvo*, p. 23.   [4] Ibid. p. 11.
[5] *Izvestiya*, 30 October 1926, no. 251. Article by 'N.A.'.
[6] Decree of Ts IK SNK, 29 August 1924, 'O samooblozhenii', SZ 1924, no. 6, art. 69.

any kind of local social needs', including maintenance of educational
and medical facilities, social security, and civic amenities. It was to
be a specific tax, raised for a stated purpose.
The response to this situation varied from area to area. Some rural
soviets did raise self-taxation themselves. Thus in Bol'shesolskii
rural soviet, Levashevsk volost, Kostroma guberniya, self-taxation
was raised to pay the forest-keeper and other local officials. Others
in the guberniya raised taxes for such purposes as 'entertaining the
peasants at the beginning of harvest', and helping the clergy.[1]
Abuses of self-taxation were widespread. Apart from being raised
directly by rural soviets, taxes were often illegal in being voluntary
in name only. In certain areas self-taxation was fixed as a specific
proportion of the single agricultural tax (for example, 35% in
Nizhnedvinsk uezd of Voronezh guberniya, 70–80% in Ostrozhsk
uezd). In Prigorodnensk rural soviet, Usmansk uezd, Voronezh
guberniya it was ordered that 'those not paying self-taxation shall
be turned over to the court'. The writer who quoted these examples
felt that illegal tax formation was one of the major infringements of
'revolutionary legality' and noted that procurators' offices had been
inundated with protests against illegal taxation. Under this pressure,
he felt, illegal tax creation was tending to go underground and take
concealed forms.[2]
In many cases self-taxation was raised by the land society, but to
finance the rural soviet. Even if specific self-taxation were not raised,
land societies frequently included in their budget items of expenditure properly the sphere of the rural soviet. Olginsk land society
(N. Ossetian Republic) included in its expenditure pay for the
militia man, lighting of the rural soviet building, pay for the watchman of the rural soviet and school buildings.[3] Not only did land
societies finance civic amenities of various kinds, but they also
paid supplements to the salary of the rural soviet chairman, and
paid his deputy and technical staff in certain areas.[4] Whilst such
statements do not in themselves imply land society influence over
the rural soviet – the reverse implication could equally well be put

[1] *Izvestiya*, 30 October 1926, no. 251. Article by P. Tadeyush.
[2] Chernyshev, 'Derevenskoe nalogotvorchestvo', *Izvestiya*, 30 October 1926, no. 251.
[3] Rezunov, *Sel'sovet i zemel'noe oshchestvo*, p. 14. He gives many similar examples in the
following pages.   [4] Kozhikov, *Na agrarnom fronte* (1928), no. 5.

on such evidence – they are quoted in a context suggesting that the land societies were exercising an influence that was undesirable from the authors' point of view.

More detailed evidence of land society budgets is scarce.[1] We may quote two examples which have been put forward as typical of the situation. In Voronezh guberniya the land societies were said to be financially independent, and Voronezh Worker–Peasant Inspectorate calculated that over 1 million rubles 'passed by' the volost and rural soviet budgets. The finance department of Rossoshansk uezd gave the following figures for expenditure by land societies of money received from exploitation of property and land, and from self-taxation for three quarters of 1926–7 financial year.[2]

Table 3.7

	Rubles	Percentage of total expenditure
Wages of agent of society	5,377	
Other expenses of agent of society	2,644	7·8
Maintaining rural postal service	23,724	23·0
Wages to rural soviet	10,338	
Other expenses of rural soviet	9,179	18·9
School needs	2,282	2·3
On political education institutions	740	0·7
Expenses of auditing commission	106	0·1
Repairs to roads and bridges	3,616	3·5
Fire precautions	4,744	4·6
Making up list of tax-payers	248	0·2
Land use measures	40,051	38·9
Total	103,049	100

Thus the land societies in that area spent about half their budget financing services which came within the scope of the rural soviet.

Even in areas where rural soviets had their own budgets, they were not always adequate. This is shown in the comparison of budgets in the area of three rural soviets in Vladimir guberniya (Krasnoselsk, Novoselsk in Byaznikovsk uezd, and Vyshelavsk Vladimir uezd) in Table 3.8.[3]

[1] Budgets of rural soviets are occasionally found in *Vestnik Finansov*.
[2] *Khozyaistvo i Upravlenie* (1927), no. 12.
[3] Ibid.

Table 3.8

	Spent by rural soviet (rubles)	Spent by land society (rubles)
Maintenance of rural soviet	1,977	315
Economic (khozyaistvennye) measures	990	3,786[a]
Cultural and social expenditure	1,067[b]	—
To agents of land society and self-taxation collection	—	309·5
Pay for chairman of mutual aid society	—	120
Hire of herdsmen	—	5,965
'Answer to Chamberlain' fund	—	37
Total	4,034	10,532·5

[a] Fire precaution, bridge and road building, purchase of bull, pay of night watchman.
[b] Schools, reading rooms, medical points.

At the XV Party Congress Molotov remarked that 'the budget is often greater in the land society than in the rural soviet'. As an example he quoted Verkhnye-Belatusk land society in Ryazan guberniya, which had a budget of 22,000 rubles in 1926–7, while the rural soviet had only 1,200 rubles.[1]

In some areas grants were made by the land societies to the rural soviets. In Gavilovsk rural soviet, Tambov guberniya, the land society income was 2,544 rubles, of which 701 rubles was given to the rural soviet. In Staro-Yureyevsk rural soviet in the same guberniya, 598 rubles of the land societies' income of 3,242 rubles was given to the rural soviet.[2]

While the general reaction to the situation was to press for the subordination of land society funds into rural soviet budgets, North Caucasus krai executive committee passed a decree which clarified the position on self-taxation, and set it in the wider context of other forms of land society income.[3] This was a decree 'to allow the land society to satisfy cultural–educational and other social

[1] *Sten. Otchet*, p. 1085.   [2] Kozhikov, *Na agrarnom fronte* (1928), no. 5.
[3] Kruglov, 'Rural social capital', in *Izvestiya*, 30 October 1926, no. 25 quotes this decree of 24 June 1926, 'On forming social capital in village and stanitsa land societies'.

needs not fully satisfied in soviet budgets'. The gathering of the land society would pass a decree on forming such a fund. The sources of capital were to be as follows:

(a) co-operative working of land plots,
(b) sale and renting of plots,
(c) exploiting land society woods, fisheries and other holdings,
(d) exploiting agricultural enterprises organised by the land society,
(e) subscription in money and kind from members of land society and others participating,
(f) subsidies from rural soviet and raion executive committee budgets,
(g) other legal sources of income.

The land society was to appoint a commission of three executives to administer this expenditure. This decision is important, as it was a recognition by an authoritative body of the inadequacies of the rural soviet, and of the ability of the land societies to organise such affairs. It is the more remarkable as the North Caucasus krai was generally regarded as an area where rural soviet budgets were developed quite strongly. Only a year later it was noted that the North Caucasus was one of the few areas where there was a rural soviet actif, a rural soviet budget, and the rural soviet led the land society.[1] It was said that the tendency for rural soviet budgets to be smaller than those of the land society was 'less noticeable' in the krai.[2] At least one commentator saw this decree as a hindrance to the development of rural soviet budgets in the area. He noted that the income of some rural soviets in the area had actually fallen, as the decree had made it quite specific that the land society should receive all income from land. Previously there had been cases where the rural soviet had received this.[3] Objection to the decree was raised by the People's Commissariat of Social Security, and the Central Committee of the Committees of Mutual Aid to the All-Russian Central Executive Committee; it was claimed that this was creating a dualism with their functions. On the other hand the People's

[1] Karp, *Isvestiya*, 15 December 1927. [2] Kozhikov, *Na agrarnom fronte* (1928), no. 5.
[3] *Khozyaistvo i Upravienie* (1927) no. 12.

Commissariats of Land, Law, and Finance found nothing illegal in this, and thought the measure useful. In October 1926 the Presidium of the All-Russian Central Executive Committee held that the objection had been groundless.[1] This was a setback for those wanting to push ahead with rural soviet expansion, and a victory for those who were more anxious to manipulate the existing situation towards Soviet ends.

The opposite solution, of the land society budget being merged into the rural soviet, is reasonably well authenticated in only one area, the Volga German Republic. It is significant that this was not an area of traditional communal land holding. On 21 July 1926 a decision was made that income from free land should be handed over to the rural soviets.[2] In the Republic, all rural soviets had had their own budgets since 1924-5. Once funds of the land societies had been included, half the income of all rural soviet budgets in the republic (387·5 thousand rubles) came from agriculture in 1926-7. The land societies' only functions were then to discuss the arable land and pasture. It was said that even where there were many land societies to a rural soviet – and there were 22 in some cases – this was successful.[3]

There are statistics which hint at the size of the problem on the national scale. It was said that research into village budgets by the All-Union Worker–Peasant Inspectorate in 1927-8 showed that the resources of land societies exceeded rural soviet budgets ten times or more.[4] At that time all self-taxation came under the land society. According to Enukidze at the XV Party Congress, the total sum of rural soviet budgets came to 16 million rubles, while the sum of land society budgets, 'and other peasant unions' (Mutual Aid Committees?) was 80 million rubles according to the People's Commissariat of Finance, and 100 million rubles according to the Worker–Peasant Inspectorate.[5] While showing an absolutely low level of rural soviet finance (if this was based, as he suggested, on 2,300 rural soviets, each would have an income of 7,000 rubles), if there were around 300,000 land societies, their average income would

[1] Kruglov in *Izvestiya*, 30 October 1926.
[2] Kozhikov, *Na agrarnom fronte* (1928), no. 5.
[3] *Khozyaistvo i Upravlenie* (1927) no. 12.
[4] Kozhikov, *Na agrarnom fronte* (1928), no. 5.   [5] *Sten. Otchet*, p. 1112.

Table 3.9   *Rural soviets with their own budgets, 17 December 1926*[a]

1st column: total rural soviets of given size; 2nd column: rural soviets of given size with budgets; 3rd column: percentage of rural soviets of given size with budgets.

	Up to 999 inhabitants		%	1000–1999 inhabitants		%	2000–4999 inhabitants	
USSR (excluding Kazakh, etc.)	25,530	207	1	24,539	511	2	17,718	917
RSFSR	22,636	195	1	17,837	417	2	11,043	642
North east area	186	—	—	297	1	—	488	24
Leningrad oblast	1,525	—	—	936	2	—	542	3
Karelian ASSR	88	—	—	71	—	—	27	—
Western raion	371	3	1	1,181	50	4	687	85
Central Industrial oblast	6,228	40	1	3,253	52	2	2,107	36
(i) Moscow Industrial sub-area	5,383	39	1	2,155	48	2	1,625	32
(ii) Ryazan-Tula sub-area	845	1	—	1,098	4	—	482	4
Central Black Earth oblast	580	—	—	1,516	1	—	1,894	14
Vyatsk guberniya	265	—	—	917	5	1	633	8
Urals oblast	596	—	—	1,572	—	—	949	—
Bashkir ASSR	808	—	—	884	—	—	245	—
Mid Volga krai	5,034	—	—	2,340	3	—	913	10
Lower Volga krai	1,205	95	8	1,013	110	11	600	88
Crimean ASSR	207	3	1	77	1	1	56	4
North Caucasus krai	269	22	8	533	95	18	749	258
Siberian krai	2,696	14	—	2,322	89	3	764	91
Far East krai	1,618	—	—	338	—	—	102	—
Belorussian SSR	270	—	—	324	—	—	1,088	12
Ukrainian SSR	1,331	12	1	4,584	88	2	4,062	258

[a] Source: Tsentral'noe statisticheskoe upravlenie, *Mestnye Byudzhety za 1926–7* (Moscow 1929), p. 10. Percentage derived by present author.

be even lower, around 300 rubles. It is possible that the figure for land society income is very incomplete.

While the debate on the proper relationship between land society and rural soviet often centred on this problem of finance, two factors combined to bring the rural soviet into a more healthy financial position. A corollary of the campaign to enliven rural soviets was increasing encouragement for them to form their own budgets. This was given support by changes in the law on self-taxation.

In 1925–6 only 3% of rural soviets in the RSFSR had their own budgets. By law only those of exceptional size were allowed to have their own budgets, and the average population of rural soviets with a budget was 3,900, while the average population of a rural

%	5000–9999 inhabitants		%	10,000+ inhabitants		%	Total		%	Population[a] per rural soviet (all rural soviets)
5	1,905	365	19	335	149	44	70,027	2,149	3	1,600
6	986	248	25	207	137	66	52,709	1,639	3	1,500
5	23	4	17	—	—	—	994	29	3	2,100
1	56	—	—	—	—	—	3,059	5	—	1,400
—	—	—	—	—	—	—	186	—	—	1,100
12	10	—	—	—	—	—	2,249	138	6	1,700
2	70	3	4	3	—	—	11,661	131	1	1,200
2	51	2	4	2	—	—	9,217	121	1	1,100
1	19	1	5	1	—	—	2,444	10	—	1,400
1	265	11	4	12	2	17	4,267	28	1	2,300
1	5	—	—	—	—	—	1,820	13	1	1,800
—	66	—	—	23	—	—	3,206	—	—	1,700
—	14	—	—	—	—	—	1,951	—	—	1,200
1	41	3	7	4	2	50	8,382	18	—	1,100
15	85	24	28	14	3	21	2,917	320	11	1,600
7	4	—	—	—	—	—	344	8	2	1,100
34	241	173	72	139	129	92	1,931	672	35	3,500
12	80	26	33	9	1	11	5,871	221	4	1,300
—	—	—	—	—	—	—	2,061	—	—	700
1	50	1	2	2	—	—	1,734	13	1	2,400
6	660	115	25	96	12	13	10,733	485	5	2,200

[a] Ibid. p. 8.

soviet in the RSFSR was 1,500.[1] The detailed picture was as shown in Table 3.9.

The regional variations are of interest. The higher weighting of budgets in the southern areas is partially explained by the larger size of rural soviet there (e.g. in N. Caucasus). This does not explain the relatively high proportion in the Lower Volga, where rural soviets were of average size: this suggests a greater strength of rural soviet activity there. The traditional commune stronghold, the Central Black Earth region, had a large average size of rural soviet, but a low proportion of rural soviet budgets.

While the legislative position did not change until 1928 and 1929,

[1] Population in rural soviets with own budgets in RSFSR, 6, 361,000; USSR, 8,374,200. Source as for Table 3.9.

The commune and soviet society

an active campaign was mounted to increase the number of rural soviets with budgets.[1] By 1927–8 the proportion had risen to 6% (3,479) of rural soviets in the RSFSR, and, helped by consolidation of rural soviets, to 14·2% (7,791) in 1928–9.[2] The process had been more rapid in the Ukraine, presumably because land societies did not offer an alternative source of finance. Thus by April 1927, one third of Ukrainian rural soviets had independent budgets.[3]

While the size of the rural soviet budgets was one problem, the pattern of expenditure was also of vital importance in making the work of the rural soviet effective. A high proportion of expenditure tended to be on administration, especially salaries for staff. An investigation in Kostroma uezd, where experimental budgets were set up in 1925/6 showed that up to 68% was spent on salaries for staff.[4] This is much higher than the following table, if this is included in 'administrative expenditure'. Over the years, campaigns to reduce expenditure on administration, and increase that on 'cultural social' needs had some success. Table 3.10 combines expenditure in volost soviets and rural soviets.[5]

Table 3.10

| | Percentage of budget spent in: | | | |
	Administration	Cultural–social	Economic-production	Other
1923–4	46·9	35·4	10·2	7·5
1924–5	42·0	41·6	8·5	7·9
1925–6	32·2	52·5	8·3	6·0
1926–7	28·3	54·2	11·8	5·7
1927–8	22·5	59·5	12·7	5·3

[1] The July 1927 law on local soviets recognised that the practice of spreading rural soviet budgets should spread provided that at least one of three conditions was fulfilled: (1) There was a fully strengthened volost or raion budget. (2) The settlements forming the rural soviet were of large size. (3) The independent sources of income of the rural soviet were large enough to cover basic expenditure. Worker–Peasant Inspectorates were instructed to report to the government on the practice of forming rural soviet budgets by 1 March 1928. Article 146: Published in *Izvestiya*, 24 July 1927, no. 167.
[2] Kiselev at XIV All-Russian Congress of Soviets, *Izvestiya*, 24 May 1929. In 1927, according to Karp, *Izvestiya*, 15 December 1927, there were still whole guberniyas such as Ulyanov without rural soviet budgets.
[3] Lepeshkin, *Mestnye organy vlasti sovetskogo gosudarstva 1921–36*, p. 188.
[4] *Izvestiya*, 30 October 1926, no. 251. P. Tadeyush.
[5] Lepeshkin, p. 188 – no source.

None the less, 74% of all expenditure from rural soviet budgets in 1927–8 was on wages.[1]

Apart from encouragement to rural soviets to have their own budgets, there was an attempt to widen the sources from which the rural soviet could draw its income, by making the rural soviet responsible for administering certain forms of local self-taxation. An All-Union decree on 'self-taxation for local needs' was passed in August 1927, and amplified in a Russian decree in January 1928.[2]

A basic distinction was made between 'compulsory' and 'voluntary' self-taxation. Compulsory taxes could only be levied for certain specific purposes such as building and maintenance of public buildings, roads and bridges, fire precautions, civic ammenities and security; it could not be levied to cover administrative expenditure, such as wages. Compulsory self-taxation was to be exacted only by a vote at the 'general meeting of citizens' gathering, thus perpetuating the unrealistic assumption that there could be such a body, consisting only of voters to the rural soviet, separate from the 'land society gathering'.[3] The rural soviet was to administer such a tax, which could be assessed in labour as well as money, although the volost executive committee would do so if a project were to be undertaken by a group of hamlets in different rural soviets.

Voluntary self-taxation was to be raised on a rather different basis, similar to the 1924 decree.[4] Such a decision could be made at the general meeting of citizens or 'other meeting of citizens' (implying the land society gathering). The rural soviet was not allowed to participate in organising or administering the tax, which could be for needs not covered by compulsory self-taxation. Only those in favour of the work for which it was collected could be assessed. The gathering itself was to apportion the tax and administer it.

The indications are that these decrees were not particularly effective. They brought self-taxation by rural soviets nearer to

[1] Kiselev at XIV All-Russian Congress of Soviets, *Izvestiya*, 24 May 1929.
[2] SZ 1927, no. 51, art. 509 and SU 1928, no. 8, art. 73. Unless otherwise, stated reference here is to the second, more detailed, decree.   [3] See above, p. 108.
[4] See above, p. 137. The All-Union decree is more detailed on voluntary self-taxation and reference is to this rather than the Russian decree, which merely mentions the possibility of such a tax.

legality, although how many discussed the matter with a 'general meeting of citizens' is a moot point. The law foundered on the artificiality of the distinction between two gatherings. It would have left the land society free to raise money under voluntary self-taxation for purely agricultural needs. The main effect on rural soviet budgets was probably to give a general impression (wrongly) that the rural soviet could now impose self-taxation. As a measure to curb the financial power of the land society, it was ineffective for the further reason that it did not touch the many sources of land society income apart from self-taxation.

Recent authors have suggested that this law marked a step towards a class-based approach to the gathering. 'Gatherings, where they took decisions on self-taxation, were transformed into an area of decisive struggle by the middle and poor peasantry against rural exploiters.'[1] The authors quoted decisions of gatherings to build schools, etc., but this was in fact nothing new. The decrees mentioned class orientation in allowing poor peasants to be exempted from taxation. Bringing self-taxation under closer soviet control reflected a firmer government line towards the gathering, but the only explicit anti-rich peasant aspect was in excluding them from voting, which merely perpetuated the unreal 1927 situation.

One objection to self-taxation was that, being enforced by the land society, the more powerful elements in the village inevitably bore less than their fair share of the burden. Rather than being based on income, in many areas it was per household, or per capita. Evidence quoted by Rezunov[2] 'from research in several guberniyas' showed that as a proportion of the agricultural tax, poor peasants paid in self-taxation 124%, the middle peasant 71·2%, and the 'rich' (bogatye) 23%. This point was also made by Kozhikov.[3] A recent history of the role of Tula Communist Party in the years before mass collectivisation suggested that kulaks and well-off tried to avoid the 'class principle' in self-taxation. An example was given of a meeting of poor peasants in the hamlet (derevnya) of

[1] Konyukhov, *KPSS v bor'be s khlebnymi zatrudneniyami v strane 1928-9*, p. 91. A similar view is taken by Podchufarov, *Tul'skiye kommunisty v periode podgotovki massovogo kolkhoznogo dvizheniya 1924-9* (Tula, 1929).
[2] Rezunov, *Sel'sovet i zemelnoe obshchestvo*, p. 13.
[3] Kozhikov, *Na agrarnom fronte* (1920), no. 5.

Volkhonovka Epifan raion. They resolved that a decree of the rural soviet on self-taxation was incorrect, as distribution was to be per capita. They were said to obtain a class approach 'by bringing it up for review at the gathering, and this decision of the poor peasantry was confirmed by a gathering of the peasantry'.[1]

While this legislative compromise on self-taxation between the commune and rural soviet was unsuccessful, the pressures on the commune were growing in other directions, political and agricultural. The rural soviets, with their growing budgets, were showing at least a minimum ability to become the sole organ of power on their own territory. The number of qualified workers was increasing. The proportion of rural soviets with their own budgets was rising. The need for a strong government-oriented body in the countryside grew with pressure for collectivisation and a class-based approach to the peasantry. The mechanism by which control over the commune was to be attempted was a budgetary one.

The problem gathered urgency with the turn of 1928–9. In the discussion on the 'General Principles of Land Holding' at the Central Executive Committee in April 1928 Milyutin had decided discussion of the budget problem was not within the competence of the meeting as legislation was pending. In December the discussion was resumed, and he admitted the need: 'the land society lords it, and the rural soviet sits on one side'. A delegate interrupted, perhaps from bitter experience, 'and has to answer for everything that goes on in the village'. To this Milyutin replied, 'true'.[2] This interchange focused very clearly the dilemma of the rural soviet.

In May 1929 the All-Russian Congress of Soviets provided the platform for discussion of the problem. The 'General Principles of Land Holding' had, at the turn of the year, placed the land societies under rural soviet administrative control,[3] but it was left until this congress for the decision to be given financial teeth. In his speech, Kiselev pointed out that while there had been a rise in the number of rural soviet budgets, they were not yet numerous enough.[4] They had risen in size as indicated in Table 3.11. Most of this rise had been by government grants, rather than rural soviets having their

[1] Podchufarov, *Tul'skiye Kommunisty*, p. 88.
[2] Ts IK SSSR, 4-yi sozyv Dec. 1928. Bull. 12, p. 21.
[3] See below, p. 154.   [4] *Izvestiya*, 24 May 1929.

Table 3.11

1925	9 million rubles
1926–7	15·6 million rubles
1927–8	24·5 million rubles
1928–9	54 million rubles

own enterprises on which to base a budget. In fact the weight of local sources had fallen from 59·4% in 1925–6 to 25·9% in 1928. A further disturbing fact was that land society and mutual aid committee incomes were also rising rapidly, as shown in Table 3.12.

Table 3.12

	Rural soviets	Land societies	Mutual aid committees
1925–6	15[a]	60[b]	41
1928–9	54	140	50

[a] This does not agree with Kiselev's earlier 1925–6 figure, but with his 1926–7 figure.
[b] He noted that no exact figures were forthcoming from People's Commissariat of Agriculture; this was an estimate based on Worker–Peasant Inspectorate Research. He does not offer any explanation why this figure should rise so steeply.

The figures in these tables show a similar position as in 1927–8 (cf. p. 143), as far as relative size of budgets is concerned. The rural soviet budget averaged 7,000 rubles, while the land society had risen to over 400 rubles. If we assume that there were on average five land societies to one rural soviet, or possibly more, in those areas where the rural soviet was large enough to have its own budget, it would seem that the rural soviet had over three times the budget of the land societies in its area. But, as we have seen (p. 143), only one in seven rural soviets had its own budget.

Kiselev's overall impression was that 'the land society has a budget three times greater than the rural soviet, and often reduces the latter to a sponger'. This was supported by delegates from Lower Volga, Vladimir, Moscow, Nizhnii Novgorod, North Caucasus and Urals.

The introduction to the decree of the XIV All-Russian Congress of Soviets 'on the position and strengthening of the lower network of Soviets' set the tone, mentioning that the struggle with the kulaks had been insufficient and the significance of collective farms underestimated. The decree was designed to ensure that local soviets were 'leaders of the economic and cultural transformation of the countryside'. The first article urged the introduction of budgets to all rural soviets, so that by 1932–3 all would have their own. One of the sources of these budgets was to be found by 'giving to rural soviets incomes of land societies received from local funds and various enterprises'. The land society was to be left the right to set up special funds for specific purposes, which had to be confirmed by the rural soviet. This was expanded by Kiselev in his concluding speech. 'If the land society collects money, for example, for a commune bull, this money should not, of course, go to the rural soviet. Also a commune collection for a shepherd or other such needs should not be given to the rural soviet.'

These summary remarks were extended by decree in October 1929.[1] By 1929–30 all 'large' (2,000 + population) rural soviets were to have their own budgets. Rural soviets were to have as sources of income, as well as land society incomes, state enterprises of local significance (for long a bone of contention), 50% of fines for non-delivery of grain, 20% of agricultural tax, and self-taxation incomes. In the event, collectivisation helped speed the process of budget formation; by July 1930, 33% of rural soviets had their own, 81% in 1931, and practically all by 1932.[2]

In discussing public administration, the problem of finance is all-important. Without financial power, no organ can exert the influence for which it is designed. This was very true in this case. None the less it is easy to fall into the position taken up by many Soviet authors who seem to use the land society budget as a scapegoat for the troubles of rural soviets. Just as power does not exist in a vacuum without budgetary support, so budgetary power is an

---

[1] 'On budget of rural soviet, and changes and additions to the decree on local finance of the RSFSR', 7 October 1929. SU no. 77, art. 751. This listed revenues from land society to be transferred. See above, pp. 137–8.

[2] Lepeshkin, *Mestnye organy vlasti soveskogo gosudarstva 1921–36*, p. 188. The decree on rural soviets of 3 February 1930 provided for all rural soviets in areas of mass colectivisation to have budgets by 1930–1.

expression of the particular groups who have control. Finance is as much an expression of influence as a source of it. While an organisation may not have influence without finance, it does not follow that the source of that influence is financial. Thus the fact that the land societies were financially more powerful than the rural soviets is an expression of a number of facts. First, the 'historical' situation; secondly, in a condition of something approaching anarchy, the land societies were able to raise funds, while the rural soviets were not. The peasantry, for whatever reason, were prepared to pay for local improvements to the land society. It was not until the process of enlivening of rural soviets had been going on a number of years, that a serious approach was made to tackle the 'problem of the land society budget'.

8 INCREASING GOVERNMENT PRESSURE IN LEGISLATION ON RURAL SOVIET–COMMUNE RELATIONS

The relatively unimpaired freedom of the commune under the Land Code of 1922 came to an end, at least in law, with the 'General Principles of Land Holding and Land Use Measures' of 1928.[1] This was an All-Union law, looking forward to Republican legislation on many points, and was therefore much less detailed than the RSFSR Land Code. While it laid greater stress on collective farming, and was consistent with the XV Party Congress approach, it insisted on the voluntary principle in transfer to collective farms. The main impression conveyed by the decree was that peasant farming was to be made more efficient through rationalisation and co-operation. There was a stronger emphasis on a 'class'-oriented approach to land use measures. The other major area in which the decree differed substantially from the land Code was in providing for stricter soviet control over the commune.

The land society was mentioned first among land holders, followed by individual households, collective and state farms. It was to decide the land holding arrangements of its members 'on the basis of current laws'. The flexibility allowed by the phrase 'and

---

[1] Postanovleniye Ts IK SSSR, 15 December 1928. SZ 1928, no. 69, art. 642. See below, p. 156ff, for discussion of the background, and Diagram IV opposite.

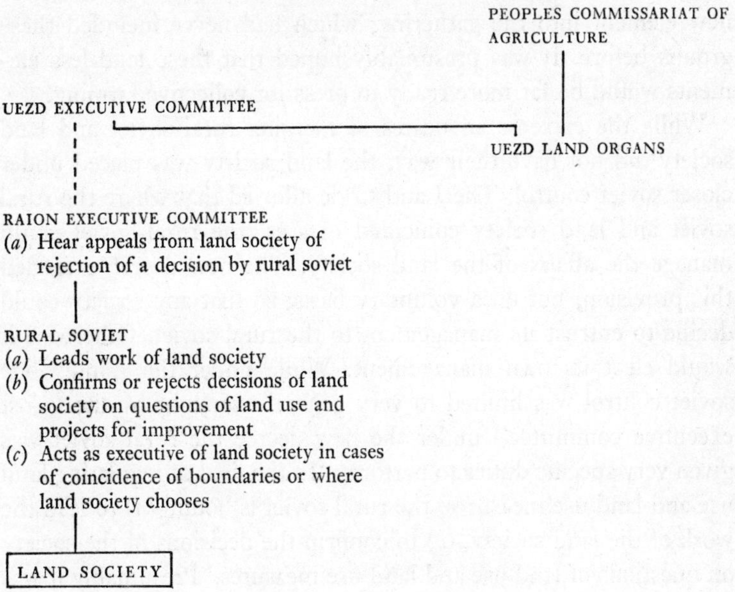

PEOPLES COMMISSARIAT OF
AGRICULTURE

UEZD EXECUTIVE COMMITTEE

UEZD LAND ORGANS

RAION EXECUTIVE COMMITTEE
(a) Hear appeals from land society of
    rejection of a decision by rural soviet

RURAL SOVIET
(a) Leads work of land society
(b) Confirms or rejects decisions of land
    society on questions of land use and
    projects for improvement
(c) Acts as executive of land society in cases
    of coincidence of boundaries or where
    land society chooses

LAND SOCIETY

Diagram IV. Administration of agriculture under 1928 General Principles of Land
Holding and Land Use Measures.

local custom' no longer appeared. There was a stronger emphasis on the role of the commune in joining co-operatives and collectives, but still no more emphatic than a statement that 'the society may take measures towards' joining one of these organisations.

In keeping with the general party approach at this time to the peasantry, there was a harder line on the activity of the rich peasants, while the 'rural proletariat' were introduced into the land society. While those excluded from voting in soviet elections were still allowed to be members of the land society, they were not to be allowed to vote in the meetings, or be elected to office. This stopped, in law at least, the anomaly of the 'kulak' holding office in the land society while being excluded from the rural soviet, which was often the weaker body. Membership was to be expanded by admitting those who were not peasants, but who 'take part with their own labour in the agriculture of a given land society, or in agricultural service trades, provided they have soviet voting rights (e.g. agricultural labourers, herdsmen and blacksmiths)'. This would bring a

F

153

new element into the gathering, which had never included these groups before. It was presumably hoped that these land-less elements would be far more ready to press for collective farming.

While the extreme advocates of merging rural soviet and land society did not have their way, the land society was placed under closer soviet control. The Land Code allowed that where the rural soviet and land society coincided in area, the rural soviet could manage the affairs of the land society. The new decree extended this provision, but on a voluntary basis, so that any society could decide to entrust its management to the rural soviet. Otherwise it would elect its own management. While under the Land Code soviet control was limited to very general oversight by the volost executive committee,[1] under the new decree the rural soviet was given very specific duties to perform. 'In the field of regulating land use and land use measures, the rural soviet is bound (*a*) to lead the work of the land society, (*b*) to confirm the decisions of the society on questions of land use and land use measures.' Presumably it was felt that this was now a practicable proposition, with the effort that had gone into enlivening the rural soviets.

All decisions of the land society had to be passed to the rural soviet for approval. Formerly only decisions on redistribution, separation of a member, and renting had to be put before a higher authority. The rural soviet was to be able to set aside a decision not only on the grounds that it infringed the rights of a member of the society, or contravened a specific law, but also if it 'contradicts the tasks of co-operation, or infringes the interests of the poor peasantry'. The society had the right of appeal to the raion or volost executive committee.

The rural soviet was to take a positive initiative in interesting a society in land use measures. While the execution of measures were the province of the land organs the rural soviets and raion executive committees were charged with exercising the closest supervision over their work in this field.

In the internal arrangements of the land society, it was stressed that a minority of members should be able to leave to organise a collective farm. Details of the size of the minority were left to

[1] See above, p. 101.

Republican legislation, as were most internal matters. It was laid down that a decision of a majority of members in favour of land use measures should be binding on the minority.

Mass collectivisation came before any Union Republic published their expansion of this decree,[1] but it is interesting as it shows the strong influence of the commune at this time through the strength of the measures to counter it. After more than ten years of Bolshevik rule they were administering the land in their hands with only minimal reference to the government. Such freedom could not last in an economy which was being increasingly centrally planned. The point of reference of the peasant had to be moved outside his home, his holding and his hamlet.

[1] The XIV All-Russian Congress of Soviets, in its decision 'on spreading the rights of local soviets' on 22 May 1929 recommended that all land society decisions be confirmed or rejected by the rural soviet, and placed land society funds under rural soviet control. See above, p. 151.

4

COLLECTIVISATION AND THE COMMUNE

I THE DEBATE ON LAND HOLDING

a *Introductory*

The problem of what form of agricultural organisation was appropriate to a socialist economy was one of the fundamental questions discussed during the twenties. Whilst most commentators up to 1928–9 paid lip service to the idea of collective farming, in the light of peasant hostility this was not seen as a practicable course until the political and economic decisions of these later years altered the perspective. Up to the summer of 1929, discussion was in terms of which forms of individual holding would make the peasant more susceptible at first to co-operation, then at a much later date, to collective working of the land. While there was a small minority of those ready to support the commune on the ideological grounds that it was a means to transfer the peasantry direct to socialism, this view was generally discounted at the centre because of the strong links of the commune with traditional peasant outlook and values. The alternative of enclosed peasant farms was hardly more attractive, with encouragement of a strong individual peasantry, but was more or less tolerated during the years of New Economic Policy. In the event, the practical way forward was a compromise, with improvements to the commune being the most common form of land use measures.

While the writings of Marx and Engels on the subject were only occasionally referred to, it is interesting to note that they did address themselves to the problem of whether the commune could be a way forward to socialism in Russia. They were rather ambivalent about the possibilities, but did not entirely reject them. Their very ambivalence meant that all sides in the debate could draw something from Marx or Engels. Engels originally conceded that the commune could possibly become the foundation of a socialist agriculture, if the proletarian revolution first came in the West and stemmed the growth of capitalism in Russia.[1] Marx's views were developed in the drafts and letter to Vera Zasulich on the practical question of whether Russian revolutionaries should seek to support the commune or hasten its demise. He felt that only a Russian revolution could save the commune, and such an initiative could not come from the commune.[2] The introduction to the Russian edition of the *Communist Manifesto* was equally cautious.[3] By 1894, Engels echoed this view, adding that the process of disintegration of the commune had gone further, and while avowedly agnostic about its possibilities, implied little faith in its usefulness.[4]

While these views of Marx and Engels are interesting, it would be wrong to exaggerate their importance to those who discussed the problems of the twenties. Only an occasional passing reference was made to them, and they could be invoked to buttress the arguments of both opponents and proponents of the commune. In this section, we review the arguments of both before describing the measures taken to improve the commune as a form of agricultural organisation, and the results of these measures.

b *Economic arguments*

On economic grounds, the supporters of transformation of the communes into enclosed peasant farms had very strong arguments. They could also look for support in some measure to Lenin's views. He was consistently scathing in his remarks about the commune and its supporters. In his pre-revolutionary criticism of the populist, Socialist Revolutionary standpoint in his *Development of capitalism in Russia*, he criticised the populists for not taking into account the fact that 'the commune has been subjected to a process of decomposition'.[5] He saw the economic pressures on the commune leading to its falling apart, and peasants being split into increasing differentiation.[6] His projects for the Party's agrarian programme did

[1] An English translation of writings by Marx and Engels on Russia is available in *The Russian menace to Europe*, P. W. Blackstock and Bert F. Hoselitz (eds) (George Allen and Unwin, London, 1953). This view is contained in a letter to Tkachev, translated on p. 210. Original in *Volkstaat*, 21 April 1875. For a useful comment on 'Marx, Engels and the Peasant', see Carr, *The Bolshevik revolution*, II, 385.

[2] Ibid. pp. 218 and 281.   [3] Ibid. p. 227.   [4] Ibid. p. 284.

[5] Lenin, *Sochineniya* (1937 ed.), III, 136.

[6] Ibid. III, 68. Article 'Chto takoe druz'ya naroda?' 1894.

not include the commune. He did not oppose the Stolypin reforms for these reasons. He was revolted by the economic backwardness of the commune, and saw no long-term solution of the agrarian pro-gramme in mixing primitive peasant ideas about equalising redistri-bution of land with contemporary socialist teaching on transfer of all means of production to common property and organisation of socialist production.[1]

Lenin maintained this view after the revolution, even though he was willing to compromise in the short term to gain peasant support. Addressing representatives of poor peasants in 1918, he said: 'We Bolsheviks were against the law on socialisation of land. All the same, we signed it because we did not want to oppose the majority of the peasantry. . . We did not want to bind the peasant to the idea which is strange to him that equalising redistribution of land is useless. Better for peasants to find it out for themselves.'[2] He was quite clear that the co-operation of individual peasants, leading eventually to collectivisation, was the way forward. This is the implication of the 'Lenin Co-operative Plan', so frequently referred to after his death. He foreshadowed it in a speech in 1919. 'We must not keep the peasant in the existing archaic commune with its fundamental scourge – redistribution – but turn each peasant onto a definite piece of ground.'[3]

It would seem reasonable to assume that both fully enclosed farms and farms with only fields enclosed would tend to be larger and have greater productivity than the households in communes in many areas. When it comes to testing this hypothesis, there is a dearth of information. While there was much research into peasant budgets in the twenties, there is very little evidence with which to compare the performance of households within and outside the commune, or of a household before and after leaving a commune.

One of the few protagonists in the debate to adduce any evidence on the question of relative economic performance was Kindeev.[4] He set out to attack what he saw as the general assumption of the land

[1] Lenin, *Sochineniya* (1937 ed.), v, 160.   [2] Ibid. (1950 ed.), xxviii, 156; similar speech p. 285.   [3] Address to VIII Party Congress, *Ibid.*, ix, 313.
[4] His book *Voprosy zemlevstroistva*, *NKRKI* (1925), based on research by NKRKI, is not easy to obtain, but his views are summarised in *Na agrarnom fronte* (1926), no. 10, pp. 77 ff., from which quotations are taken here.

organs, that the commune formed the best means of transition to collective farming. He criticised the arbitrary decision to do only work directed to improve the commune, rather than help peasants leave the commune, taken regardless of local conditions. He gave Leningrad guberniya as an example.[1] He felt that it was not Marxist to say that a given form of land holding could of itself lead to a change in social and economic relationships. On the question of economic performance he had strong, but limited evidence. He showed yield and productivity in all cases in his samples to be lower in the commune than in the enclosed farm. Unfortunately, his approach was a static one, which left unanswered the question whether those peasants who were in enclosed farms of either kind produced more or less when they were members of a commune.

In Smolensk guberniya he showed that yields of peasants in fully enclosed farms exceeded those of commune householders in rye by 22%, in oats by 18%, and in buckwheat by 70%. They had a higher number of animals for a given area – 19% in the case of cattle, 20% of pigs. The percentage of peasants sowing clover varied, according to uezd, between 3·2 and 28% for commune households, and between 27 and 60% for peasants in fully enclosed farms. One would expect these figures in an area where geographical factors clearly favoured the enclosed farm.

He was able to show superiority in Volokolamsk uezd in the north west of Moscow guberniya, probably an area with substantial commune holdings, but still in natural conditions far from favouring the commune (see Table 4.1).

Something of a dynamic approach was adopted in comparing levels of agricultural technique in a sample investigation of 219 households in Leningrad guberniya. Comparison was made between those households which, as land use measures, had transferred to a commune with broad strips, and those which had transferred to a farm with only fields enclosed (see Table 4.2).

The only figures which Kindeev gave for the RSFSR as a whole related to crop rotation. The three-course system was maintained on 95·8% of the sown area of all communes, on 28·7% of fully enclosed farms and 21·8% of farms with only fields enclosed.

---

[1] See above, p. 31.

Table 4.1

	Commune households	Farm with only fields enclosed	Fully enclosed farm
Harvest: quintals per desyatina			
Rye	56	77	71
Oats	64	70	75
Potatoes	708	876	944
Percentage of waste ground	9·6	3·7	3·5
Value of agricultural production per desyatina of ploughed land (gold rubles)	132 (100)	183 (139)	151 (115)
Percentage of households in co-operatives	48	90	100

Table 4.2

	Households transferring to	
	Commune with broad strips %	Farm with only fields enclosed %
Engaging in multi-course rotation	31·5	61·4
Percentage with ploughed area of 3+ desyatina	Fell by 36	Rose by 48
Percentage with ploughed area of 1–3 desyatina	Rose by 38	Fell by 29·4
Cows per household	Fell by 2	Rose by 2–4
Number of ploughs per household	Rose by 3·5	Rose by 33
Number of households in co-operatives	Rose by 27	Rose by 103

While such evidence did support the view that productivity tended to be higher in the enclosed farms than in the communes, it is on the whole drawn from areas where conditions did not favour the commune. He does not compare holdings of similar size. It is unfortunate that Kindeev was almost alone, among those debating the problem of what form land use measures should take, who produced evidence on economic performance to support their argument. The most extreme of the published supporters of the commune, Sukhanov, minimised the economic inefficiency of the commune, rather suggesting that he had not much of a case by suggesting that, even if it were shown that the enclosed farms were more efficient, they should not put economic development before the more important criterion of progress towards socialism.[1]

It would, of course, be possible to argue that even if an efficient household increased its output by leaving the commune, output in a given area could fall if the influence of the more efficient peasant were withdrawn from the commune.

c   *Co-operatives*

One of the major points of discussion was whether the 'Lenin Co-operative Plan' could be more effectively realised if peasants were weaned away from the commune into enclosed forms of holdings. The argument was that peasants in co-operatives were more likely to become members of collectives, although there was little evidence that this happened. Kindeev used this as one argument in support of the development of enclosed farms. From his researches the peasants with enclosed holdings were more likely to join agricultural co-operative organisations than the peasants in communes. In Smolensk guberniya, the percentage of commune members in agricultural co-operatives was 34·3%, while for peasants in fully enclosed farms it was 53·7% and in farms with only fields enclosed, 64%. In Troitsk uezd, Leningrad guberniya, in eight volosts where the commune was the predominant form of holding, 34% of households were in co-operatives, while in eight volosts where farms with only fields enclosed predominated, 53% of households were co-operative members. These figures should be taken with caution when considering the general situation, as they refer to areas where the commune was less strongly developed. However, there is evidence to suggest that, in general, it was the better-off peasants who most frequently became members of co-operatives; if this group also left the commune more readily,[2] it would seem likely that peasants with enclosed farms did become co-operative members more readily. This was presumably because they had more drive to take advantage of schemes which could help them to improve their husbandry. It seems that the assumption that because they participated in co-

[1] Sukhanov, *Na agrarnom fronte* (1926), no. 11–12, pp. 98–109.
[2] See below, p. 167.

operatives, they would, at some time in the distant future, be ready to participate in collective farms, misunderstood their motives for joining co-operatives. Indeed, the 'co-operative' argument was, for Kindeev, mainly concerned with the efficiency of the peasant household, rather than long-term possibilities in line with the N.E.P. Support for Kindeev's view came, by implication, from Gurov, who remarked that in his five years with the People's Commissariat of Agriculture, he had never heard of a commune becoming a collective, except where the commune was already in an advanced state of disintegration.[1] Kubanin argued that uniting peasants as 'small commodity producers in an old, class organisation' hindered them from uniting in the only 'acceptable' way, co-operatives.[2] Sukhanov argued that eventually the communes could become members of co-operatives, but admitted that this would not happen as long as the stronger peasants left the commune, as they were more likely to join the co-operatives.[3] More moderate protagonists of the commune as useful in particular areas as a transitory stage, such as Dubovskii,[4] saw the 'co-operated' commune as the way forward, but admitted that the communes had a lower proportion of their members in co-operatives than enclosed farms.

d *Social differentiation and the commune*

The 'social' composition of the commune was a major point in the discussion of the future. The question of the social composition of the commune, and of the underlying social dynamics, were never properly examined in the Soviet period. On the one hand, the commune was seen as a device whereby the rich peasant maintained his superiority, on the other as a curb on his attempts to dominate the poorer peasantry. The assumption was, on nearly all sides, that there was a fairly clear stratification of the peasantry into three major groups – rich (kulak), middle and poor.

The question of peasant differentiation is one into which we cannot enter at length here. The broad picture is that, up to the

[1] Debate at Agrarian Section of Communist Academy. *Na agrarnom fronte* (1926), no. 9, pp. 81 ff.　　　　　　　　　　　[2] Kubanin, *Ibid.*, no. 11–12, pp. 111ff.
[3] Sukhanov, *Na agrarnom fronte* (1926), no. 11–12, pp. 98ff.
[4] *Ibid.*, no. 11–12, p. 142 (contribution to debate at Communist Academy); (1926), no. 5–6 (article).

mid-twenties, the 'middle' size of holding grew most, with a narrowing of extremes, with differentiation growing in the later twenties. This view is shared by most of those who used various criteria to define categories of peasant. Among the typologies used were value of production (People's Commissariat for Worker–Peasant Inspectorate),[1] income, combined with length of time hiring labour (Council of People's Commissars' Commission, headed by Frumkin, included Strumilin).[2] With collectivisation, and the policy of 'liquidisation of the kulak', certain official categories came into being. The decree of 21 May 1929 gave the following 'marks of kulak households': (*a*) systematic use of hired labour for agricultural work; (*b*) ownership of a mill, creamery, or a variety of other simple 'industrial enterprises' which used motor, wind or water power; (*c*) hiring out mechanically propelled machinery 'systematically'; (*d*) hiring buildings; (*e*) participation in trade, money lending, commissional middle-man work, or receiving non-labouring income (e.g. church services); (*f*) in addition to above conditions household with income of over 300 rubles per capita but not less than 1,500 rubles for whole household.[3]

There was some refinement of the concept of 'rich peasant' on political lines. The Commission on Collectivisation of the Politburo divided kulaks into three groups:[4]

(1) Those actively opposing the new social and economic order, engaged in counter-revolutionary work;
(2) those less actively opposing collectivisation, who refused to submit to widespread collectivisation;
(3) those ready to submit and be loyal to Soviet power.

While a variety of economic and political criteria for stratification of the peasantry have been devised, it is not possible to comment

[1] < 400 rubles 'smallest'; 400–1400 rubles 'part smallest, part middle'; 1400+ rubles 'largest'.
[2] SNK SSSR. Results of their research 'Otchet SNK SSSR izuchenii nalogovoi nagruzki na naseleniyu', pp. 30–1, quoted by Molotov, XV Party Congress. *Sten. otchet*, p. 1053. On this basis, 3·7% peasant households kulak in 1926–7 (p. 1054). For an invaluable study of this problem cf. M. Lévine, article in *Soviet Studies* (1966), and his book, *Russian peasants and Soviet power* (Allen and Unwin, London, 1968).
[3] 'Postanovlenie SNK SSSR', 21 May 1929. SZ, 1929, no. 34, art. 301.
[4] Quoted by N. A. Ivnitskii, 'O nachal'nom etape sploshnoi kollektivizatsii', *Voprosy istorii* (1962), no. 4.

effectively on the influence of social structure on the working of the commune until much more is known about the nature of peasant differentiation. This warning note must be sounded before going on to discuss the arguments based on differentiation which were used by those who attacked the commune as a social institution. One has to accept that much of this argument starts from a view of peasant stratification in economic terms which may be accepted, although many of the dividing lines are quite arbitrary. In discussion of the effects of differentiation, an equally important factor is the subjective view of peasants, whether these categories are meaningful in terms of prestige or power of categories of peasant. Here there is almost no evidence.

It is difficult even to attempt any discussion of the significance of stratification for the peasantry, or to attempt any kind of model of social prestige within the peasant community. On the one hand is the fact that the kulak was by definition the wealthiest peasant in the village. The source of his wealth was probably twofold. First, he would be producing a higher share of his output for the market, and, secondly, and related to this, he would have the capital to buy inventory which he could hire to other peasants. He may also have indulged in other forms of renting and lending. We will see that there probably was no one clear-cut group, but it seems likely that the extreme cases stood out as the most prosperous peasants. In most areas this would be a relative term, and natural calamity could change a family's circumstances drastically. It may well have been that the kulak in this sense did not arouse great hostility, as he represented what most other peasants would like to be (and, possibly, could be, or had been – there is some evidence of cyclical mobility, based on the demographic structure of the peasant household changing over time).[1] However, it is a mistake to impose upon the Russian peasant in this period a kind of Western 'protestant' ethic. He was probably not an 'economic man', interested in maximising output – the state of the market did not encourage this, even had he been interested in other than subsistence farming. It may well be

---

[1] A. Chayanov, *Organisation of the peasant farm*, published in Russian, Moscow 1925, translation by R. E. F. Smith. Chayanov in this study largely assumes the peasant to be a commune member, but does not discuss change of system of holding, although he sees 'vertical integration' through marketing co-operatives as the force for change.

that the word 'kulak' was a way, in some areas, of describing the exception to this.

While Soviet writers probably over-played the degree of peasant differentiation or, rather, its significance to other peasants, there was no doubt some element of opposition to those who had become unduly successful, especially if this was felt to be at the expense of others. While the policy of 'liquidation of the kulaks' may be seen as a means of exerting pressure on the peasantry as a whole to support the collectivisation campaign, there was also an element of trying to find some grounds for the majority of the peasantry to support the campaign. Stalin misjudged the temper of the peasantry and by increasing outside pressure closed the ranks of the peasantry rather than drove a wedge between them. This is not to say that antagonism between groups of peasants did not exist – perhaps a more subtle approach would have added to them, instead of the crudeness of Stalin's policies giving all peasants common cause.

While it is difficult to assess the significance of the term 'kulak' to the peasant, to the Soviet government it virtually became a term for peasants opposing Soviet aims. Since this was true of most peasants, one feels that the 'kulak' became a scapegoat for the feelings of the party about the peasantry as a whole. Similarly, many of the arguments about communes being under kulak influence were simply a way of saying they were more powerful than the rural soviets. Probably the most revealing definition of a kulak was that of Yenukidze: 'if we take economic criteria, we have a motley picture ...but we can now speak of the kulak as "that element which, by its farming and by its behaviour, disturbs the implementation of that basic task of transfer to large-scale socialist agriculture".'[1]

One of the problems when discussing social differentiation within the commune is the extent to which the richer peasants remained in the commune. Kindeev[2] implied that they tended to leave for enclosed farms in some areas, although this is by no means conclusive. Kubanin felt it was not necessarily the rich peasants who could use the commune for exploitation, but rather the more energetic who wanted to rid themselves of the restrictions of the system.[3]

[1] XV S'ezd KPSS. *Sten. Otchet*, p. 1119.   [2] See above, p. 161.
[3] Kubanin, *Na agrarnom fronte* (1926), no. 11–12.

The supposition that it was on the whole the more prosperous peasants who left the commune can to only a limited extent be supported by other statistics. In Moscow guberniya, it would appear that fully enclosed households were significantly larger in terms of area than commune households, but that households in farms with only fields enclosed were slightly smaller.[1]

Table 4.3

	Desyatinas per household	per mouth
Hamlet with 'pure' commune	5·0	0·92
Hamlet with only fully enclosed farms	7·4	1·24
Hamlet with only farms with only fields enclosed	4·7	0·87
Hamlet with both enclosed forms	5·9	1·13

Table 4.3 was in a sample of households where 93·4% were in communes, 5·9% farms with fields only enclosed, 0·8% fully enclosed farms. In this area it would seem that those households going into the most usual form of enclosed farm were in fact slightly smaller in terms of both absolute size and area per head than commune households. In Ivanovo-Voznesensk guberniya, which shared many of the characteristics of Moscow guberniya, the position was similar. The commune and farms with only fields enclosed were of similar size, 3·8 and 3·9 desyatinas of *arable* land respectively, while the fully enclosed farm held 5·5 desyatinas. However, in five out of eight uezds the farms with only fields enclosed held 'significantly more' land than the commune householder.[2] In these areas it would seem that the larger-scale peasant enclosed his land fully if outside

[1] Gurov, 'Predvaritel'nye itogi zemleustroistva', *Na agrarnom fronte* (1925), no. 10. Research by guberniya executive committee in 1924, p. 83.
[2] Ivanovo Voznesenskii Gubernskii RKI, *Zemleustroitel'naya pomoshch'krest'yamskomu naseleniyu*, p. 31. It is worth noting that in a very dissimilar area, Irkutsk okrug in Siberia, farms with only fields enclosed were smaller than commune households.

	Hectares per household	per mouth
Commune	46	8.3 (may include waste ground)
Farms with only fields enclosed	38	6·5
Fully enclosed farms	60	8·0

Zemlepol'zovanie i sel'skoe khozyaistvo Irkutskogo okruga v tsifrakh (Irkutsk, 1928).

the commune. Perhaps the smaller-scale peasant who left the commune could not afford to do so. No information about other areas was available to the present writer. On an all-Russian scale, there possibly were 13 hectares to each commune household, and 38 hectares to each enclosed household.[1] No comparative figures of land per head are available.

On *a priori* grounds it would seem that the more efficient peasant would wish to leave the commune, and that the enclosed farms would be most efficient.[2] However, there is remarkably little statistical evidence to support this view. If those outside the commune were more efficient than those inside, there is no conclusive evidence whether it was because those who left the commune were in any case more efficient, or whether their efficiency increased on leaving the commune, or both, or what were the relevant factors involved.

There is very little information on who did in fact leave the commune for enclosed farms when this was possible. There seems to have been no research published in the twenties on this problem. Danilov, using archival sources, suggests that the richer peasants, as one would expect, left the commune more frequently than the middle peasants. There is no evidence to suggest what proportion of peasantry of a given economic group left the commune.

As one would expect, the middle and poor peasant left the commune more frequently in the north west and west, where natural and economic conditions were more favourable to the enclosed farm, than in other areas. Thus in Kirillov uezd of Cherepovets guberniya, a majority of poor peasants opting to take land use measures in 1924

[1] Assuming Milyutin's figure of 211,000 enclosed households of both types to be correct (see above, p. 11), and that fully enclosed farms accounted for 2 million, and farms with only fields enclosed 6 million hectares (see above, p. 22), assuming that there were 17 million households in communes, and 222 million hectares held in communes. In 1916, according to the entry 'Khutor' in the *Bol'shaya Sovetskaya Entisiklopediya* (1st ed.), the position in certain areas was as follows:

| | Desyatinas per household | |
	fully enclosed farm	commune
Tver'	23·6	14·4
Moscow	10·7	7·5
Kostroma	11·8	10·1
Poltava	26·7	7·7
Ufa	25·5	16·0

[2] Even as staunch an advocate of the commune as Sukhanov was willing to admit that enclosed peasants tended to have better economic performance.

chose to leave the commune for enclosed farms; the richer peasants showed the same tendency to a greater extent.[1]

Table 4.4

Percentage of all households in given group subject to land use measures	Poor	Middle	Rich
Transfer to enclosed forms	57·9	58·3	81·6
To improve commune	30·3	31·5	14·7
To group settlement (gruppoye vyselki)	11·8	10·2	3·7

In Krasnodar raion (*sic*) of North Caucasus, middle peasants formed the bulk of those who transferred to enclosed forms in 1923–4. We have no comparable figure for the distribution of these categories among the peasantry of the areas as a whole, but it would seem likely that richer peasants were over-represented and poor peasants under-represented among those transferring to homesteads.[2]

Table 4.5

Percentage of households taking land use measures	Remaining in commune	Transferring to enclosed forms
Rich (well-to-do and kulak)	6·9	25·6
Middle	46·2	46·8
Poor	46·3	27·9

While a higher proportion of wealthy peasants transferred to enclosed forms of holding than of middle or poor peasants, the latter on occasion expressed a wish to leave the commune. A survey of 140 communes in Moscow guberniya showed that 50% of peasants would have liked to transfer to homestead farming.[3] Such a view is

[1] Danilov, *Voprosy istorii* (1960), no. 8, p. 111. He also gives the result of a survey in Siberia (Ishim okrug), where the professed aim of peasants transferring to enclosed farms was given as 'to get land in one piece', 'get the best land', 'to be on one's farm the full boss who doesn't have to depend on anyone'. There were accusations that the dwellers on enclosed farms managed to get more than their fair share of land. Ts GAOR i SS, f 4, ob 5, op 9, d 34, l 108.
[2] Danilov, op. cit. p. 110. Ts GAOR i SS, f 478, op 59, d 305, l 35.
[3] Gurov, *Na agrarnom fronte* (1925), no. 10, p. 83. Also, poor peasants in Kuraginin

difficult to evaluate without knowing the precise question, and the circumstances under which it was asked. While it is no doubt true that the cost of transferring to enclosed forms of holding was a deterrent to certain households which would otherwise have transferred, this cannot be a main explanation of the enclosed forms being mainly found probably among the wealthier peasantry. In many areas there was a return to the commune after the revolution, possibly suggesting that social factors outweighed the purely economic in the view of most peasants. Little is known at present of the motivating forces for change in a peasant household. In the 1920s in Russia external factors do not seem to have been a powerful enough incentive for radical change within the commune over most of European Russia. In the central grain-growing areas, the enclosed farm had least hold, suggesting that the grain market was not a sufficient incentive for change. In areas near conurbations, and in areas producing industrial crops, market forces did undermine the commune to a much greater degree, and there a group of substantial peasants with enclosed farms emerged.[1]

The opponents of the commune dismissed it as a mechanism for the wealthy peasant to ensure his superiority. One speaker described it as 'a primary vetcha, or parliament, in which the class struggle is carried on over the division of land'. He thought it merely a new form of populism to think that communes could be a possible way to collective farming. In his view they had no real organisation, and his verdict was that collectives would only come from those who left the 'land society'.[2] This view was supported by Chernov, who remarked that 'all the land society amounts to is the old feudal commune'. In his opinion the commune tended to be a union of poor peasants, who couldn't leave, and rich peasants, who ensured that they didn't. He felt it was not the kulak, but the progressive peasant, who left. However, he admitted that peasant opinion should first be sounded out before any attempt was made to get rid of the

volost, Perm okrug, told representatives of Worker–Peasant Inspectorate 'everyone wants to leave the commune, but they have not got the means' (Danilov, *Voprosy istorii* (1960), no. 8, p. 109).
[1] See also above, p. 36.
[2] Pashukanie. Debate at Agrarian Section of Communist Academy, 30 September–4 October 1926. Printed in *Na agrarnom fronte* (1926), no. 9, pp. 81ff.

commune.[1] Most positive advocate was Gurov. His research on land use measures had led him not only, as we have seen,[2] to question the economic effectiveness of the commune. He remarked that in his five years with the People's Commissariat of Agriculture he had never heard of a commune becoming a collective, except where the commune was already in an advanced state of disintegration. In his view it was worthwhile going so far as to forbid redistribution in order to encourage peasants to concentrate their land on one plot. The farm with only fields enclosed was, in his view, far from being a step back from socialism, a vital step along the road.[3] Presumably he favoured this form of enclosed farm as with a fully enclosed farm a collective would need a further removal of dwellings, and also it would encourage to a greater degree a sense of the land being owned by the peasant if he lived as well as worked on it. Kubanin attempted to place this discussion in a more specifically Marxist context. In the past the commune had been a progressive force, 'just as small, petty-bourgeois holdings were an advance on feudal latifundia'. However, the demise of the commune was now not leading towards a 'farmer' agriculture, as it would under capitalist conditions. It was easing the way to co-operation among poor and middle peasants.[4]

We have already seen that one of the arguments against the commune was that the richer peasant was able to influence rural soviets, as he held the commanding position in the commune, which dominated the rural soviet. The official view of the 'class' structure of the commune was put succinctly in the *Great Soviet Encyclopaedia* in 1933 thus: 'in the process of the class struggle in the countryside, the kulak tried to separate the land societies from the system of soviets, take charge of them and guide the development of land in a capitalist way. The position of the kulak found its expression in the theory of the "autonomy" of the land society.'

[1] *Na agrarnom fronte* (1926), no. 9. Similar points were made in this discussion by Uzhanskii, Kubanin and Lisitsin. The last-named remarked that there was no compulsion that the backward members of a commune should follow the more advanced. All that happened was that leading peasants would struggle with winter grazing, but the cattle were allowed to wander over the clover.
[2] Article in *Na agrarnom fronte* (1925), no. 10.
[3] Debate at Agrarian Section of Communist Academy. *Na agrarnom fronte*, (1926), no. 9, pp. 81 ff.
[4] Kubanin, 'Obshchina pri diktaturoi proletariata' (otvet N. M. Sukhanovu), *Na agrarnom fronte*, no. 11–12, pp. 111–26.

There was a body of evidence to suggest that rich peasants did use the commune to further their own ends. Opposition to the commune on these grounds was one of the principle lines of argument. A long article by Kubanin summarised this position. His argument is typical of others.[1] He distinguished between the well-to-do peasant, who left the commune because of its inefficiency, and the kulak who had more to gain by staying and deriving his wealth from 'parasitic' renting and hiring. He quoted observations from local newspaper correspondents which suggested the kulaks were against land improvement schemes. At times they indulged in practices which land societies had power to stop, and he interpreted their failure to do so as evidence of their being under kulak influence.

While the statistics supporting his argument, based on uncertain returns from newspaper correspondents, are so vague as to be of little use, certain concrete examples are worth noting. *Stepnaya Krest'yanskaya Gazeta* (3 January 1926) stated that kulaks tended to be against land use measures because where there was frequent redistribution the kulak could always be certain of having the best of the land. Not only poor peasant timidity was to blame, but also apathy at times. *Zabaikal'skii Krest'yanin* (17 January 1926) told of one village where the poor peasantry had agitated for a nine-year long partition (razdel), but this met with kulak opposition and few poor peasants turned up at the gathering, with the result that the kulaks got their way. This may point to a general feeling that the gathering was useless anyway with the kulak being so influential behind the scenes. *Bednota* (15 June 1926) cited examples of kulaks occupying land left by peasants who went to work temporarily in the town, and then refusing to return it. The argument of the kulak for distribution of pasture land by cattle, rather than by number of members of the household was strikingly put in a phrase by one of their number who said 'people don't eat hay' (*Izvestiya*, 28 July 1926).

The threat of physical force being used by the kulak was a real one, according to Kubanin, but more insidious was the way in which the kulak was able to get round the administrative structure. Thus,

[1] Kubanin, op. cit.

171

in one rural soviet (Krapivna in Bezhets uezd) the chairman, instead of obeying the decisions of the volost land commission on land use measures, called the land society gathering (in itself an indication of the flexibility of the arrangements at the local level at this time) and there argued against any measures which might result in the poor peasants receiving more land. He then drew up minutes to this effect and made everyone sign them before they left the hut (*Bednota* 23 September 1926).

Kubanin argued that it was not those who wanted to enrich themselves who left the commune. It was rather those who became tired of the restrictions and pettiness of the system. A peasant wanting to enrich himself easily would not be so stupid as to leave the commune, as he would have more chances inside. *Bednota* had organised a discussion on these problems, and all correspondents had been against the commune as it was organised at that time.[1]

The inferences he drew from his investigation were that the commune influenced the development of social relationships in the countryside in three ways. First, it slowed the cultural and economic growth of the poor peasant. Secondly, it united small commodity producers in an old, class organisation, and hindered their uniting in the only acceptable way, in co-operatives. Thirdly, capitalist relations did not develop purely, but in the old kulak, trade-usurer way. This was because the most progressive elements were denied the choice of form of land-use. Those wanting to get rid of the commune were from all classes, poor, middle and well-to-do (zazhitochnye) but not the kulak. The well-to-do were the potential bourgeois small farmers, and as such were to be circumscribed by the soviet state, and by co-operatives enlisted in the struggle against the kulaks and against the commune. He admitted that doing away with the commune could lead to 'some petty capitalist trends', but that socialist relationships could be established in the countryside only once the commune had been abolished.

This view was not substantiated by Rezunov, in the most thorough research on commune–rural soviet relationships published. He felt it was difficult to make a judgement on the social composition of the

[1] Unfortunately he is not specific as to date, but he has quotations from *Bednota* 15 June 1926 and 28 October 1926.

gathering. While he noted examples of kulak 'malpractice', reports which he had gathered from many localities suggested that the middle peasant played the most important role in discussions at the gathering.[1] Central attempts to exclude rich peasants from an active part in gathering discussions had proven fruitless.[2] In any case, it was probably not the rich peasant who did most work for the commune. While he could influence gathering decisions so that, for instance, self-taxation may be imposed per head or per household rather than by income or other criteria related to wealth, the day-to-day running of the commune was probably in the hands of the middle peasants, who were the largest group.

The commune, by ensuring equal distribution of land between households acted in some ways as a curb on richer peasants. This was no doubt true in those areas where the basis of differentiation was amount of land held. In villages of Don okrug, it was said, 'the land societies take an active part in defending poor peasants from the rich in distribution of land'.[3] However, the inconveniences of communal tenure were, proportionately, a lesser problem to the larger peasant. Data from peasant budgets showed that expenditure, proportionately, on carting for households with a sown area of up to 2 hectares was 45% more than for households of over 10 hectares, 38% more for households with 2–6 hectares, 15% more for households with 6–8 hectares.[4] The more substantial peasants could use a number of devices to further their own ends. Even where there was reasonable equality in size of holding, rich peasant households tended to have strips two to three times larger than those of poor peasants.[5] This they arranged by exchanging strips, and other means, which allowed them to use their implements to some effect. The unrationalised commune with a large number of small strips could help the larger peasant, as the poorest were forced to give their holding up because their strips were too small to use. From a technical point of view, it was probably in the interests of the more

[1] Rezunov, *Sel'sovet i zemel'noe obshchestvo*, p. 40. [2] See above, p. 109.
[3] 'Soveshchanie pri Ts IK SSSR po voprosam sovetskogo stroitel'stva', *Materialy komissii po ukrepleniyu raboty sel'soveta i vika*, p. 56.
[4] Danilov, *Voprosy Istorii* (1960), no. 8, p. 114. Quoting N. K. Zem, *Materialy po perspektivnomu planu razvitiya sel'skogo khozyaistva*, ch. 5, p. 23.
[5] Danilov, *Voprosy Istorii* (1960), no. 8, p. 105. Quoting ibid. ch. 1, p. 42.

efficient peasant to leave the commune, if he wished to maximise production. Given the wider political influences at any given time, the major criterion of whether the richer peasant would leave the commune was presumably the importance of production for the market in the area, and the strength of the communal organisation in local affairs. It may be that a peasant wishing to have a strong influence in an area would remain in the commune, especially as thereby soviet organs could also be influenced. This would be more likely if the prosperity of the rich peasant were derived from using his capital and investing rather than from farming. Without greater knowledge of the local situations, one cannot make any general statement.

From the evidence available, it is not possible to assess the effect of economic interdependence among the peasantry on the commune. The effect of other economic considerations could more than outweigh the tendency to equality implicit in redistribution of land. The picture as a whole must have been a fairly complicated one. The Soviet stereotype was of a commune under the power of one or two rich peasants, who held more land than others by easing the rules on redistribution, but whose main power lay in their capital, and the consequent dependence of both poor and middle peasant on them.

Here we can do little more than point out the complexity of the situation, rather than attempt an analysis of the economic relationships within the peasantry. As far as renting of land was concerned, it has been suggested that about half the land used by rich peasants in the central land-working areas was rented.[1] Total area of land rented out in European USSR reached 10·9 million hectares in 1926, but before the war had been 41·1 million hectares.[2] However, it was not a practice of the rich peasant only. In the North Caucasus, rich peasants rented just over half the fund of rented land, but those middle peasants who rented land increased their sown area by 25–30%.[3] Research in 1926 by Worker–Peasant Inspectorate showed

---

[1] Renting of land for up to two rotations was allowed from April 1925 onwards by Plenum Ts K KPSS. *KPSS v rezolyutsiyakh* (1954), II, 120. Reduced to one rotation in July 1928 by decree of Ts IK SSSR, SZ 1928, no. 44, art. 394, foreshadowed in decision of the October 1927 Plenum of the Party. *KPSS v rezolyutsiyakh* (1954), p. 428, which noted that growth of renting had 'undermined nationalisation of land'.
[2] Danilov, *Istoriya SSSR* (1958), no. 3, p. 97.   [3] Ibid.

how complicated the situation was[1] (see Table 4.6).

Table 4.6

	Percentage of those renting out land	Percentage of rented-out land
Poor peasant	19·9	9
Middle peasant	67·0	60·5
Rich peasant	13·1	30·5

In Samara guberniya, 45% of households were involved in renting or renting out land.[2]

The most common reason for renting out land was lack of means of production (72·4% of Worker–Peasant sample quoted above). A substantial minority rented out their plots because the land was too far away, or the strips too small to be worked economically (18·9%), and a small number (7%) did not have sufficient labour power. Evidence in Lower Volga krai suggested that middle peasants rented land often because their allotment was too far away to be worked economically with the capital at their disposal.[3] A study of patterns of renting would be invaluable. Over-all generalisations are likely to be unhelpful as differences between areas were so great. A substantial proportion of all peasants were involved in renting land – Danilov estimates 36·9% of peasant households in RSFSR in 1927.[4]

Where labour was hired with the land, dependence was obviously increased greatly. It is not clear how often a household would hire out one of its members as well as rent out land. About half the peasants were involved in hiring labour – 35·4% hiring out, 19·8% hiring, although there may have been some overlap. Probably over half of poor peasants sold their labour power, and one third of middle peasants hired.[5] In Samara guberniya 9% of households hired labour for a prolonged period. It is difficult to establish which stratum of peasants did the hiring, as hiring of labour over a certain

[1] Ibid. p. 96.   [2] Kritsman at XV Party Congress. *Sten. Otchet*, p. 1198.
[3] V. K. Medvedev, 'Likvidatsiya kulachestva v Nizhne-Volzhskom Krae', *Istoriya SSSR* (1958), no. 1, p. 16.
[4] In *Istoriya sovetskogo krest'yanstva i kolkhoznogo stroitel'stva*, ed. M. P. Kim (Moscow, 1963), p. 60.   [5] Ibid. p. 62.

number of days became in itself a mark of a kulak household. Quite a large proportion of households were involved in short-term hiring by the day – for example in 1927 in Samara guberniya, 30% of households hired, 23% hired out, and 5% did both. In Moscow guberniya in 1925, 62% of peasants were involved in hiring labour.[1]

The picture is even less definite with hiring of inventory and cattle. The classical picture is of the kulak hiring them out at usurious rates. That there was a widespread lack of capital is well enough established. In one okrug of Lower Volga krai, half the poor peasant and 14% of middle peasant households had to hire inventory and cattle.[2] The extent to which these relationships permeated the countryside was shown in Samara guberniya, where 11% of households hired out cattle or machines, 43% hired them, but 35% did both – only 9% neither hired nor hired out. In Moscow guberniya the latter figure was 11%.[3] This was to some extent countered by hiring points, some of which were built by communes, and by co-operatives. Where there was an effective tractor column hiring was transferred to this new form. For example, the tractor column of Pavlovsk, Aleksandrovsk and Fomino-Svechnikovsk claimed not only a fall in renting of inventory, but also of land. In 1927 it was said 4704 hectares of land were rented, but this had fallen to none by 1929.[4]

This bare outline of renting and hiring arrangements is enough to suggest that a simple model of kulak domination could not be adequate. The economic relationship underlying the social structure of the commune must have been more subtle, but our knowledge is not sufficient to start to construct such a model. Economic influence through renting and hiring was not a simple pyramid, with the kulak dangling puppets who went through the motions of organising a commune according to the strings he chose to pull. Most house-

---

[1] Quoted by Kritsman, *Na agrarnom fronte* (1927), no. 2. His sources: for Samara, Vermenuchev, Gaister, Rayevich, *710 Khozyaistv Samarskoi gubernii*. TSU, SSSR (Moscow, 1928); for Volokolamsk uezd, Moscow guberniya, Anisimov, Vermenichev, Naumov, *Proizvodstvennaya kharakteristika krest'yanskikh khozyaistv razlichnykh sotsial'nykh* grupp (Moscow–Leningrad, 1927).

[2] Medvedev, *Istoriya SSSR* (1958), no. 1, p. 16.

[3] Kritsman, *Na agrarnom fronte* (1927), no. 2.

[4] M. I. Ovchenikov, 'Rol' traktornykh kolonn i MTS v kolkhoznom stroitel'stvo na Severnom Kavkaze v 1929, *Nauchnye doklady vysshei shkoly, istoricheskie nauki* (1960), no. 3, p. 21.

holds became by turn loaner and loanee, according to economic conditions, chance happenings, time of year and degree of specialisation.

e *Conclusions*

There were theoretical arguments both for and against the commune as a means of developing agriculture in the USSR. The opponents of the commune stressed the inefficiency of redistributed communal holding, and felt that improvements to the system could bring about only marginal increases in output. They tended to dismiss the arguments for the commune as idealistic, as taking no notice of the social stratification which was taking place in the commune through renting and hiring. Opposition to the commune led, logically, to support for individual peasant farming if collectives were not an immediate prospect. The dilemma was to some extent solved by arguing that the individual 'farmer' peasants could more easily be brought to co-operatives, which could extend a long-term influence to collective forms of farming. The prospect of a strong peasant agriculture becoming a social problem was glossed over.

The extreme case for the commune had been put by Sukhanov, seeing it as possibly growing into the 'smallest Soviet state unit', virtually replacing the rural soviet as well as running the land communally. He saw it as the ideal means for transition to socialist agriculture, and rather dismissed arguments against its inefficiency by stressing its idealogical potential.[1]

The economic arguments, such as they were, favoured the enclosed farm. Social and political arguments to some extent counterbalanced these. With collective farming apparently impracticable, much of the discussion in the twenties tended to be based on negative arguments. Those who supported enclosed farms were often anti-commune rather than pro-enclosure.

One of the main problems when reviewing discussion of the social structure of the commune is that the terms 'rich' 'middle' and 'poor' peasant were used fairly indiscriminately without a really serious attempt to define them. This is particularly serious when these

[1] N. Sukhanov, *Na agrarnom fronte* (1926), no. 11–12, pp. 98–109. He was a Menshevik who had been a Socialist Revolutionary. His article was evidently printed with some trepidation and was 'balanced' by one by M. Kubanin, based on a reading of his manuscript.

terms were used as if they meant the same in all areas of Russia. So-called 'class' arguments were used by both defenders and attackers of the commune. While we have called in question the categories used, we have had to accept them in describing the debate, as these were in terms in which it was undertaken. It is far from clear in fact in which light it is most realistic to view peasant differentiation. Study of the effect of differentiation on the commune can thus do little more at this stage than raise questions, and reject oversimplified models of both 'kulak-dominated' and 'egalitarian' commune put forward by the protagonists of this period.

The main stream of thinking about the commune in the twenties was more empirical. It was accepted that on the one hand encouragement of the individualistic forms was politically undesirable, and on the other that the commune could not, in itself, be a socialist institution as it stood. It was felt that the commune could, in the first place, be improved in its organisation of agriculture and land holding. This would ease the worst inefficiencies, and be acceptable to most peasants. The hope was that this would lead to a peasantry more ready to participate in co-operation and, ultimately, in collective farming.

The dilemma was most cogently put by Lyashchenko. He noted that Lenin made little distinction between types of individual peasantry, whether they were commune or enclosed peasants. He lumped them together as 'individual peasants', as opposed to those who were in societies for joint working of the land, artels, or soviet farms. Lyashchenko admitted quite frankly that, from the point of view of production, the fully enclosed farm was the most rational and progressive form, but at the same time it was least adaptable to collective farming. While concentration on enclosed or settlement forms of holding was being excused by stressing their potential for developing co-operatives, there were countervailing factors which were being ignored. Differentiation of the peasantry, and the fact that co-operation probably most benefited the strongest, suggested that the argument for encouraging enclosed farming was a specious one. The result could be not collectives, but a worse individualism.[1]

[1] P. Lyashchenko, *Na agrarnom fronte* (1925), no. 1.

This line of argument was supported by Dubovskii. He saw the 'co-operated' commune as the way forward to collectivisation. The shortcomings of the commune, such as smallness of plots, could be countered by fiscal measures and normative rules. He stressed that talk in generalisations was unhelpful because of the regional differences in land holding. In north western oblasts the enclosed farm joining co-operatives was emphasised more readily as the way forward. He was at pains to show that neither commune nor enclosed farm could be considered as anything other than a transitory form. In his own area, the North West krai, the commune was fairly rare, and it would be reasonable to liquidate the commune entirely and concentrate on forming new small settlements, and, less desirably, fully enclosed farms. He conceded that such a policy would be quite inappropriate in other areas.[1]

There was some discussion whether the disincentive to improving one's holding implicit in redistributional holding could not be dealt with. Some suggestions were made that, since redistribution was essential to maintain equality of holding between households, it should be allowed as and when there was a need, occasioned by, for example, marriage and death. This could be on the basis of small re-adjustments, and not wholesale redistribution.[2] The general weight of opinion expressed in discussion was against small re-adjustments, and favoured re-partition only at long intervals.[3] Some speakers favoured outright abolition of redistribution.[4] There was no great enthusiasm for the schemes of compensation mooted.

This theme was extended to discussion whether inter-village land use measures should cease. Some suggested fixing a definite date after which there would be no more equalising redistribution of land between communes.[5] This was opposed by those who, for example, felt it unfair that in one commune there should be five

[1] *Ibid.* (1926), no. 11–12, pp. 142 ff. (contribution to debate at Communist Academy). 'Sovremennoe malozemlya' in *Na agrarnom fronte*, no. 5–6.
[2] For this view, expressed at Conference of Peasant Members of Central Executive Committee, see Balabanov (Kursk), and a Black Earth delegate. *Na agrarnom fronte*, no. 11–12, pp. 127 ff.
[3] Ibid. Speakers from Tver, Siberia, Ivanovo Voznesensk, Ulyanov, Voronezh, Pskov, N. Caucasus. In April 1928, Milyutin supported this view at Central Executive Committee, *Na agrarnom fronte* (1925), no. 11–12, pp. 726–7.
[4] E.g. Hauke, *Na agrarnom fronte* (1926), no. 10, p. 69.
[5] E.g. KZP project, Hauke, loc. cit.

eighths of a desyatina per member and only three eighths in another.[1] It was pointed out, however, that this could not be an endless process throughout the country which would result in chaos. Only the more glaring anomalies should be removed.[2]

Another view which was not in the end embodied in the legislation was that norms of fragmentation should be laid down, so that households would not fall below a certain size. The point was left for Republican legislation. One speaker made the interesting point that such a measure should be withheld while there was still unemployment.[3]

There was some call for minimum standards of efficiency to be forced on peasants. As it was, those who used land 'harmfully' could be punished under the Land Code, but some (e.g. Hauke, *Na agrarnom fronte*, 1926) thought more positive measures were needed. This was rejected by those who felt that such a measure would antagonise the poor peasantry at a time when the government was trying to enter into an alliance with them.[4]

It was pointed out that the tax system worked unfairly for those who were in communes, as all land was taxed equally, no matter what quality. Those who had the largest plots did not necessarily have the highest production potential, as allowance was made for quality in repartition. This would be a disincentive to taking land use measures, if one's holding were to increase in area, but not in quality.[5]

One of the abuses to which the fully enclosed farm had given rise was that dealing in land was frequently undertaken in the guise of buying and selling houses. These fetched two and three times their real value, as the main purpose of the deals was to buy the land surrounding the house. Rural soviets had no legal power to investigate such cases, and the land organs tended to be weak.[6] This happened often where peasants left the countryside to work in the towns.[7] One delegate to the Central Executive Committee went so

[1] E.g. Syryev, *Na agrarnom fronte* (1926), no. 11–12, pp. 127 ff.
[2] Volkov, ibid.
[3] Sambanov, *Na agrarnom fronte*, no. 10, pp. 77 ff.
[4] E.g. Pashukaniya, *Na agrarnom fronte*, no. 9, pp. 81 ff.
[5] Cf. Platov and Zurylin, *Na agrarnom fronte*, no. 10, pp. 77 ff.
[6] Central Executive Committee, December, *Bulletin* 17, p. 20, Uzvekov.
[7] *Ibid.* 17, p. 37. Sosin.

far as to ask why there was any provision at all for allowing new
fully enclosed farms in the proposed 'general principles'.[1]

The rather artificial distinction between 'land society' and 'commune' was made by a number of speakers. Rudin noted that arguments against the 'land society' confused the land society with the
commune. The land society could include other forms, including
enclosed farm, but he was ready to admit this was rare. The essence
of the distinction, however, lay in the land society being a commune
which had improved its holding arrangements. He admitted that
'our agricultural development for many years to come will consist of
transfer from the 3-field, narrow strip system to the improved
commune with wide plots'. Splitting communes into enclosed farms
would, in his view, destroy the small element of co-operation (in, for
example, crop rotation) which existed in the countryside, and put
back the possibility of collectivisation for many years.[2] In winding
up the debate at the congress of peasant members of the Central
Executive Committee, November 1927, Milyutin also made the
point that the land society should not be confused with the commune
'in its old form with low socialist potential'.[3] This formula was
virtually a face-saving device for continuing to encourage communal
holding, albeit improved and rationalised.

Twelve months later Milyutin was more decisively anti-enclosure;
in the debate at the Central Executive Committee in April 1928, he
did not come out decidedly in favour of any particular form of land
society. He was content to say that he thought no form should be
mechanically abolished, but that unviable forms of tenure should be
left to die of their own accord.[4] By the time the December debate
came round he was much more conscious of the need, from a political point of view, to exert pressure on the enclosed farm. He reported
that 'from almost everywhere' had come the demand that land use
measures should not take enclosed forms, but concentrate on
improving the commune to broad strips.[5]

[1] *Ibid.* 17, p. 43. Baskakova.
[2] *Na agrarnom fronte* (1926), no. 10, pp. 69 ff. This view, in support of the commune,
was also held by Sviderskii, ibid. (1926), no. 11–12, pp. 142 ff. and Platov, pp. 127 ff.
[3] Ibid. pp. 127 ff.
[4] Milyutin at Central Executive Committee, April 1928, 4.ii sozyv, 7-oe zasedanie, p. 724.
[5] Milyutin at Central Executive Committee, December 1928, loc. cit. *Bulletin* 12.

2 LAND USE MEASURES

a *Legislation*

The 1922 Land Code contained no reference to what forms of peasant holding were desirable. There was no indication that the collective farm was an end to be aimed at, or that any particular form of land use measures were preferable. One form was 'transfer of all or some holdings of a land society to enclosed farms'.[1] There was no reference to differentiation between groups of peasants, according to their economic or social position. In short, the Land Code reflected the political decisions about the peasantry taken with the New Economic Policy.

The disquiet about enclosed forms of holding which we have seen reflected above in discussion was probably even more marked at local party level. A circular of the People's Commissariat of Agriculture as early as October 1924 to all land organs was quite clear. 'Not only should transfer to fully enclosed farms not be made a positive task... active measures should be taken to stop further transfers to fully enclosed farms, and the population be attracted to other forms of land holding from which transfer to collective farming would be less difficult.'[2] Application by a whole settlement to transfer to enclosed farming was to be refused. This was presumably in response to the upsurge in transfer to enclosed forms after 1922 (see Table 4.7).[3]

Table 4.7 *Proportion of land use measures taken (by area) involving transfer to enclosed forms*

1919–21	1922	1923	1924	1925	1926	1927	1928
0·03	7·3	9·8	6·0	5·3	3·6	2·2	0·8

This was reflected in a number of areas. Gurov, a protagonist of the enclosed farm, noted that there was administrative pressure to prevent peasants leaving the commune for enclosed holding in a

[1] Land Code. Clause 166d.
[2] Archive, quoted by Danilov, *Istoriya SSSR* (1958), no. 3, p. 112.
[3] N. K. Zem. RSFSR. *K voprosu ob ocherednykh zadachakh raboty v derevne*, p. 112, and *Sel'skaya zhizn'* (1929), no. 32–3, p. 32. Quoted by Danilov, op. cit. pp. 112–21.

number of areas. Urals Obkom had decreed that fully enclosed farms should not be set up, except where natural conditions excluded other forms. The position was similar in Pskov guberniya. Moscow guberniya land department noted that 'credits will not be granted in cases of land use measures undertaken to transfer to fully enclosed farms, and only in some cases to a farm with only fields enclosed. The commune is the transitional form in Moscow guberniya to collective farming'.[1] This made for difficulty in areas where the commune was not such a well established form. Kindeev quoted the case of Leningrad guberniya. An investigation by Leningrad Worker–Peasant Inspectorate had shown that 'the resolutions of the Third Congress of Soviets on the need to observe strictly the right of peasants to a free choice of form of land holding accorded by the Land Code, is not being fulfilled by the land organs'. They tended to implant just one form – the commune with broad plots. The guberniya land department had struck out work on transferring peasants to enclosed forms in its plan of land use measures. At uezd level this was seen in action. Petitions by peasants for transfer to farms with only fields enclosed received the reply that it was suggested they turn to broad-plot communes, otherwise no land use measures would be sanctioned.[2] He reported, even more surprisingly, a similar situation in Smolensk guberniya, stronghold of enclosed holdings, and in Pskov guberniya.[3]

Other areas followed the spirit of the Land Code more closely. Ivanovo-Voznesensk guberniya Congress of Land Workers passed a resolution in March 1926 that 'the best forms of land holding are the commune with broad plots, and the farm with only fields enclosed, but no administrative pressure is to be exerted for the introduction of this or that form, giving the population freedom of choice and recommending only the form which is economically most profitable'.[4]

Central party policy was ambivalent. The April 1925 Plenum of the Party emphasised the need to maintain freedom of choice, forbidding

---

[1] Gurov, *Na agrarnom fronte* (1925), no. 10, p. 80. There was a similar move in the Ukraine – cf. Volf, speech to Conference of Agrarian Marxists (*Sten. Otchet*, p. 215).
[2] Kindeev, *Na agrarnom fronte* (1926), no. 10. Cf. p. 31.
[3] See above, p. 31.
[4] Ivanovo Voznesenskii Gubernskii RKI, *Zemleustroitel'naya pomoshch'*, p. 35.

administrative methods of struggle against enclosed farms. However, it mentioned that the task of the Party was to 'help growth of those forms of holding most favourable for co-operation and mechanisation [settlements – poselki i vyselki]'.[1] While this was slightly less emphatic than the 1924 People's Commissariat for Agriculture circular (which in turn reflected the conclusions of a Central Committee commission on work in the country), the drive against the rich peasant initiated by the XV Party Congress in 1927 brought a rejection of further transfers to enclosed farms. The decision on land use measures enjoined the party to 'help in all ways the growth of such forms of land holding as are most favourable to the development of agriculture [settlements – poselki i vyselki], curbing the practice of separation to the farm with only fields enclosed, and especially to the fully enclosed farm, completely stopping this where they lead to the growth of kulak elements'. An identical decision had been made at the October 1927 Plenum of the Party.

In most areas there was an immediate fall in the transfer to enclosed farms (cf. above, p. 182). There were areas where the process continued to grow, but on a very small scale. Thus in Tula guberniya, 135 farms with only fields enclosed were set up in 1928, 145 in 1929, and 239 in 1930.[2]

The 1928 'Basic Principles of Land Holding and Land Use Measures' followed a similar line to the Party Conference. This law had been debated since two projects were published after the 1924 Constitution of the USSR had pointed out the need for such a law, especially as the RSFSR Land Code was inappropriate to many areas.[3] One was prepared by the Commission on Legislative Proposals of the Council of People's Commissars of the USSR (hereafter referred to as KZP), and the other by the Council of People's Commissars of the RSFSR (SNK). It[4] is interesting to follow the history of the projects.

They were very different in conception. The KZP project was fairly detailed and ran to 11 pages, whilst the SNK one was in most general terms, and ran to only 3 pages. The former followed the

[1] *KPSS v rezolyutsiyakh*, II, 121.
[2] Podchufarov, *Tul'skie kommunisty v periode podgotovki massovogo kolkhoznogo, dvizheniya 1924–9*, p. 78.   [3] Article 1 h.
[4] Published in *Na agrarnom fronte* (1926), no. 5–6, pp. 94 ff.

RSFSR Land Code quite closely, while the latter left much broader areas to republican legislation.

The introduction to the KZP project stated that they wanted to change the RSFSR Code as little as possible, as the RSFSR Land Code had been the only piece of Soviet legislation in which the peasant had shown any interest. It was thought that the peasantry would view with suspicion any attempts to alter radically the Land Codes. On the 'land society', the KZP project virtually repeated the RSFSR Land Code's provisions, whilst admitting that a wide field should be left to the Union Republic. There were some minor additions and some clarifications. There was a more satisfactory definition of a land society as 'a union of households for establishing and regulating their way of land holding [zemlepol'zovanie]. It can also have as its aim joint use of fields or subsidiary holdings'. Republics were left free to forbid land holding outside a society. There was some contradiction within the project, as the commune was not included in the list of land holders, yet communal holding was recognised as one form of 'working the land for own use': presumably the distinction was intended that although this was a legitimate form of land holding, the household was the user, as it worked the land. The commune was not a land-user as it did not work the land communally.

The SNK project had very few references to the land society. It was included in the list of 'unions of labouring users of land and cattle' to which the use of land was to be granted. It was to be left to republics to decide which types of union should have the right to use land. The only reference to communal holding was that republics were to decide upon a date after which further compulsory equalisation would not be allowed.

The discussion which followed the publication of the projects has already been mentioned. Two themes are relevant here. First, there was the discussion whether a more, or less, detailed statute was required, and how much autonomy the republics should have in determining form of land holding. There was considerable criticism that the KZP project was too long. While some thought, like Gremoi,[1] that it was unthinkable that such vital matters affecting

---

[1] *Na agrarnom fronte*, no. 7–8, pp. 11 ff.

land relations in the USSR as relation between household and land society, between individual and collective, should be decided at any but the highest level, the general feeling was opposed to this view. Hauke[1] pointed out that other federated countries did not even attempt to produce a central land law, even a country as small as Switzerland did not do so. He thought the KZP consisted only of lawyers, and had no agricultural specialists. They were guilty of centralism, of trying to impose the RSFSR land code on all the Union. The section on state law of the Communist Academy favoured the SNK project as 'this is not supposed to be a Code, but general principles'.[2]

The second relevant point was the discussion whether a land society should be counted as a land user. Much of this discussion was taken up by those who mistakenly thought the KZP project did not allow for communal holding. Milyutin[3] made this accusation when winding up the debate. The SNK project merely stated that all citizens with political rights had the right to hold land if they worked it. The confusion on the KZP project, which we noted earlier, was to some extent dissolved by the reality which Hauke[4] injected into the discussion. The naming of the household as land holder rather than the land society might be excellent in Roman law principles of having no two owners of the same piece of land, but this did not correspond to the realities of the commune, whose pasture was used directly by the commune as a whole, and where it was far from clear who was the land-user.

The Presidium of the Communist Academy adopted the SNK project, in the light of the discussion in the agrarian section of the Communist Academy, and at the Congress of peasant members of the Central Executive Committee. The resolution reflected the changing political climate. The KZP project was rejected as too detailed, not leaving sufficient discretion to the republics, and had not made the land society a land user. While the SNK project was favoured, it did not give any encouragement to collectivisation. Neither project had a clause which aided the socialisation of the

[1] *Na agrarnom fronte* (1926), no. 10, pp. 69 ff.
[2] *Na agrarnom fronte*, no. 9, pp. 116 ff.
[3] *Na agrarnom fronte*, no. 11–12, pp. 127 ff.
[4] *Na agrarnom fronte*, no. 10, pp. 69 ff.

countryside. The SNK article should be re-worked from this point of view. Also, the question of membership of the land society should be made explicit, showing that rural workers could join. The position of rural soviet-land society relationships was to be clarified. The main points where the presidium recommended change were to give the project more political bite. 'The principle of preference for collective and state farms should run through the decree.' Questions of land holding and land use measures should be decided from a class point of view, with the rights of the poor peasant fully secured, and the social composition of the land society made plain.[1]

The SNK project was considerably reworked before being laid before the All-Union Central Executive Committee for debate in April 1928. The April session passed the project on to the December session, when the final 'foundations' were passed, differing little from the project discussed in April. This new SNK project differed considerably from that approved, with reservations, in January 1927. The political climate had further intensified pressure on the peasantry, and, in meeting the requirements of a stronger 'class' line, the project had more than doubled in length, running nearer to the KZP one in terms of detail.

The detailed provisions on land society–rural soviet relationships and membership of the land society are mentioned elsewhere. From the point of view of land use measures, the most significant point was that while it was to respect the right of the population to a free choice of form of land holding, it should help the general development of agriculture, co-operation and collectivisation.[2] The general tone is summed up thus: 'Requests for land use measures directed to the foundation of enclosures are undertaken last in turn, and not executed when foundation of enclosed farms leads to growth and strengthening of the kulak.'[3] This decree was barely in force before the decision on collectivisation made it obsolete, and no corresponding Republican legislation appeared. We now turn to the actual work undertaken to 1929.

[1] *Na agrarnom fronte* (1927), no. 1, p. 100. Decree of Presidium of Communist Academy, 15 January 1927.
[2] *Obshchie nachala zemlepol'zovaniya i zemleustroistva*. SZ 1928, no. 69, art. 642, clause 5.
[3] Ibid. clause 18.

b *Practice*

The vast bulk of land use measures undertaken concerned the commune. Of this, the most widespread single type of work was

Table 4.8 *Weight, by area, of land use measures undertaken in RSFSR by 1 January 1928*[1]

	Division of large land societies	Transfer to wide strips	Founding collective farm	Enclosed farms	
				With only fields enclosed	Fully enclosed
North region	44·4	23·0	12·6	9·4	3·1
Leningrad oblast	17·7	25·4	2·4	35·5	19·0
Western oblast	36·9	9·8	2·4	18·0	32·9
Central Industrial oblast	36·6	36·1	4·1	20·6	2·6
Central Black Earth oblast	69·5	25·5	3·9	0·7	0·4
Vyatka oblast	75·5	10·4	11·5	1·5	1·1
Urals oblast	64·9	18·8	12·5	2·2	1·6
Mid-Volga krai	61·8	18·0	19·5	0·3	0·5
Lower Volga krai	80·9	6·3	11·9	0·7	0·2
North Caucasus krai	39·7	52·5	5·6	1·4	0·8
Siberian krai	41·6	49·9	5·2	2·5	0·8
Far East krai	29·7	43·2	12·2	13·4	1·5
Total	46·1	37·4	6·6	6·5	3·4

sorting out intermingled holdings between communes, so that each commune had its holdings in a minimum number of separate places, and not mixed with holdings of other communes. This covered a far larger area than all the other works undertaken put together. One third of all cultivated land in the RSFSR in April 1928 had received this attention, compared with one fifth which had been the subject of all other types of land use measure (cf. Table 4.9).[2] Up to and including 1925, this had comprised the major part of the work each year. Of 83·7 million desyatinas subject to land use

[1] Ts IK SSSR, *sozyv 4-yi, sessiya 4-ya, 4-oe zasedaniye* (December 1929), *Bulletin* 13. Basis of areas not specified – apparently Gosplan.
[2] At the XV Party Congress in December 1927, Molotov remarked that only 12% of land area of the RSFSR, and 15% of the Ukraine had been subject to intra-commune redistribution.

Table 4.9 *Land subject to land use measures as a percentage of total agricultural land on 1 April 1928*[a]

	Division of large land societies	Transfer to wide strips	Founding collective farm	Transfer to enclosed farms		
				With only fields enclosed	Fully enclosed	Inter-village
North region	2·5	1·3	1·1	0·6	0·2	
Leningrad oblast	3·1	5·3	0·5	7·4	4·0	22·9
Western oblast	12·4	3·3	0·8	6·1	11·3	28·8
Central Industrial oblast	7·8	7·7	0·9	4·4	0·5	56·7
Central Black Earth oblast	17·3	6·4	1·0	0·2	0·1	80·0
Vyatka oblast	4·2	0·6	0·6	0·05	0·05	4·5
Urals oblast	4·7	1·3	0·9	0·1	0·1	33·3
Mid-Volga krai	9·95	2·9	3·1	0·05	0·1	23·4
Lower Volga krai	9·8	0·8	1·4	0·08	0·02	39·9
North Caucasus krai	16·1	21·9	2·3	0·5	0·3	56·5
Siberian krai	9·6	11·5	1·2	0·6	0·1	12
Far East krai	0·8	1·3	0·27	0·4	0·03	20·1
Total	9·0	7·4	1·3	1·2	0·7	33·3

[a] Ts IK SSSR, *sozyv 4-yi, sessiya 4-ya, 4-oe zasedaniye* (December 1928), *Bulletin* 13.

measures by then, 64·6 million was subject to inter-volost or inter-commune redistribution.[1]

A summary of land use measures undertaken is provided by Table 4.8.

The division of large communes into smaller, more manageable units were the main land use measures undertaken within the commune. This work was most concentrated in the Black Earth and south east regions, where the problem of distance from plots was at its most acute.[2]

This process seems to have taken two basic forms. In the one,

[1] 'Post. Komakademii po dokladu Milyutina', 15 January 1927. Total area on which land use measures were undertaken each year in the RSFSR:

1919	1920	1921	1922	1923	1924	1925
3·5	10·1	14·5	12·2	10·7	13·9	18·5

(million desyatinas)

[2] A drastic cutting down in size in the Central Black Earth region, from several hundred household communes to 'poselki' of 20–30 households, was recommended by Yakovlev in *K voprosu, sotsialisticheskogo pereustroistva sel'skogo khozyaistva*, p. 88.

Table 4.10 *Percentage of land use measures completed by 1 January 1928 undertaken in a given year*[a]

Land use measure	1919	1920	1921	1922	1923	1924	1925	1926	1927
Inter-village [*sic*]	2·8	9·9	14·2	9·8	7·9	19·2	14·3	15·2	12·7
Division of large societies to smaller	0·1	0·54	2·04	6·88	11·04	3·45	15·95	26·3	33·7
Transfer to wide strips	0·0	0·0	0·02	3·3	8·58	10·0	13·7	25·4	39·0
Setting up collective farms	2·5	7·4	19·1	12·1	10·3	7·4	8·0	13·5	19·7
Transfer to farms with only fields enclosed	0·0	0·01	0·07	15·2	15·1	19·3	18·8	18·2	13·32
Transfer to fully enclosed farms	0·03	0·01	0·04	23·0	20·0	17·1	11·2	18·7	9·52

[a] Ts IK SSSR, op. cit. (December, 1928), *Bulletin* 13.

the existing settlement pattern continued, but the single large commune, comprising a number of settlements, was split into two or more communes which joined a smaller number of settlements.

The other form was to change the actual settlement pattern, forming new, more compact communes. This 'new settlement' form of measure increased in popularity to 1929; presumably it was so favoured by the party not only because it offered the most economically efficient form of the commune, but also because it offered some break-up of existing communes with the possibility of a resulting change in the social relations within those communes. The definition of this form is not without its ambiguities, as there seem to have been few detailed studies of the process.[1] We have seen that from the time of the People's Commissariat of Land circular in 1924 onwards,[2] there was considerable central pressure for this form of land use measure.

The distinction between 'poselki' and 'vyselki' as forms of land use measure is nowhere made completely clear. It may be that the distinction was along the lines outlined below[3], with 'poselki' being a

[1] See Glossary.   [2] See above, p. 182.   [3] See Glossary.

re-grouping of the land of an existing commune between existing settlements, with the 'vyselki' involving either re-shaping of the settlement pattern in a given area of land, or the establishment of new settlements on new land outside the existing used land, or a combination of both. This hypothesis is not, however, confirmed by Danilov's use of the terms. He notes that 'there was division [razdel] of the holding [nadel] of large communes into separate parts', and, as a different process, 'dispersion [rasselenie] of the commune to settlements [poselki]'.[1] He does not attempt to explain the term 'vyselki', which would seem to correspond to his use of the term 'poselki'.

The economic effects of splitting up very large communes into smaller units were probably beneficial, but empirical evidence is scarce. Danilov quotes the results in 3 volosts of Saratov guberniya in 1927-8. The number of settlements (seleniya) with an area of over 10,000 hectares was halved, while the number with up to 500 hectares was increased from 128 to 199, and with 500–3,000 hectares from 56 to 102. It is curious that this was in terms of settlements; hectares per commune would be a more useful measure, and one suspects this is what was meant. It was claimed that over half the 'settlements' transferred to improved rotations. Arable area rose 14–15% in the first year. An increase in value of produce per household of 23·9% was claimed.[2] Without more details, it is not possible to say whether this improvement was due entirely to the change in size of commune having beneficial effects on the constituent households, or also to a general rise in interest in improved techniques resulting from the presence of surveyors and agricultural officers. While the latter effect cannot be discounted, it is likely that a smaller unit would be more susceptible to change of technique, especially if it were a newly formed one, where resistance to change would be less.

A less radical form of improvement to the commune was rationalisation of the field and strip pattern within an existing commune, which accounted for one third of the work by area. (This work was also done when large societies were divided up, but was counted as part of that work.) As extreme interlocking of plots was a

[1] Danilov, *Istoriya SSSR* (1958), no. 3, p. 112. See Glossary.
[2] Danilov, op. cit. p. 113. Ts GAOR i SS, f 3983, op 1, d 45, ll 172-80.

191

problem of the north, north west, and west, the largest proportion of this work was done in those areas, although parts of the Central Black Earth region also shared this problem, and a substantial proportion of land there also underwent this form of rationalisation. The exception to this rule, as with division of large societies, is the North Caucasus, where one would have expected more emphasis on division of large societies than on transfer to wide strips.

Only one tenth of the work, by area, was concerned with separation of households from communes into enclosed farms. In Leningrad oblast, 54% of work by area consisted of founding both forms of enclosed farm. None the less, this only touched 11·4% of the total worked land area. This area had been less subject to withdrawal from enclosed farming after 1917 than the country as a whole. Similar considerations apply to the Western oblast, where 50% of land use measures by area was of a similar nature, covering 17·4% of agricultural land area. The Central Industrial oblast was the only other area with a significant transfer to enclosed farming, largely to farms with only fields enclosed.

The low absolute level of land use measures undertaken is striking, with only 9% of agricultural land being in the hands of communes which had been divided into smaller units, and 7·4% in the hands of communes with wide strips. The principal agricultural areas were those which supported land use measures the most, but, even so, only the North Caucasus had over a quarter of its land in improved communes (38%), with the Central Black Earth region coming second (23·7%). The second most intensive area of land use measures as a whole was the Western region, where improvements to the commune were combined with transfer to enclosed forms (total 33·1% of agricultural area).

The main reason for this low level of work was a lack of staff and funds, rather than a lack of demand. While these were the main reasons, others were put forward. It was suggested that land use measure officers tended to be too precise, taking a long while to deal with hundredths of a hectare.[1] This, however, was not new to areas where arguments were traditionally carried on over small strips.

[1] Kotelnikov, speaker from Bashkiria at Central Executive Committee debate, December 1928, *Bulletin* 16, p. 7.

Collectivisation and the commune

Lack of workers was a long-standing problem. In 1916 there were 7,000 land use measure officers, and they were unable to cope with the volume of work.[1] The numbers did not reach their post-war level until after 1925 (see Table 4.11).[2]

Table 4.11   *Number of land use measure officers*

1918	1919	1920	1921	1922	1923	1924	1925
							about
3,226	3,666	3,696	3,761	4,379	4,351	4,916	6,000

In December 1927, there were 11,500 and they were overwhelmed with work.[3]

As far as cost was concerned, government subsidies were available for part of the cost of land use measures from 1924–5 onwards. Before then it had been entirely at the peasant's expense. It was not until after October 1927 that a substantial proportion were enabled to have work done free, with grants made on a 'class' basis.[4]

The type of land use measures undertaken each year reflected the political trends we have already noted. While all forms of work, besides setting up collective farms, were increased in 1922, work on setting up enclosed farms rose over ten-fold with the 'wager on the strong'. It was not until 1927 that a serious downward trend in setting up enclosed farms is noticeable, apart from a curious fall in the formation of fully enclosed farms in 1925. Over half the work of improving communes completed by 1927 was done in 1926 and 1927, reflecting a very rapid growth in this work as increased funds became available.

In this section we have seen the practical results of the theoretical discussions, and the way in which the work undertaken reflected the decisions taken. The work was largely based on improving the commune to the extent that pressures for improvement from within the commune allowed. While these pressures could be influenced in a negative way, for example by refusing to undertake certain kinds of

[1] B. D. Brutskus, *Agrarny vopros i agrarnaya politika* (Petrograd, 1922), p. 168.
[2] Gurov, *Na agrarnom fronte* (1925), no. 10, p. 78.
[3] Yakovlev, XV Party Congress, December 1927.
[4] Shchuleikin, 'Razvitie zemleustroistva', *Na agrarnom fronte*, February 1928, no. 2, pp. 84 ff. See also Danilov, *Istoriya SSSR* (1958), no. 3, p. 121.

work, and excesses were noted in some areas, on the whole there was no question of compulsion by government organs for communes to change against their own wishes. We now enter the final period of the commune's history, when the conflict of interests leads to government action in collectivisation.

3   THE COLLECTIVISATION CAMPAIGN

a   *Legislative pressure*

In this final section, we examine the effects of the collectivisation campaign on the commune. The attempt to use the commune for Soviet ends was reflected in legislation at the close of the twenties. An attempt at use of the gathering as a platform for discussing and disseminating central policies is exemplified by the decree, 'On measures to increase the harvest' of late 1928.[1] This ordered all raion, volost, okrug and uezd Congresses of Soviets to publish decrees compelling the use of certain simple agricultural techniques. Such decrees were to be published only after discussion of these questions in the agricultural commission (section) of the rural soviet, 'and at the gathering'.

While most legislation on matters such as taxation or improvement of technique tended to be directed straight at the household, in the late twenties it came to be recognised that the land society could possibly be used to encourage the activity of its members towards a more rational agriculture. In early 1929, the land society was encouraged to take improvement measures as a unit in a decree 'on the single agricultural tax, and lightening the tax burden on the middle peasantry'. The agricultural tax in each household in a society where all members took such measures was to be reduced by 10%, or by 5% if not by all members.[2]

The gathering was called upon to aid the grain delivery campaign in a series of decrees in 1929. In June the 'general meeting of citizens' was encouraged to take upon itself delivery of a given quantity of grain, which was binding on the whole village. Those households

[1] Ts IK SSSR, 15 December 1928. SZ no. 69, art. 643, clause 14.
[2] SZ 1929, no. 10, art. 95, art. 5a, 8 February 1929.

which did not fulfil the quota allotted to them were to be fined up to
five times the amount due, or have property confiscated if unable to
pay. Refusal to deliver could be met with criminal proceedings.
25% of the sum realised from fines was to be allotted to funds 'for
the cooperation and collectivisation of the poor peasantry'.[1] By a
later decree a similar proportion was to be given to funds for
households 'suffering from kulak oppression'.[2] This control was
formalised by the formation of 'commissions for helping with grain
collection under the rural soviet' in September 1929, which were to
be elected at the gathering.[3]

The gathering was also called upon to mark the 'day of harvest and
collectivisation' (14 October 1929) with intensive effort to 'mobilise
the middle and poor peasantry for the development and socialist
reorganisation of agriculture and attack on the kulak'. Gatherings
were to discuss targets for the day.[4]

Land societies were encouraged to undertake delivery contracts.
From December 1929, the gathering of the land society could decide
to make by a simple majority a contract which would be binding on
all members. The gathering was to divide up the obligation between
households. In cases of non-fulfilment by a household the rural
soviet would recover 'administratively' the produce not delivered.
The rights of the rural soviet were the same as those mentioned above
for grain delivery.[5] Contracting by land societies had been mentioned
in July 1928 by a decree on contracted delivery of grain crops of the
autumn sowing campaign of 1928. By this 'agreements on contracted
delivery of...grain are concluded with whole land societies, pro-
ductive unions, and groups of sowers on the basis of voluntary
agreements'. Such contracts were made 'exclusively through the
network of agricultural cooperatives' – an interesting indication that
land societies may have been corporate members of co-operatives,

1 SU 1929, no. 60, art. 589. 'On spreading rights of local soviets in helping fulfilment of
state tasks and plans.'
2 SZ 1929, no. 71, art. 763, 16 November 1929. SZ 1929, no. 76, art. 728, 14 December
1929 went into greater detail. Amended slightly by SU 1930, no. 8, art. 102.
3 SU 1929, no. 70, art. 681, 9 September 1929.
4 Postanovlenie Ts K VKP(b), 23 August 1929. Printed in Sharova (ed.), *Kollektivizatsiya sel'skogo khozyaistva* (Akad. Nauk. 1956), p. 195.
5 SU 1929, no. 90, art. 900, 31 December 1929. SZ 1929, no. 65, art. 610, 7 October
1929.

rather than their members being individually in co-operatives. At that time there was no mention of disciplining societies and households not fulfilling their quota, neither was there any indication whether the contract would be binding on all members of the society.[1] It is not easy to judge how far the commune did come to discuss such topics. Danilov suggests quite extensively. He noted that in contracted delivery of winter sowing of 1928, 14,238 communes took part. While this is a small proportion of all communes, this was a quarter of all organisations, and represented 40% of all peasants participating. He notes that minimum agricultural measures were taken in 125,000 land societies in the RSFSR. Over 75% of land societies in the North Caucasus and Lower Volga oblast took such measures.[2] It is impossible to assess whether these were just paper figures to show that local authorities were attempting to carry through central policy, or whether this area of minimum agricultural measures was one where a degree of peasant co-operation proved possible.

By whatever means, in certain areas, certain communes did come to take a 'soviet-centred' view of their work. In Novo-Titarovsk Stanitsa, Kuban okrug, the 'general meeting of groups of poor peasants and executives of the land society' took a decision that 'we will count all concealers of grain as enemies of our Soviet power, and, branding them with disgrace, we will exclude them from membership of the land society, and give the land to honest, hard working peasants'.[3] The same author gave as a 'model' example of the work of the land society in the grain delivery campaign the Stanitsa Poltskaya of Slavyansk raion, Kuban okrug. In June an expanded plenum of the stanitsa soviet decreed that villagers with a surplus should take it to collection points during June. A meeting between agricultural society, (sel'skokhozyaistvennoye obshchestvo), delivery organisation and the soviet decided on control figures for each hamlet. People with a surplus were summoned to the stanitsa soviet, 500 in all, and Soviet policy was explained.

[1] SZ 1928, no. 46, art. 412, 21 July 1928.
[2] Danilov, *Istoriya SSSR* (1958), no. 3, p. 122, quoting *Sel'skokhozyaistvennaya gazeta*, 21 May 1929 and 10 July 1929.
[3] Quoted Konyukhov, *KPSS v bor'be s khlebnymi zatrudneniyami* (Moscow, 1960), p. 135.

(Members of the soviet were responsible for producing a given quantity of grain, and faced dismissal from the soviet if they did not do so.) The gathering of the stanitsa passed a resolution which said that the meeting was revolted by the grain-concealing activities of named peasants. It declared all grain growers must give up their surpluses and unmask those who concealed. Those found concealing were named and expelled from the land society. A group of lesser offenders were warned.[1]

In Tula guberniya the gathering was, ideally, used by the Party organisation in 1928 as a means of fulfilling the grain delivery plan. A resolution of the Guberniya Party Committee called for systematic work to exert social pressure on households hiding grain by using poor peasant meetings, or village gatherings to unmask people hiding grain, to conclude with them agreements on delivery of grain.[2] We will later see that in this area, the gathering was used as an assembly for Party agitation to put forward the virtues of collectivisation.[3]

There were attempts to involve communes in the movement for socialist competition. While it was December 1929 before a decree to this end was published,[4] it seems that 'socialist competition' between land societies was organised in the Central Black Earth region in spring 1929. Besides State farms, collective farms, and tractor columns, land societies also were engaged in competitions for raising yields and collectivising. For example, Talovsk raion challenged Mineralny Vody raion of the North Caucasus. In 1929 the competition in the raion included besides 12 rural soviets, and 52 collectives, 35 land societies.[5] Whether this meant anything other than purely paper participation cannot be judged from the article.

The combination of the 'General Principles of Land Holding' and of the decision of the XIV All-Russian Congress of Soviets on budgets brought the land society under close soviet control in legislation at least. One interpretation of the effects of this is given in a letter from Krasnoyarsk okrug executive committee to all raion

[1] Ibid. pp. 140–1. [2] Podchufarov, *Tul'skiye kommunisty*, p. 23.
[3] See below, pp. 199ff.
[4] 10 December 1929. SU 1929, no. 87/88, art. 865.
[5] P. N. Sharov, 'God velikogo pereloma v Ts Ch O.', *Istoricheskie zapiski*, no. 41, pp. 232–3. (Identical article also in no. 51, pp. 216–17.)

executive committees and rural soviets.[1] According to this, the rural soviet was now to take detailed interest in the agricultural affairs of the land society. Increasing sown area was to be a first priority. The raion executive committee was to send control figures of sown area to rural soviets, with tasks for increasing it. This was to be worked out by the rural soviet section, but the letter noted that 'such work should not only be done in the rural soviet. It is only complete when continued in the gathering and in the households'. Thus the gathering was to discuss sown area – but in order to find ways of fulfilling requirements from above. In 1928–9, the People's Commissariat of Agriculture had ordered that reduction of sown area was one of the most blatant of kulak manœuvres, and that article 60 of the Land Code should be brought against such households. They noted the unwillingness of land societies to do this, and evaluated this in terms of their class basis being unsuitable for a socialist agriculture.[2]

One means of exerting rural soviet pressure on the land society was to be the 'production conference'. This was an extension of the agricultural sections of rural soviets proposed at the XIV All-Russian Congress of Soviets into a more broadly based organ which had as its aims 'working out measures for the socialist reconstruction of agriculture, for increasing sown area, raising yields. . . on the basis of the class policy of the Soviet power'.[3] The production conference was to be composed of members from most rural organisations – rural soviet members, state and collective farms, representatives, co-operative delegates, executives of land societies, 'agro-agents', agronomists, surveyors, vets, Peasant Mutual Aid, and Trade Union representatives, teachers, librarians, and komsomol activists. Among the many tasks of this body was 'helping land societies' to transfer to multi-course rotation, and generally keeping watch of the land-use of the land society. 'Agro-agents' were elected to lead the work of the land societies, and they were to work under the direct leadership of the production conference, under the guidance of the agricultural officer. These agro-agents were to be elected by a special meeting of land society members from candidates put forward

---

[1] *Zadachi sel'sovetov v dele razvitiya i pereustroistva sel'skogo khozyaistva.* Published as a pamphlet (Krasnoyarsk, 1929).
[2] Danilov, *Istoriya SSSR* (1958), no. 3, p. 126. Ts GAOR i SS, f 5201, op 6, d 76, l 12.
[3] 10 December 1929. SU no. 87/88, art. 865.

by the production conference. They were to be accountable not to
the land society, but to the rural soviet, and were thus instruments of
the new soviet control over the land society. A further decree detailed
their work.[1] This made it clear that they were the executives of the
agricultural production conference to the bodies who elected them.
(This decree mentioned co-operatives and collective farms, but
not land societies.) They had a right to call a 'general meeting of
citizens' gathering, and report there on their work.

Whether such officials did exist is difficult to establish. Once the
drive for collectivisation had started, the focus of discussion on the
countryside changed, and little more was heard of the land society
as an institution.

b *The campaign and the commune*

The commune structure seems, on the whole, to have been disregarded by those who were sent from the centre to carry out collectivisation. While they use the words 'settlement', 'village' and
'gathering' in those reports which are accessible, there is hardly an
instance of the word 'commune'.

There had been a number of experiments in guiding communes
in a collective direction, centred around 'tractor columns'. The
essence of these was that mechanical equipment was made available
to a commune on the understanding that holdings were rationalised
so that best use could be made of the equipment. By the time of the
XVI Party Conference in April 1929, there were 45 such 'tractor
columns', serving 200 'land societies' with an area of 750 thousand
acres. They were run by the grain co-operative system. For example,
Talovskaya tractor column in the Central Black Earth region
(Borisoglebsky okrug) had led 11 land societies to agree to common
working of land. Balks were eliminated, multi-course rotation
established, and selected seed used.[2] This way forward was advocated at the Conference by Kalinin. In return for seed and use of

[1] 'Polezhenie NKZ RSFSR', 20 January 1930.
[2] '16-ya Konferentsiya KPSS', *Sten. Otchet*, pp. 403–6. Speech by Belenkii. See also
A. Lozovoi in *Na agrarnom fronte* (April 1929) for a description of columns run by
sovkhozy and other predecessors of MTS. Danilov, in *Sozdanie materialno-tekh-
nicheskikh predposylok kollektivizatsii* (1957), pp. 348–9, points out the impracticability
of tractors being used on strip farms unless the whole commune agreed.

tractors, the peasants provided labour and undertook to 'fulfil exactly the directives of the agricultural officer and mechanics'. Rotation on the newly consolidated land was to be decided by representatives of the peasants in agreement with the specialists. He stressed that this combined voluntary co-operation, and, in fulfilling the demand for machinery, introduced a vital new element into the commune – co-operative labour.[1]

The tractor brigades, in their drive for voluntary co-operation, based themselves on the assumption that there was a strong demand among the peasantry in general for tractors. This assumption is questionable, as it suggests a desire to increase the output of the peasant household, not always the case in the state of the development of the market in Russia at this stage. Even if the peasant economy had been responsive to market conditions, there would have been little incentive to increase output in the market conditions of 1927–8, with virtually static grain prices, and industrial goods almost impossible to obtain in the countryside.[2] Further, tractor working involved undermining the whole holding pattern of the commune, and it would seem there was little general demand for this at this time. While the tractor was no doubt an object of curiosity and wonder, it seems unlikely there would have been any general demand. The concept of a commune tractor may not have been an impossible one, as there was already sharing of some capital equipment. However, most of the implements used in day-to-day work were the property of the household; sharing a machine of such general usefulness would have presented problems which specifically seasonal equipment and, for example, bulls, did not. In the event the 'commune tractor' was never tried, not least because technical knowledge in the commune was too low. Tractors remained in the hands of centrally-based columns. A decree forbade sale of tractors to 'small peasant unions' except in exceptional circumstances, and allowed sale only to state and collective farms large enough to utilise them, Machine and Tractor Station (MTS) and co-operatives.[3] This tightened up a previous decree[4] which

---

[1] *Sten. Otchet.*, p. 292.   [2] Cf. M. Dobb, *Soviet economic development since 1917*, pp. 218–21.   [3] 21 December 1928. SZ 1929, no. 5, art. 5.
[4] 15 June 1928. SZ 1928, no. 41, art. 375.

allowed for distribution of tractors to peasant mutual aid societies, once the needs of state and collective farms had been met. Probably the only peasants who wanted, and could have used, a tractor were those who left the commune for enclosed holdings, and they were increasingly in disfavour. The tractor became increasingly used, not only as a means of effecting improvement in the commune, but of speading the campaign for liquidation of the rich peasant, and wholesale collectivisation. The fact that there were not enough tractors was certainly a hindrance to the work of the columns, but the problem lay deeper than that.

The 'workers' brigades' sent out from the towns were faced with rather similar problems to the tractor columns, but suffered by being even more remote from the countryside in their composition. The aim was that workers from the towns would offer their skills in repairing and servicing agricultural implements, and use the relationship thus established to persuade the peasantry of the value of collectives. The method of sending workers to the countryside to conduct propaganda had been a common strategy in the twenties, and may have had some influence on the rising vote in rural soviet elections. The repair brigades had a more difficult message to try and convey, but offered certain skills in return. How far these skills were needed is questionable, in view of the fairly primitive equipment used by most peasant farmers. The movement was at its height from the spring sowing campaign of 1929 to 1930, and 72,402 men took part in 10,422 brigades throughout the USSR in this period.[1]

It is difficult to evaluate the reception given to these brigades as described by post-war secondary sources. Resistance to the brigades is described as kulak influence. For example, a grain delivery brigade of three bolsheviks from Sverdlovsk station went to the village of Vorobyevsk in Tyumen okrug in October and November 1929. Their work is described as follows:

arriving in the village, the workers organised a general meeting on the question 'The Five-Year Plan and Grain Delivery', then went from household to household. The position in the village was tense.

[1] V. I. Mukhachev, 'Rol' rabochikh brigad v kollektivizatsii Ural'skoi derevni v 1929–31', *Nauchnye doklady vysshei shkoly. Istoricheskie Nauki* (1960), no. 3, pp. 10 ff.

The commune and soviet society

The kulaks had formed a false collective farm. There was no party cell or komsomol in the village. The brigade formed a group of poor peasants into a komsomol cell, and worked with middle peasants, using the support of the mass of villagers to develop a struggle with the kulaks. The kulak group, headed by the chairman of the false collective, was overthrown. In reply the kulak group made an armed attack on the brigade, but were arrested, and a new collective farm was formed.[1]

This kind of report is typical of many in the press at the time, and quoted in secondary sources.

This stereotype is also perpetuated in descriptions of the work of the 'twenty-five thousanders', workers who were sent from factories with the aim not only of helping in the collectivisation campaign, but also of staying on in the countryside to be leaders of the collective farms, rural soviets, and Machine and Tractor Stations.[2]

A series of letters from workers in Tambov guberniya throw some light on the situation.[3] Not surprisingly they do not differ greatly from the pattern of work laid down by the okrug committee of the Party.[4] Work on collectivisation was to be connected with the struggle against the kulaks. The aim was to get the *gathering* (skhod) to pass a decision that kulak inventory be seized, and a collective formed. While the gathering is thus mentioned, stress is mainly on organising groups of poor peasants, and calling meetings of middle and poor

[1] Mukhachev, op. cit. p. 14. Also, on the work of these brigades, see article by E. Zombe in *Voprosy istorii* (1947), no. 5, which includes several local reports. A useful collection of local reports is provided in *Istoricheskii arkhiv* (1955), no. 2 by Gribkov and Lenekin.
[2] The 'twenty-five thousanders' were sent from factories to the countryside by a party decision of 25 November 1929. Articles, with some documentation of their work appeared in *Istoricheskii arkhiv* (1956), no. 1, pp. 99 ff. – article by N. A. Ivnitskii on Moscow workers, which includes a number of fairly frank letters from twenty-five thousanders outlining their difficulties; V. M. Selunskaya, *Voprosy istorii* (1954), no. 3, p. 209, a general article; E. Zombe, *Voprosy istorii* (1947), no. 5, p. 5, a general review; Gribkov and Lenekin, *Istoricheskii arkhiv* (1955), no. 2, participation of metal workers in collectivisation in spring 1930 (on workers' brigades); a collection of materials in *Materialy po istorii SSSR*, 1, 390. Among books on this theme: A. P. Sandakov, *Kommunisticheskaya partiya – organizator pomoshchi rabochego klassa v derevne v osushchestvlenii kollektivizatsii sel'skogo khozyaistva* (Moscow, 1956); B. Abramov, *Organizatorskaya rabota partii po osushchestvleniyu Leninskogo kooperativnogo plana* (Moscow, 1956); N. Spektor, *Partiya – organizator shefstva rabochikh nad derevnei* (Moscow, 1957); V. Ya. Rozenfeld, *Dvatsatipyatitysachniki* (Moscow, 1957).
[3] Published in *Materialy po istorii SSSR*, 1 (Akad. Nauk, Moscow, 1955).
[4] Ibid. p. 338, Document no. 7.

peasants for every 25 households. (Possibly to undermine the existing commune?) After preparation, a general meeting (obshchee sobranie) of the village was to be called, from which those excluded from voting in elections would be barred. A resolution would be passed at this meeting on forming a collective farm. It is notable that most of these letters do not refer at all to the commune. Their work was centred on rural soviets, but they held meetings at the level of the settlement or hamlet (poselok and derevnya). These meetings are everywhere referred to as 'general meetings', rather than 'gatherings', perhaps reflecting the town workers using the term from the legislation, rather than the locally used word.

These workers from outside the village often organised general meetings on the lines suggested by the 1927 decree, with the kulak excluded. Exclusion was often by force – e.g. letter of A. N. Egorov, where 'to prevent the general meeting being broken up, a wealthy peasant was arrested',[1] and in another village one Garnishchev reported that 'there was much kulak opposition at some settlements [poselki] to collective farms; there are counter-revolutionary outbursts at general meetings, for which they are all arrested'.

While this may have been used for the commune meeting, in the sense of the geographical area covered, from the tone of the letters it seems unlikely that the gathering was called as part of the commune business. In any case the distinction between meetings at the hamlet level was probably fairly blurred. There is only one case of a conscious attempt to use the commune directly. A worker in Novodvizhensk rural soviet reports that besides the usual meetings of komsomol, of groups of poor peasants, and of collective farmers, at each land society 'shock initiative groups' were set up. It is notable that these consisted of school teachers and rural soviet members rather than peasant leaders. The rural soviet plenum would pass a resolution on joining a collective farm, and all members were attached to land societies to work on collectivisation. These nuclei in the land societies, under the guidance of a workers' brigade, held meetings for poor peasants, middle peasants, women and young people. From 27 December 1929 to 13 January 1930, three land societies joined a collective farm, and issued a challenge to the two

---

[1] Document 14, entry 27 December.

remaining land societies.[1] What pressures were used to bring about these results is not clear.

'General meetings of citizens' were not only called by workers from the towns. Some rural soviets used this method in their collectivisation campaigns. Again, it is not clear whether these were called on the basis of communes; this is not made explicit. A fairly typical example is the following account of the history of a collective farm in Saratov guberniya. The village of Kozlovka had 1313 households, 87 kulak, 512 middle peasant, 507 poor peasant, 207 workers and employees. In November 1929 the rural soviet and Party cell began agitation work for collectivisation. A number of general meetings of citizens were called, also poor peasant meetings, and meetings for groups of poor peasants. A group of 40 poor peasant heads of household voted to organise a collective. Later the rural soviet took a unanimous decision that all rural soviet members should join the collective farm. In early December, a general poor peasant meeting voted that all poor peasants should join the collective, making a total of 270 households. 'There was then counter-action by kulaks. Where kulaks did not succeed in persuading individuals against the collective farms, they tried to disrupt the general meetings of citizens by means of those under their influence [podkulachniki].' For example, in February 1930 the question of the sowing campaign came up at the general meeting of citizens. Those under kulak influence protested against any form of collective sowing. Poor peasants were for it. Middle peasants were incited to leave the meeting by those under kulak influence. A fight broke out and kulaks killed a former commander in the Red Army. On 15 February 1930 there was a raion party organisation directive to increase the speed of collectivisation, ordering the whole village to be in a collective farm by March. The question was put to a general meeting of citizens: 'who is against the collective farm?' A minority raised their hands, so the collective farm was organised. 'This administrative way aroused middle and poor peasant antagonism', and there was a retreat with the appearance of Stalin's 'Dizzy with success' article in March. Liquidation of kulaks as a class was implemented by the rural soviet drawing up a list of kulaks, which was discussed at

[1] Document 14, p. 381. Report by V. S. Stepanov.

groups of poor peasants and confirmed by 'general meeting of citizens'.[1]

It would seem that such 'general meetings of citizens' bore only a tenuous relationship to the commune. It may be that the tradition of peasant meetings to discuss affairs at least helped to create an atmosphere for the rural soviet to call such meetings. While they had existed on paper for two years, they seem to have been used by rural soviets only after the beginning of the collectivisation campaign, in so far as rural soviets were prepared to take a part in the campaign – frequently they were not. A similar instance of use of a 'general meeting of peasants' is reported in Tula guberniya, where such a meeting was called at the rural soviet building to counter 'meetings of believers' at the church where the idea of collectivisation was rejected.[2] The idea of using the commune as a transitional form, previously implicit in Party policy, had proved impossible, given the need for rapid collectivisation. One legal lever which could in theory be used against a commune in the collectivisation campaign was a revision to the Land Code in December 1929, where land society land being used 'harmfully' could be used to organise or strengthen collective farms or state farms. Land organs could take such land as a land use measure. (Alternatively the land could be given by the raion executive committee to members of the society having too little land, presumably to counter-balance 'unfairness' in the re-distribution.)[3] The communes would not provide a platform for speakers to persuade them to turn themselves voluntarily into collectives. Indeed this policy does not seem to have been attempted in most areas. This could be interpreted as insensitivity of Party workers to the existing social structure, but, more likely, as a realisation by them that headlong confrontation with the peasantry could not force whole communes to become collectives. Indeed the policy was largely to make the most of assumed divisive elements in the countryside, and foster the group interests of the poor peasant, rather than approach the commune as an entity.

[1] *Saratovskaya partiinaya organizatsiya v periode nastupleniya sotsializma po vsemu frontu – sozdaniya kolkhoznogo stroya. Dokumenty i materialy* 1930–2 (Saratovskoe knizhnoe izdatel'stvo, 1961). Document 41 – report on position of collective farm 'Comintern' of village of Kozlovka.   [2] Podchufarov, *Tul'skie kommunisky*, p. 116.
[3] SU 1930, no. 1, art. 1, 30 December 1929.

CONCLUSIONS

We have been concerned with the last five years of communal land holding in Russia. Collectivisation marked the end of a phase in Russian peasant land holding. Redistributional strip holding was encouraged before the abolition of serfdom in 1861 by the system of poll taxes. The 1861 reforms further strengthened the land-holding basis of the commune. The effects of the Stolypin legislation in breaking up communal holding were not as extensive as was often suggested. The return of the peasantry in many areas after the revolution meant that at the start of our period communal holding had returned to pre-Stolypin proportions. Communes retained most of their pre-revolutionary local government functions in the absence of any other authority in the countryside in the post-revolutionary years. Our task has been to indicate the nature and extent of communal land holding in the final years, and the pressures for change upon the commune.

In setting about this task, we have been very conscious of the gulf between peasant society as it actually was, and as it was seen and interpreted by those at the centre. Materials on this whole problem are scarce enough, but those that we have nearly all come from central sources. Almost by definition, peasant society leaves no written account of itself, and we rely on the observations of others. In this period there were serious studies of the economics of the peasant household, but nothing on peasant social institutions, and very little serious published work on the commune. Many of our sources are the observations of politicians or administrators. Legislation has been quoted at length as a reflection of government attitudes. While it is interesting to see this view of the problem, only occasionally have we been able to see beyond with direct evidence from the countryside. The peasant's concept of the world, and, indeed, of time, was in this period only beginning to be changed by contact with the wider world beyond the village. Production was still largely subsistence farming for the household. There had

206

always been demands for surpluses to pay the landlord, or to pay taxes, but production for the market had made comparatively little inroad into the peasant economy in many areas of Russia. Contact between the peasant culture and that of the towns and government had been growing under the Stolypin reforms. For some time peasants had left the villages for temporary work in the towns. Most of all, the war and civil war took peasants away from their villages to the army, and at the same time brought armies to the countryside. None the less, the gulf between the two cultures was still very wide.

The problem was only in part that of a lack of sympathy by the Bolsheviks for the peasantry. This was in itself a reflection of the deeper division between the Russian peasantry and the culture of the urban, and governing circles. The peasantry had for ages been divorced from the government based on land-owning, court circles. The divide between them and the urbanised Bolsheviks was also great, although many urban workers came from peasant families.

With this general background in mind, we may turn to specific questions. There was no direct correlation between the number of settlements and communes in most areas. In some areas the commune consisted of a large number of settlements. This was so in the north west, where many communes were made up of very small settlement, and where the land of each commune was interspersed with that of other communes. A rather different pattern of multi-settlements commune existed in the south east where one commune was often a very large institution consisting of a number of settlements along a river. By contrast, in other areas there could be more than one commune to each settlement. Our understanding of the commune as a social institution would be greatly enhanced by a study of the relationship between the settlement, the unit of habitation, the household, the unit of work, and the commune, the unit of land holding. Unfortunately we have only the most sketchy evidence about the physical size relation, and none at all about the functioning of the large multi-settlement commune. From the point of view of local administration it would seem the commune, rather than the settlement, was the most important unit in most areas.

The actual land-holding patterns of communes varied greatly.

In areas where there was pressure on arable land, strips tended to be narrow, and any household might hold a large number. This was especially so in grain importing areas. In the Volga region and the south east the problems were rather those of distance between the household and its land, which was not held in a very large number of strips. These broad physical differences have considerable implications for the working of the commune, but no evidence was available to specify these further. Enough evidence was available to sound a warning against looking upon the Russian commune as a uniform institution in all areas. Variations were considerable not only between broad geographical regions, but within quite small areas.

One important point which arose in our study of land-holding was that commune membership was not necessarily defined by a hard and fast line. The commune was essentially an institution concerned with the holding of arable land. Thus if arable holdings were not the major part of a household's economy, membership of the commune was only a subsidiary factor in the management of that household's economy. Thus figures for commune membership varied because they were not necessarily using the same criteria. In most areas with arable farming this did not lead to a serious discrepancy, but in the north west and west was an important factor to consider. A further point is the extent to which households which had left the communal holding for enclosed holding still participated in the commune. Since the commune had a variety of non-land-holding functions, it seems likely the divorce could not be complete, and that commune membership depended upon the particular function of the household and commune being considered.

Redistribution was still extensively practised in the period we are dealing with. One of the incentives to redistribution before the revolution, equalisation of obligations to the government, still existed in modified form. The commune was no longer the unit of taxation, but the agricultural tax was, at the start of the period, virtually based on area held. The commune continued to fulfil its major function of reconciling conflict over land holding in a period when new areas of land had been seized from the landlord by the peasantry, and the break-up of large households called for readjustment of holdings within the commune. While full redistribution of whole communes were not so common, adjustments for size of family continued in most areas. Of the other agrarian functions of the commune, we have been able to discern little. Communal rotation, usually three-field, was widespread, but we have no evidence how this worked.

Having given some indication of the nature of communal holding in the period, the second half of our work was concerned with the pressures for change acting on the commune in its final years. The land-holding and administrative functions were subject to rather different pressures, and were considered separately for the sake of clarity. While a warning against generalisations was made when discussing land holding, it did not prove possible to examine the commune further on an area basis when discussing its non-agricultural functions.

A number of internal pressures were beginning to affect the commune's land holding. The number of households was increasing as large families split up into smaller units. Younger men thereby came to be heads of households, and attended the gathering. Numbers of peasants had served in the wars or worked in towns. In such ways urban values were at least coming to the notice of peasants. There was a steady pressure, especially in areas near the towns, from households to take up enclosed forms of holding.

This was reflected in the external pressures on communal land holding. Economically, it was generally assumed that enclosed holding would be more efficient, although there seems to have been remarkably little empirical evidence to support, or deny, this reasonable-sounding hypothesis. Politically, the development of a small-farmer type of agriculture was distasteful to the government. Whether the conditions were in any case suitable for the development of such an agricultural economy is a debatable point. Enough is not known of the motivating forces for change in a peasant household, but it seems unlikely that, for example, the provision of tractors would have impressed the peasantry either for or against the government in view of the low level of their techniques although production for the market was growing, albeit slowly. While some work was done in creating new enclosed holdings in the twenties, this was strongly discouraged in most areas as politically undesirable. There are hints that there was a substantial demand, but the evidence is not very strong. In terms of practical work done, the land-holding agencies seem to have reached a compromise with the peasantry, and concentrated on easing the most inconvenient features of communal holding. Most of the work involved breaking down the largest communes into smaller units. Very little of this process has been recorded, but the fact that it was done suggests that in these areas the significant social unit was smaller than the commune as a whole. The vast bulk of communes remained stable and unchanged, except for possibly having their land consolidated into one area rather than interlocking with another commune. Land use measures encouraged a pattern of fairly small communes, with each household having a small number of large strips, not too far away from the home. While there were arguments in the centre as to which form would encourage co-operation, and which lead to collectivisation, actual work was directed to improving the existing method of holding.

The political discussion of the commune both as a land-holding and an administrative unit was largely in terms of a 'class' analysis of the peasantry. The assumption was that the commune was used by the rich peasant to manipulate the rest of the peasantry, who were indebted to him. It has been no part of our task to discuss questions of differentiation within the peasantry, and we have found virtually no direct evidence on the internal social dynamics of the commune. We have, however, had to question this approach. We can agree that the equalisation of land holding between families need have been no bar to differentiation based on other criteria. Indeed, there is evidence that inefficiencies of strip farming hit the family with the smallest holding hardest. However, the evidence is far from clear that there was a particular group of peasants who did all the renting, hiring out and money-lending within one commune. The question of function must be raised again, and it seems likely that many households were by turn hirers and hirers out. In the smaller commune, with its face-to-face relations, group leadership may well have changed according to function. This is not to deny that at the extreme end of the spectrum there was the kulak as depicted in

Conclusions

Soviet terms. However, definition is far more elusive than was suggested by Soviet writers, and, one suspects, his influence was not so all-pervasive. One of the most important criteria, the subjective views of peasants themselves about differentiation, is hard to discover. It must remain a question of speculation whether the 'Soviet' kulak was not the aim to which all peasant households aspired. Evidence on cyclical mobility suggests attainment of this was even a possibility. What is certain is that the Bolshevik approach to the peasantry, at least after 1927, in practice united the peasantry. Within the commune, it seems likely there was a subtle balance between the majority of households, and those which were distinctly more prosperous. As pressure from the government increased, it would seem that community of interest grew stronger.

The local government of the countryside was virtually in the hands of the communes in the mid-twenties. While it was in a sense true that this was the pre-revolutionary commune strengthened rather than weakened by the revolution, there was an important difference. The commune was no longer related to the official system of government, and was no longer responsible for raising taxation for the state. The rural soviets had taken over the functions of the commune in relationships with the government. The commune was very much more independent than it had been in any previous period. The more unpleasant functions had thus, from the point of view of the peasantry, been split off on to the soviets.

While government policy towards the land-holding functions of the commune was quite tolerant from 1922 to 1929, there was never any questioning at the centre of the policy that the soviets should take over all those functions of rural administration undertaken by the commune. The philosophy behind the rural soviets suggested peasant involvement in the wider society. This was largely interpreted as an educative process, an awakening of the peasantry to the wider society, rather than a looking for a peasant contribution to that society. This begged two questions – first, whether the Russian peasantry at that time were interested in, or able to comprehend, integration into any Russian state system, and secondly, whether they could in any case be enthused by the particularly Bolshevik

Conclusions

flavour of the new system. In the event, one may be surprised at the numbers of peasants participating in the rural soviet elections, and standing for office. One feels this must be interpreted in terms of an interest in trying to obtain as sympathetic interpretation as possible of central policy at the local level. Information on the motives of peasant members of rural soviets, and what they did, is very scarce. Even more scarce is information on peasant party members. It is evident that a substantial number were drawn from the better-off peasantry. It seems likely that they were often younger members of households, perhaps expressing their discontent with the patriarchal family, although this was not now so rigid, and with the backwardness of peasant life. However, few remained actively engaged in agriculture and their quality was always considered suspect in a proletarian party.

Many devices were used to try and increase the influence of the rural soviets. Their financial weakness, compared with the strength of the communes, was used as a scapegoat to account for their poor performance. This financial weakness reflected the feeling at the centre that the rural soviets would have been unable to make good use of funds entrusted to them. Peasants supported the commune financially, while the rural soviets made exactions for purposes only dimly understood by the peasant tax-payer.

Collectivisation was a decision made, we assume, mainly on economic grounds. However, it cut through the problems which the commune presented. The, for the Bolsheviks, gloomy alternatives of either encouraging a 'farmer' peasantry, or supporting an institution which tended to conserve rather than discourage peasant values, were laid aside in collectivisation. The lack of administrative control over the peasantry expressed in the persistence of the communes as the effective grass-roots level of local government would be solved. The collectivisation campaign highlighted the weaknesses of the rural soviets. They had been too far away from the peasantry both geographically and in spirit to influence the peasantry towards taking part in the wider society. However, they were too close to the peasantry to be of use in enforcing collectivisation. The main work was done by the town workers, and collectivisation expressed the swamping of the rural culture by the urban. The commune as a land-holding system was swept away, but just what elements are continuity and which change in the system of collective farms it is perhaps too early to say as collective farming itself undergoes change.

However, we must reject the view that the collective farm represented some sort of logical successor to the commune for the peasantry. It has been suggested that the transfer from one form of communal organisation to another, although at first an unwelcome one, was not a radical one. The tradition of being prepared to subordinate his own interests to those of the commune in land holding must certainly have meant that the collective farm was not completely strange to the peasant. It has been argued that the commune prevented the development of a concept of a certain piece of land being the property of one household – but there was a concept of right to a certain amount of land. This, however, is a slight element of continuity when compared with the changes. The commune reconciled conflicting interests, but collective farming was based on an assumption of active co-operation. In the commune, a household held a few strips which were to all intents and purposes its own for a period. Once the household entered a collective farm its members worked in the collective fields, and had only a vegetable garden of their own. Only holding, and certain broad decisions about cultivation, were communal in the commune: in the collective farm there was compulsory collective labour. In the commune the peasant had his own inventory and livestock, in the collective farm these were largely the property of the collective farm. This all meant a completely different approach to work – it was no longer an individual decision within the household, but involved a labour discipline external to the household. It may have been that the peasants felt no regret at the departure of the more objectionable kulaks, but the chairmen of the new kolkhozy were usually strangers, and often townsmen. In the commune the households responded as an individual unit to the pressures to produce, but in the collective farm production was centred on output for others' use. Physically, it seems certain the collective farms were not usually based on the old land-holding units.[1]

While communes possibly continued to exist until collectivisation

[1] See Appendix B.

Conclusions

was complete, we have no direct evidence of their existence beyond 1930. The rural soviets continue to call general meetings called 'gatherings' to this day. Nominally, these meetings are to discuss many of those affairs of local importance discussed formerly by the commune gathering, although agricultural matters are the province of the collective farm general meeting.[1] Just how widespread they are, and how much real autonomy they have is very doubtful.

In conclusion, one must take up the introductory point about the nature of the commune as an institution. Its organisation was informal in the extreme, although the wealth and size of some communes in the period suggests a degree of formal organisation. From certain Soviet sources, one gains the impression that the commune was used consciously by the peasantry as an instrument to oppose the rural soviets. The commune never took on this function. It was the existing way in which the peasantry organised themselves at the time of revolution, and the rural soviets were rarely strong enough to take over their functions. When the collectivisation campaign began, we have no evidence to suggest that the commune itself became the focal point of peasant resistance.

The revolution had in many ways a less profound impact on the town than the countryside. The urban worker still went to the same factory after the revolution, performed the same tasks. The agrarian revolution from above of 1929 meant the peasantry had to adjust to having the land they had held removed from the control of the household, to their work being directed to the collective fields, to a new concept of production. The interaction of urban and peasant culture in Russia is still continuing. The phase we have described must mark the end of the peasant society's isolation from the urban.

We have continually had to point out the need for further research. This has been a study of the land-holding basis of the commune and its administrative functions. There is a great need to enliven these bare bones with a study of the social structure of the

[1] On this, see D. A. Borodin, 'K voprosu o sel'skikh skhodakh', *Sovetskoe gosudarstvo i pravo* (1960), no. 12; K. S. Sladkov, *Sel'skie skhody* (Gosyurizdat 1955), reviewed in *Izvestiya* 8 October 1955; a description of a skhod in Kuibyshev oblast, *Izvestiya*, 19 October 1960; D. S. Karev (ed.), *Yuridicheskii spravochnik deputata mestnogo soveta* (Moscow, 1960), p. 114. I. M. Raznatovskii, *Sel'skie sovety – organy sovetskoi vlasti* (Gosyurizdat 1957) (in series V pomoshch' rabotnikam sel'skikh sovetov, ed. B. M. Babyi).

commune, and the dynamics of its working. Perhaps the materials for this will one day come to light. An adequate understanding of the working of the commune would be based on the techniques of peasant agriculture at this time and their implications for co-operation between households, for example, use of draught-power. One can but assume this aspect changed but little after the revolution but studies of peasant economy need not only to be conducted in terms of yield and output, but also what the methods used implied in social terms. The importance of kinship in the commune and in the Russian peasantry has not been explored. Many questions remain about the economy of the peasant household, especially the attitudes underlying the statistics. One hopes that Soviet workers can take advantage, before it is too late, of the memories of peasants who were in commune households in their youth. Aerial archaeology could provide valuable information on the physical layout of the commune. These are questions at random. More detailed ones have been raised in the text. Further research can not merely provide answers to historical questions, but illuminate a crucial question for our time of the nature of the peasantry and its response to changing conditions.

GLOSSARY

For fuller explanation, see Russian word.

Additions (and subtractions): Nakidki (skidki)
Agent: Upolnomochennyi
Agricultural labourer: Batrak
Agricultural officer: Agronom
Agro-agent: Agroupolnomochennyi
Allotment: Nadel
Artel: *see* Commune (artel)
Balk: Mezhnik
Centre of population: Naselennyi punkt (cf. selenie)
Collective farm: Kolkhoz (cf. zemlepol'zovanie)
Collective farm (commune): Kommuna (cf. zemlepol'zovanie)
Collective farm (artel): Artel' (cf. zemlepol'zovanie)
Collective farm (TOZ): TOZ (cf. zemlepol'zovanie)
Commune: Obshchina
Commune (mir): Mir
Contracting: Kontraktatsiya
Course: Polya (also field)
Crop rotation: Sevooborot
Declaration of non-fragmentation: Deklaratsiya nedrobimosti
Distribution: Raspredelenie
Division: Razdel
Elder: Starosta
Enclosed forms of holding: Khutor i otrub
Farm with only fields enclosed: Otrub
Field: Polya (also course)
Fully enclosed farm: Khutor
Garden plot: Usadba
Gathering: Skhod
General meeting of citizens: Obshchee sobranie grazhdan
Hamlet: Derevnya (*see* selenie)
Head of household: Domokhozyain

Appendix A

Household: Dvor
Intermingled strip system: Cherespolositsa
Land holding: Zemlepol'zovanie
Land society: Zemel'noe obshchestvo
Land use measures: Zemleustroistvo
Land use measures officer: Zemleustroitel'
Long distance from home to plots: Dal'nozemele
Middle peasant: Serednyak
Mir: Mir (cf. obshchina)
Multi-course rotation: Mnogopol'e
New settlement: Poselok; vyselok
Non-redistributable forms of holding: Uchastkovye formy zemlepol'zovaniya
Peasant Mutual Aid Society: KKOV
Poor peasant: Bednyak
Redistribution: Pereraspredelenie, peredel
Redistribution units: Razverstochnye edinitsy
Rich peasant: Kulak
Rural society: Sel'skoe obshchestvo
Rural soviet: Sel'skii sovet
Separation: Vydel
Settlement: Selenie
State farm: Sovkhoz
Strip: Polosa
Subtraction: Skidki (see Addition)
Surveyor: Zemlemer
Village: Selo
Village executive: Sel'skii Ispolnitel'
Well-to-do peasant: Zazhitochnyi krestyanin

RUSSIAN–ENGLISH

AGRONOM   Agricultural officer

AGROUPOLNOMOCHENNY   'Agro-agent'. Land society member acting as agent of the rural production conference from December 1929. Very doubtful whether any were in fact elected. See p. 198.

ARTEL   *see* Kolkhoz.

BATRAK   Landless agricultural labourer.

BEDNYAK   Poor peasant.

Glossary

CHERESPOLOSITSA   Intermingled strip system. Often used in sense of *excessive* intermingling of plots. Not necessarily redistributable.

DAL'NOZEMEL'E   Long distance from home to plots, and between plots in strip system.

DEKLARATSIYA NEDROBIMOSTI   Declaration of non-fragmentation. A declaration by a household that it would not split up into several smaller households.

DEREVNYA   Hamlet (*see* Selenie).

DESYATINA   Unit of area – 2·7 acres.

DOMOKHOZYAIN   Head of family.

DVOR   Household.

GUBERNIYA   Largest unit of local administration in pre-revolutionary Russia, retained to the mid-twenties, when replaced by the larger oblast and krai. Average population in RSFSR 1924, 1·38 million.

HECTARE (GEKTAR)   Unit of area – 2·47 acres.

KHUTOR   Fully enclosed farm. Holding of a household outside the commune where land and house were consolidated on one piece of land. Where khutor and otrub occur together 'enclosed farms' is used for brevity to cover both.

KKOV (Krest'yanskii komitet obshchestvennoi vzaimopomoshchi) Peasant Mutual Aid Society.

KOLKHOZ   Collective farm. Types of collective farms, sometimes known as collective forms (tovarishcheskie formy):

Kommuna: Here translated as collective farm (commune), to avoid confusion with obshchina. Fully communalised collective farm, with all land, animals and capital under control of the collective farm, with no individual household economy.

Artel: Collective farm (artel). Principal land animals and capital under control of the collective farm, but individual households retained small private plots.

TOZ: (Tovarishchestvo dlya obshchestvennoi obrabotki zemli) Collective farm (TOZ). Society for collective land working. The least socialised form of collective farm, with land cultivated jointly, but no other communalised aspects.

KOMMUNA   *see* Kolkhoz.

KON   cf. Pole.

KONTRAKTATSIYA   Contracting. A forward contract to sell agricultural produce at a fixed price – often with a counterpart supply of industrial goods; often involved an agreement by peasant to use improved techniques.

KRAI Along with oblast, largest unit of local administration, replacing the guberniya from the mid-twenties onwards. Same size limits as oblast, distinguished therefrom by having autonomous oblasts within its territory.

KULAK Rich peasant. Russian occasionally retained to make the sense clear.

MEZHNIK (also Mezhi, mezhpolose) Balk. Border strip between strips of different households in intermingled strip system.

MIR Commune (mir). The Russian is retained as this word can often be used interchangeably with obshchina. The dictionaries of Smirnov and Aleksandrov equate the two words. There is some difference in emphasis, best shown by Ushakov, who suggests that mir is 'commune with its members'. Obshchina can be used in a narrow sense relating to the particular form of land holding, while mir is not used thus. Mir is not often used in Soviet writing. When it is used, it is to associate the commune with the old and traditional. It suggests a spirit as well as an institution.

MNOGOPOL'E Multi-course rotation (of more than three courses).

NADEL Allotment. An allotment of arable land under any form of land holding.

NAKIDKI 'Additions'. Used in 'skidki i nakidki', 'subtractions and additions', together translated as minor readjustments (of holdings in commune, as opposed to any major repartition between members).

NASELENNYI PUNKT Centre of population – cf. Selenie.

OBLAST' Largest unit of local government, replacing the guberniya in the mid-twenties. Population varied from 5 to 10 million in RSFSR.

OBSHCHEE SOBRANIE GRAZHDAN General meeting of citizens – cf. Skhod.

OBSHCHINA Commune. Used both to denote the particular form of land holding, intermingled re-partitional strip farming, as well as the general village community which held the land in common. Cf. Mir, Zemel'noe obshchestvo. Terms used in communal tenure – Cherespolositsa, Dal'nozemel'e, Nakidki, Peredel, (Pere)raspredelenie, Razdel, Razverstochnye edinitsy, Skidki, Vydel, for which see appropriate heading.

Glossary

OKRUG   A middle unit of local government between the raion and oblast, which replaced the uezd, but was abolished in 1930. Population of approximately ½ million in 1929.

OTRUB   Farm with only fields enclosed. Holding of a household outside the commune where the land was consolidated in one place, but apart from the house. When khutor and otrub occur together, 'enclosed farms' is used for brevity to cover both.

PEREDEL   Redistribution. Used when strips of commune redistributed among member households. Could be partial (chastichnyi), involving only part of the land of each household, or full (polnyi), involving all the land of each member of the commune.

PERERASPREDELENIE   Redistribution (as peredel), but occasionally used in sense of a once and for all redistribution, as opposed to a redistribution at regular intervals.

POLE   Field, or course of a rotation. Could be sub-divided into yarusy, kony and polosa. See p. 7.

POLOSA   Strip. Unit of holding in commune. Shirokie polosy – broad strips, where rationalisation had meant each household had fewer, broader, strips. Cf. Pole.

POSELOK and VYSELOK   New settlement. In general, poselok means a new settlement of any kind, including, for example, a housing estate. Vyselok is used as a new rural settlement made as a result of land use measures. Hived-off settlement is a possible translation. The distinction, if there is one, between the two terms is not clear in the countryside.

Both terms can mean not only a pattern of settlement, but also a method of land holding. Thus, at the XV Party Congress it was resolved to 'help the growth of forms of land holding most favourable to development of co-operative mechanisation of agriculture (poselki, vyselki, etc.), curbing the practice of separation into enclosed farms'.[1] The implication is clearly that the new settlements were to have communal land holding, possibly with strips of a more rational size without redistribution. Thus Milyutin envisaged that new settlements would not redistribute their land.[2]

It would seem that when a large commune was subjected to land use measures and divided up three basic patterns were

---

[1] Resolution 'On work in the countryside', article 5b, *KPSS v rezolyutsiyakh*, II, 257.
[2] Speech to Central Executive Committee of the USSR, '4-yi sozyv, 7-oe zasedanie, April 1928'. *Sten. Otchet*, p. 726.

possible. First, the existing settlement pattern could be retained, but the land redistributed between the members of the old commune so that the existing settlements could form the basis of two or more new communes. The other two processes would involve not only changing the pattern of land holding, but also the pattern of settlement. In the one, the whole of the existing commune would be divided up into smaller units, but rather than retain the existing settlement pattern, new settlements would be created to correspond more closely to the new land-holding units. The land would thus be largely that of the old commune. This possibly corresponded to poselki. The final pattern would be where a group of members left the old, large commune, to new land outside the commune territory. This possibly corresponded to the vyselok, the hived-off settlement. This view is purely hypothetical, as there is little evidence on which to make generalisations. It seems to have some support in Danilov's description in *Istoriya SSSR* (1958), no. 3, p. 112, and Kovalev, *Sel'skoe Rasselenie* (Moscow, 1963), pp. 121 and 173.

While new and hived-off settlements were usually farmed with an improved strip system, this was not necessarily so. It was said that in the north west new settlement (poselkovoe) land holding predominated, and communal was rare, implying that the new settlements were based on farms with fields only enclosed.[1] Likewise, small poselki had been advocated, and attacked, as a method of developing peasant holding in Belorussia, where enclosed forms of holding predominated.[2]

It thus appears that the words are used, in relation to the countryside, in two senses. The general one implies setting up of new small settlements with any method of land holding. In a narrower sense, as used in the XV Party Congress resolution, it implies breaking up a large commune into smaller ones, or hiving off of a new small commune from a large one. (See also p. 191.)

RAION Unit of local administration immediately superior to the rural soviet area and, until its abolition, below the okrug.

[1] Dubovskii, speaking at Agrarian Section of the Communist Academy. Quoted in *Na agrarnom fronte* (1926), no. 11–12, p. 142.
[2] Cf. Pinchuk's attack on Kislyakov at Conference of Agrarian Marxists, December 1929. *Sten. Otchet*, pp. 176 ff.

Replaced the former volost, but was larger in area. Average population 40–50,000 in 1930.

RASPREDELENIE Distribution (as Pereraspredelenie).

RAZDEL Division. Used of household splitting up into smaller units, or commune being broken either into smaller communes or to enclosed forms of holding.

RAZVERSTOCHNYE EDINITSY Redistribution units. The norm to be used by commune when distributing land between member households. Land could be allotted according to size of household, number of males, number of cattle, or other criteria.

SELENIE Settlement. There is some confusion in the terms used for settlement. A tentative outline of their relationship is suggested below.

General words	*Translation*	*Comment*
Poselenie	Settlement	General terms describing any group of dwellings from a city to isolated dwellings. Thus either term may be used to describe these below.
Naselennyi punkt	Centre of population	
Selenie	Settlement	General term for a *rural* settlement, thus includes any term below. (In pre-revolutionary times some-equated with derevnya, but has general use in Soviet times.)
Specific words		
Selo	Village	In pre-revolutionary times, usually a settlement with a church.
Derevnya	Hamlet	Smaller than selo – in pre-revolutionary times usually without a church.
Poselok	New settlement	Can be used in urban as well as rural sense.
Vyselok	Hived-off settlement.	

Appendix A

SELO Village. Cf. Selenie.

SEL'SKII ISPOLNITEL' Village executive. An official appointed for maintenance of law and order in village by rural soviet. Two-month term of office, one for 25 households. Not very often commented upon – rarely appointed?

SEL'SKII SOVET (SEL'SOVET) Rural soviet. Lowest level of local administration in countryside – did not necessarily cover area of village, usually rather larger.

SEL'SKOE OBSHCHESTVO Rural society. A pre-revolutionary unit of rural administration, covering a rather larger area than the commune.

In Soviet times, occasionally used wrongly, when zemel'noe obshchestvo or obshchina is plainly intended.[1]

SEREDNYAK Middle peasant.

SEVOOBOROT Crop rotation.

SKHOD Gathering. The meeting of the commune. In law, from 1927 there was a distinction between the gathering of the land society, and the gathering 'general meeting of citizens' (obshchee sobranie grazhdan), which was to be attended only by those with soviet electoral rights. Also used loosely by Soviet writers to describe meeting of villagers called by outsiders – e.g. Party, volost officials, MTS, State Farm, Repair brigades, workers from towns. Meeting of KKOV (*q.v.*) usually referred to as Skhod.

SKIDKI Cf. Nakidki.

SOVKHOZ State farm.

STAROSTA Elder. Elected head of commune, a term not officially used in Soviet times.

TOZ (Tovarishchestvo dlya Obshchestvennoi Obrabotki Zemli) *See* Kolkhoz.

UCHASTKOVYE FORMY ZEMLEPOL'ZOVANIYA Non-redistributable forms of land holding (cf. Zemlepol'zovanie). Included not only khutor and otrub, but also strip holdings which were not redistributed communally.

UEZD Middle level of local government in pre-revolutionary Russia, retained until mid-twenties when superseded by the larger okrug. Average population in RSFSR in 1924, 180,000.

[1] Cf. Law on Socialisation of Land, 31(18), January 1918, passed at III Congress of Soviets, art. III B(5) mentions sel'skie obshchestva amongst those with a right to use land. Law 'On repartition of land', of 1 July 1919 (SU 1919, no. 36, art. 362) perpetuates this use of the word, as does that of 30 April 1920 (SU 1920, no. 35, art. 170). See also pp. 88 and 98.

Glossary

UPOLNOMOCHENNYI Agent (of land society). Soviet term for official of commune. Not to be confused with agro-upolnomochennyi.

USAD'BA Garden plot. Non-redistributable holding of member of commune.

VERSTA Unit of distance – 1·1 km.

VOLOST' Lowest level of local administration in pre-revolutionary times, below the uezd. In Soviet times above the rural soviet. Replaced in mid-twenties by the larger raion. Average population in 1924 in RSFSR, 14,500.

VYDEL Separation (of household with land from commune).

VYSELOK New settlement, formed by splitting off from existing settlement. See Selenie, Poselok.

YARUS Cf. Pole.

ZAZHITOCHNYI KREST'YANIN Well-to-do peasant.

ZEMEL'NOE OBSHCHESTVO Land society. Term used by 1922 RSFSR Land Code to include groups of land-users of all kinds, including communal, non-redistributable and collective. While the term was used in this broad sense – all peasant households in the Ukraine were bound to be members of a 'land society' – it came to be used in practice, at least in the RSFSR and in most Soviet discussion, as equated with the commune. Where this is quite obvious I have translated the word commune, leaving 'land society' for direct quotations and places where there is a doubt. Some commentators tried to suggest that the Soviet land society was in some way different from the pre-revolutionary commune, but this seems to have been a mere form of words.

ZEMLEMER Surveyor.

ZEMLEPOL'ZOVANIE Land holding. Literally 'land-use', but applies to the method of holding, and not to the crops grown. Methods of holding are summarised in Table A1. Trudovoe zemlepolzovanie means not only use of land for farming, but implies making one's living from land by one's own efforts.

ZEMLEUSTROISTVO Land use measures. Any work involving physical re-organisation of land, such as by irrigation, drainage or re-organisation of holding. It is with the last we are mostly concerned here. It includes work such as redistribution of land between villages, division of large communes into smaller, transfer of commune to fewer, larger strips, thereby alleviating

Appendix A

Table A1

Russian	English	Land holding
OBSHCHINA	Commune	Communal – redistributable among members
UCHASTKOVYE FORMY	Non-redistributable forms of holding	
(i) KHUTOR	Fully enclosed farm	Individual household
(ii) OTRUB	Farm with only fields enclosed	Individual household
(iii) UCHASTKOVO-CHERESPOLOSNOE	Farm with intermingled strips outside the commune	Individual household
KOLKHOZ	Collective farm	
(i) KOMMUNA	Collective farm (commune)	Communal
(ii) ARTEL	Collective farm (artel)	Communal
(iii) TOZ	Collective farm (TOZ)	Communal
POSELOK, VYSELOK	Settlement	Communal, formed from a larger existing commune. Redistributable?
SOVKHOZ	State farm	State

excessive interlocking of strips and excessive distance between strips; setting up collective farms and transferring households to enclosed forms.

ZEMLEUSTROITEL' Land use measures officer.

226

Glossary

Layout of fields	Dwelling	Labour
Strips plus non-redistributable garden plot	Apart from strips	Individual household on own strips
Consolidated	With the fields	Individual household
Consolidated	Apart from the fields	Individual household
Strips, non-redistributable	Apart from strips	Individual household
Consolidated	In settlement	Collective
Consolidated	In settlement	Collective
Usually consolidated	In settlement	Collective
Small number of strips per household	Apart from strips	Individual household on own strips
Consolidated	In settlement	Wage

APPENDIX B

COMMUNE AND COLLECTIVE FARM:
PHYSICAL RELATIONSHIP

It is not clear whether there was geographical continuity between
commune and collective farm. It seems unlikely that this was so
before mass collectivisation began. Average size of collective farms
was much smaller than average commune size. Wesson gives the
following figures (Table B1) for collective farm size in the USSR,
1926–30, in households.[1]

Table B1

Type of collective farm	1926	1927	1928	1929	1930
Commune (collective farm)	12	18	19	28	71
Artel	11	18	12	16	73
TOZ	13	21	12	17	57

We have already suggested that average commune size in the RSFSR
was approximately 50 households.[2]

From this evidence alone, it is clear that it was not a usual pattern
for whole communes to transfer to collective farming. Indeed this
would seem likely from the general climate at this time. There may
have been a number of isolated instances of this happening. Milyutin
hinted in 1928 that there was evidence of 'land societies changing
into societies for co-operative land-working, artel, commune etc.
and undertaking communal working of land'.[3] This was put forward
in a speech arguing that improved land societies were the correct
way forward to collectivisation. There seems to have been no published evidence of this happening in the pre-collectivisation period.

There may well have been some confusion in statistics as to
where a 'society for co-operative land-working' began, and a commune ended. While these figures for size probably reflect no such

[1] Robert G. Wesson, *Soviet communes* (Rutgers University Press, New Jersey, 1963),
p. 123. An invaluable study of the commune-type collective farm.
[2] See above, p. 12.
[3] Speech at Ts IK, December 1928. *Bulletin* 12, p. 23.

confusion, it is possible that many of these societies were also included in the figures for communes. While there is little evidence for this, it may be that many communes were counted as collective farms by becoming regarded as societies for co-operative land-working. While Wesson's evidence, on size grounds, points to these societies and communes being distinct, the fact that some statistics in the early twenties graded holding as including commune, artel, and commune (collective farm), suggests that societies for co-operative land-working could have been counted still as communes.[1] While it would be an interesting hypothesis that such societies then developed into artels, and thus supported Milyutin's contention, there is no evidence that this happened.[2]

Commune members leaving to form a collective farm did not necessarily have this land consolidated into one area. Indeed one of the problems of many early collective farms was that their land was intermingled with commune land.[3] This problem was perhaps not such a great one for a society for co-operative land-working, although obviously it meant less rational use of labour. The problem was more serious for artels and communes. It appears that a fairly substantial proportion of collective farms formed before 1928 had consolidated their land (in part, presumably, because they were not on former commune land). Milyutin gave the following percentage of non-consolidated collective farms in the RSFSR (Table B2).[4]

Table B2

	Society for co-operative land-working	Artel	Commune
Organised before January 1928	48	13	4
Organised between 1 January 1928 and 1 May 1928	73	50	16

[1] See above, pp. 23ff.
[2] Indeed it would be valuable to examine the dynamics underlying statistics of forms of collectives to see whether, before 1930, collectives did change their form.
[3] At close of 1925, 46% of collective farm communes, 52% of artels, 56% of societies for co-operative land-working, on average 52·3% of all collective farms were not consolidated. *Istoricheskii arkhiv* (1960), no. 1, p. 49. 'Materialy k sodokladu TSKK-RKI o kolkhozakh', 15 June 1926.
[4] Quoted in *Pravda*, 8 December 1928. In Ts IK discussion (December 1928, *Bulletin* 17), interjection in speech by Rozit, he admits second set of figures to relate to period I have quoted.

Commune and collective farm

Apparently there was a campaign to consolidate collective farms in the summer of 1928, so that by 1 November 1928 the percentage of non-consolidated collective farms was as follows:[1]

Table B3

	Society for co-operative land-working	Artel	Commune	All
Organised before April 1928	2·2	2·1	0·6	2·1
Organised between April and 1 November 1928	27·8	25·5	9·6	25·8

Thus, at least until 1928, there was a high degree of inter-locking of plots of members of communes and societies for co-operative land-working. This was true to a lesser extent with artels. From these figures it is apparent that collectives could not immediately separate from the commune. Indeed, one commentator remarked that new collectives had to wait until the land society decided to undertake land use measures before they could be consolidated.[2]

We have already seen that those conducting collectivisation at local level do not often appear to have tried consciously to found collective farms on existing communes. There had been some discussion as to whether this was desirable at the XVI Party Conference in April 1929. Before the policy of liquidation of the kulaks as a class had been decided upon, some speakers suggested that it was useful to have whole land societies becoming collective farms, including the kulak, so that he would be under the thumb of the collective, rather than away forming his own homestead, which could be a springboard for capitalism.[3] Two speakers with experience of working on tractor columns were more hesitant. One remarked that he had organised 11 tractor columns in the Central Black Earth region, and some 'large collective farms' had been formed where whole land societies did transfer. He felt the kulak was too disruptive. He was supported by another speaker from the same area, who also had seen land societies transferred at least to collective land-working *en bloc*.[4]

---

[1] Rozit. Ts IK discussion, December 1928, *Bulletin* 17, p. 36.
[2] Schur, speaking at Ts IK December 1928, *Bulletin* 15, p. 37.
[3] Contributions by Zaitsev (p. 369) and Kalinin. *Sten. Otchet.*
[4] Contributions by Vareikis (p. 334) and Belenkii (pp. 403–6). *Sten. Otchet.*

Appendix B

While the transfer of whole communes to collective farming in one move seems to have been the exception, we may ask whether once collectivisation was complete in an area, the collective farm occupied the same area as the former commune. Kovalev, in his work on rural settlement, suggests the position was as follows:

Collectivisation did not result in a massive reconstruction of the network of points of population in most regions, as collective farms were organised on the whole on the basis of existing rural settlements [poseleniya]...in these [pre-war] conditions 'single settlement' [selenie] collective farms predominated, or a village [selo] and its surrounding new settlements [vyselki]; also centres of population [naselennye punkty] with several collective farms are not rare in southern steppe regions.[1]

While this suggests settlement patterns remained the same after collectivisation, this does not necessarily imply that the units of land holding remained the same.

We can find no definite confirmation of this in particular areas. In Moscow guberniya in 1928–9 the average size of a commune was about 50 households.[2]

The size, in households, of the collective farms of Moscow oblast is given in Table B4.[3]

Table B4

Year (on 1 July)	Average number of households per collective farm	Percentage collectivisation (of households)
1927	20	0·5
1928	15	0·7
1929	16	1·8
1930	30	7
1931	35	36
1932	37	48
1933	—	—
1934	49	74·4
1935	55	89·9
1936	60	—

Thus, in the pre-collectivisation period, collective farms were considerably smaller than the land societies, in terms of households.

[1] S. A. Kovalev, *Sel'skoe rasselenie*, MGU (Moscow, 1963), p. 123.
[2] See above, p. 37.   [3] *Sotsialisticheskoe stroitel'stvo SSSR* (1936).

Commune and collective farm

At the time of most rapid collectivisation, 1930–2, the number of households per collective farm was well below the average for the 1928–9 land society. As more collective farms were formed, average size grew, suggesting a growth in size of existing collective farms. By the time of nearly full collectivisation, the average size of collective farm was rather larger, in terms of households, than the 1928–9 land society. While the difference of 10 households is not large, one may have expected the collective farm size to have been smaller, not larger, if the two were to be based on the same geographical area, to allow for migration to the town. However, migration was possibly by individuals, rather than whole households, which would not influence size in terms of households. Dekulakisation could have led either to a fall in number of households, due to deportation, or a rise if households were split up.

In the Mid-Volga region, we have seen that there was a wide range of size of commune,[1] from 58 to 139 with an average of 80 households. Average size of collective farms in the region was as shown in Table B5.[2]

Table B5

	Households
1 June 1928	16
1 June 1929	18
May 1930	77
1 July 1931	132

As the collectivisation rate increased in following years, collective farms became *on average* much larger than size of commune, but collectivisation may well have been concentrated in areas with large communes.[3]

However, measurement of size by household numbers is not a good method of testing physical identity. Thus over the RSFSR as a whole once collectivisation was nearly complete in 1935, average size of collective farm was 62 households.[4] We have seen that commune size was probably 50–5 households. However, the number of collective farms when there was nearly full collectivisation was little more

[1] See above, p. 45.
[2] In May 1930, 20·5% of households were collectivised. *Narodnoe khozyaistvo SSSR 1932* (Moscow, 1932). [3] Ibid.
[4] *Sotsialisticheskoe stroitel'stvo SSSR* (Gosplan, 1936), p. 278.

than half the number of communes in 1928. Were the number of peasant households in 1928 related to the number of collective farms in 1935, a figure of around 100 households per collective would be reached.

Thus the apparent similarity of the commune and complete collective farm in size in terms of households does not indicate a physical geographical identity, as there was a fall in the number of peasant households from 1928 to 1935. We simply do not have the evidence to suggest how collective farms were formed, and detailed studies of particular areas are needed. It does seem certain that there was no general tendency for collective farms to be based on existing communes.

While there appears to be no link between communes and the collective farms which succeeded to their territory, it is worth investigating whether there is any connection between communal holding and the rate of collectivisation. On the one hand it could be argued that areas of communal holding might pave the way for collectivisation as a result of experience of a degree of co-operation between peasants, or on the other that the commune would act as a focal point for peasant resistance. Not surprisingly, comparison of figures for collectivisation with what is known of communal holding shows no definite results.

While we can see that the areas of most intensive collectivisation at this stage in the campaign in the RSFSR were the areas with the highest proportion of communal holding, this is no indication that there is a direct relationship. Collectivisation was concentrated in grain growing areas in order to try and raise marketed produce, and administrative methods were often used to obtain high percentages of collectivisation. The commune was strongest in these grain growing areas and therefore most exposed to collectivisation. The lower rate of collectivisation in the west and north west is not so much a reflection of resistance engendered by enclosed forms of holding being more firmly entrenched, but rather of the collectivisation campaign being less intensive at this stage in these areas. Some confirmation of this is suggested by the high rate of collectivisation at this time in the Ukraine, with its mainly enclosed holding.

These may seem rather negative results with which to conclude, but it is important to establish where the break between continuity and change came, as we have until now emphasised continuity in so many ways. The collectivisation campaign ignored and broke up the existing pattern of land holding units, just as it had largely ignored the organisational structure which was based on communal holding. The evolutionary process was at an end for the commune, but the revolution which overtook it was one from above, reflecting the wider problems of the process of growth of the country.

APPENDIX C

THE COMMUNE AFTER 1930

Collectivisation overtook the communes in 1930. Little is heard of the actual situation in areas which remained outside collectives. All our evidence for the continuing existence of the commune at least until 1931 is based on the fact that new legislation continued to provide for 'land societies'.

The guiding light was the decree on re-organisation of rural soviets in February 1930.[1] In 'areas of widespread collectivisation', land societies were to be liquidated and their rights and duties transferred to rural soviets. In areas where there were still land societies, the rural soviet was entrusted with directing the work of land societies on their territory, directing their work towards the socialist reconstruction of agriculture. The rural soviet was to have the right to cancel, alter and confirm decisions of the land society. There was to be a separate 'general meeting of citizens', called by the rural soviet, which would select questions for discussion there.

This was in the spirit of earlier legislation subordinating the land society to the rural soviet, and for the first time made it an explicit duty for the rural soviet to direct the land society towards collectivisation.

This was amplified in a decree 'on the liquidation of land societies in areas of mass collectivisation' in July 1930.[2] Land societies were to be disbanded if over 75% of the households within an area were collectivised. Their management was to be handed over directly to the rural soviets, who presumably would not allow these households to remain long outside the collective. It would be difficult to imagine a rural soviet organising a redistributional commune whose fields probably lay within the boundaries of collective farms. (An indication of the methods used 'to attract single peasants to collective work' is provided in a report on the progress of the harvest in collective farms of Lower Volga krai, 27 July 1930.[3] Many collective farms 'by all means strive to attract to the collective harvest the

---

[1] 'Osnovnye polozheniya ob organizatsii sel'skikh sovetov'. Article 14–30. *SZ SSSR*, no. 16, art. 172.
[2] Post. V. Ts. IK SNK. 30 July 1930. SU no. 51, art. 621.
[3] Document 66 of *Saratovskaya partiinaya organizatsiya*. Cf. p. 205, n. 1.

Appendix C

single peasant households. Single peasants often organise voluntarily collective harvesting on the example of the collective farm, single peasants also organise their shock brigades, taking over collective farm methods, join with collective farms, and collect the harvest together with collective farmers.' It was said that 9,000 harvest brigades of collective farms and single peasants took part in the campaign. In one area, general threshing floors were organised both for collective and individual peasants. Overall, the result was said to be a flow of single peasants into the collectives.) All holdings and property of the land society were to be handed over to the rural soviet. The extensive list gives some idea of the work of the communes at this time.[1] Agricultural capital was to be handed directly to the collective farm, and those remaining outside the collective not allowed to use it. They could still use common land. The debts of the society remained the responsibility of the former member households. The burden of the debt was to be distributed among households by the rural soviet according to their ability to pay. Obligations undertaken for contracted delivery were to be laid upon individual households after the liquidation of the society. The actual process of liquidation was to be carried out by the rural soviet, on a decree of the raion executive committee, who set a time limit for the operation.

This law was amended slightly in November 1931, re-defining areas of mass collectivisation as those with 68–70% of middle and poor peasant households in collective farms, including no less than 75–80% of sown area.[2] This was the last reference to the land society in Soviet legislation. In 1930 there were a number of pieces of minor legislation which allowed for the existence of land societies. Thus, in January 1930, audit commissions of rural soviets were also entrusted with reviewing land society finances.[3]

In June 1930 there was a decree on 'working of peat deposits by collective farms, agricultural societies, land societies and other working land users'.[4]

A decree on 'village judges' of October 1930 mentioned that quarrels involving collective farms and land societies did not come under their jurisdiction—incidentally, these officials were to be elected at the 'gathering (general meeting of citizens)';[5] a companion

[1] Quoted above, p. 137.   [2] SU 1931, no. 65, art. 645, 10 November 1931.
[3] Ibid., no. 4, art. 42, 20 January 1930.   [4] Ibid., no. 28, art. 372, 6 June 1930.
[5] Ibid., no. 51, art. 629, 10 October 1930.

decree of the same date on settling land disputes provided 'if one of
the sides is a land society'.[1] When the section of the Land Code dealing with redistribution of land under rationalisation schemes was
revised in September 1930, the land society was involved. 'With
repartitions [razverstki and razdely] and separation [vydel] from
societies, the amount of land partitioned to the household is determined by the number of redistribution units belonging to the
participant in rationalisation.'[2]

That communes continued to exist well into the thirties is
suggested by the fact that it was only by mid-1931 that it was claimed
half of peasant households were collectivised, and by July 1934 that
three quarters of peasant households in the RSFSR were collectivised.[3] They are never mentioned in the literature as a problem,
and there is no indication of their organisation. It seems quite
likely that they were quite firmly under the control of higher
organs, with the most stubbornly anti-collective members having
been deported.

[1] *Ibid.*, no. 51, art. 623, 10 October 1930.
[2] *Ibid.*, no. 50, art. 596, 20 September 1930, confirmed by Ts IK on 30 December
1930 in SU 1931, no. 3, art. 35.
[3] *Sel'skoe khozyaistvo SSSR* (1935), p. 633.

BIBLIOGRAPHY

WORKS IN ENGLISH (INCLUDING TRANSLATIONS)

Balzak, Vasyutin, Feigin, *Economic geography of the USSR* (trans.), Macmillan, N.Y., 1949.

W. R. Batsell, *Soviet rule in Russia*, Macmillan, N.Y., 1929.

A. Baykov, *The development of the Soviet economic system*, Cambridge U.P., 1946.

F. Belov, *History of a Soviet collective farm*, Routledge and Kegan Paul, London, 1956.

Bienstock, Schwarz, Yegow, *Management in Russian industry and agriculture*, Oxford U.P., N.Y., 1944.

P. W. Blackstock and B. F. Hoselitz, *The Russian menace to Europe* (a selection of writings of Marx and Engels on Russia), George Allen and Unwin, London, 1953.

Jerome Blum, *Landlord and peasant in Russia*, Princeton, 1961.

E. H. Carr, *A history of Soviet Russia: Socialism in one country*, Parts I and II, Macmillan, London, 1958 and 1959.

G. B. Carson, *Electoral practices in the USSR*, Praeger, N.Y., 1955.

Alexander Dallin, *German rule in Russia 1941–5*, N.Y., 1957.

H. S. Dinerstein, *Communism and the Russian peasant*, Free Press, Glencoe, Ill., 1955.

M. Dobb, *Soviet economic development since 1917*, Routledge and Kegan Paul, London, 1948.

M. Fainsod, *How Russia is ruled*, Harvard U.P., 1953.

—— *Smolensk under Soviet rule*, Macmillan, London, 1958.

S. N. Harper, *Civic training in Soviet Russia*, Chicago, 1929.

J. Hazard, *The Soviet system of government*, University of Chicago Press, 1957.

M. Hindus, *Broken earth*, Jonathan Cape, London and N.Y., 1926.

—— *Humanity uprooted*, Jonathan Cape, London and N.Y., 1929.

—— *Red bread*, Jonathan Cape, London and N.Y., 1931.

L. E. Hubbard, *The economics of Soviet agriculture*, Macmillan, London, 1939.

N. Jasny, *The socialized agriculture of the USSR*, Stanford, California, 1949.

R. D. Laird, *Collective farming in Russia – a political study of the Soviet kolkhoz*, University of Kansas, 1958.

239

Bibliography

M. Levine, *Russian peasants and Soviet power*. Allen and Unwin, London, 1968.

P. I. Lyashchenko, *History of the national economy of Russia* (trans.), Macmillan, N.Y., 1949.

B. W. Maxwell, *The Soviet state*, N.Y., 1934.

J. Maynard, *Russia in flux*, Gollancz, London, 1941.

—— *The Russian peasant and other studies*, Gollancz, London, 1942.

J. H. Meisl and F. S. Kozera, *Materials for the study of the USSR*, Ann Arbor, 1950.

D. Mitrany, *Marx against the peasantry*, Chapel Hill, N.C., 1951.

B. Moore, *Soviet politics. The dilemma of power*, Harvard U.P., 1951.

L. Owen, *The Russian peasant movement 1906–17*. Owen, King, London, 1937.

B. Pares, 'The new land settlement in Russia'. *The Russian Review*, Liverpool, vol. I, no. I, January 1912.

Ratner, *Agricultural co-operation in the Soviet Union*, Routledge, 1929.

G. T. Robinson, *Rural Russia under the old Régime*, Longmans, N.Y., 1932.

L. Schapiro, *The Communist Party of the Soviet Union*, Eyre and Spottiswoode, London, 1960.

R. Schlesinger, *History of the Communist Party of the Soviet Union*. (Manuscript at Glasgow University. Published in Italian.)

D. J. R. Scott, *Russian political institutions*, George Allen and Unwin, London, 1958.

S. Shidlovsky, 'The Imperial duma and the land settlement', *The Russian Review*, Liverpool, vol. I, no. I, 1912.

Y. Taniuchi, *The village gathering in Russia in the mid-twenties*, Monograph no. I, Centre for Russian and East European Studies, Birmingham, 1968.

V. P. Timoshenko, *Agrarian Russia and the wheat problem*, Stanford, 1932.

J. Towster, *Political power in the USSR 1917–47*, Oxford U.P., N.Y., 1948.

N. Vakar, *The taproot of Soviet society*, Harper, N.Y., 1962.

F. Venturi, *Roots of revolution* (trans.), London, 1959.

L. Volin, 'Peasant household under Mir and Kolkhoz', in *Foreign Agriculture*, vol. IV, no. 3, March 1940 (U.S. Dept. of Agriculture, Washington, D.C.); also in Ware (ed.), *Cultural approach to History*, American Historical Association.

Bibliography

Vucinich, *Soviet economic institutions*, Stanford U.P., 1952.

M. Wallace, *Russia*. Editions from 1877 on. Cassell, London.

B. and S. Webb, *Soviet Communism – a new civilisation?* W.E.A., London, 1935.

R. G. Wesson, *Soviet communes*, Rutgers U.P., New Brunswick, 1963.

WORKS IN RUSSIAN

On land holding aspects

Agrarnaya sektsiya komakademii (Agricultural Section of the Communist Academy), debates printed in *Na agrarnom fronte*, 1926, nos. 9, 10, 11–12.

Baranskii, *Ekonomicheskaya geografiya SSSR* (4th ed.), Moscow, 1926.

B. D. Brutskus, *Agrarnyi vopros i agrarnaya politika*, Petrograd, 1922.

A. Chayanov, *Organizatsiya krest'yanskogo khozyaistva*, Moscow, 1925. (English translation, *Organisation of the peasant farm*, by R. E. F. Smith.)

Cherny, 'Zemleustroistvo v Kubane', *Na agrarnom fronte*, 1927, no. 11–12.

Ts. V. Chernyshev, *Sel'skoe khozyaistvo dovoennoi Rossii i SSSR*, Moscow–Leningrad, 1926.

V. P. Danilov, 'Zemel'nye otnosheniya v sovetskoi dokolkhoznoi derevne', *Istoriya SSSR*, 1958, no. 3.

—— 'K itogam izucheniya istorii sovetskogo krest'yanstva i kolkhoznogo stroitel'stva SSSR', *Voprosy istorii*, 1960, no. 8.

L. I. Dembo, *Krest'yanskii dvor i zemel'noe obshchestvo*, Leningrad, 1925.

N. Druzhinin *et al.*, *Khozyaistvennye raiony SSSR, Tsentral'naya promyshlennaya oblast'*. *Sbornik statistik*, Gosizdat, Moscow–Leningrad, 1927.

Dubovskii, 'Sovremennoe malazemelya', *Na agrarnom fronte*, 1926, no. 5–6.

L. Grigoriev, *Ocherki sovremennoi derevni, kniga 2-ya*, Moscow, 1925.

P. Gurov, 'Predvaritel'nye itogi zemleustroistva', *Na agrarnom fronte*, 1925, no. 10.

Bibliography

Irkutskii okruzhnyi zemotdel, *Zemlepol'zovanie i sel'skoe khozyaistvo Irkutskogo okruga v tsifrakh*, Irkutsk, 1928.

Ivanovo Voznesenskii gubernskii RKI, *Zemleustroitel'naya pomoshch' krest'yanskomu naseleniyu*, Ivanovo-Voznesensk, 1927.

Kazantsev (ed.), *Zemel'noe pravo*, Moscow, 1958.

Khozyaistvennye raiony SSSR, *Tsentral'naya promyshlennaya oblast'*. Sbornik statistik, Gosizdat, Moscow–Leningrad, 1927.

Kindeev, *Voprosy zemleustroistva*, Moscow, 1925. 'O proektakh obshchikh nachal zemlepol'zovaniya i zemleustroistva', *Na agrarnom fronte*, 1926, no. 10, p. 89.

E. Kochetovskaya, *Natsionalizatsiya zemli v SSSR*, Gospolizdat, Moscow, 1952.

Konferentsiya agrarnikov marksistov, *Trudy*, Moscow, 1929.

N. I. Kozlov, *O zemel'nom obshchestve*, Moscow–Leningrad, 1926.

L. Kritzman, 'O proektakh obshchikh nachal zemlepol'zovaniya i zemleustroistva', *Na agrarnom fronte*, 1927, no. 2.

Kryukov, *Osnovy sel'sko-khozyaistvennoi ekonomiki*, Petrograd, 1923.

Kubanin, 'Obshchina pri diktaturoi proletariata', *Na agrarnom fronte*, 1926, no. 11–12.

Kubanskii statisticheskii otdel, *Kubanskii statisticheskii sbornik za 1924–6*. Tom 1, Krasnodar, 1928.

V. I. Lenin, *Sochineniya* (1937): iii, 68, 136; v, 60; ix, 313; xii, 419.

—— *Sochineniya* (1950): xxvi, 226–9; xxviii, 156, 285.

Moskovskaya oblast, statisticheskii otdel, *Moskva i Moskovskaya Oblast' 1926/7–1928/9*, Moscow, 1930.

Narodnyi Komissariat Raboche-Krest'yanskogo Inspektorata RSFSR, *Vyvody i predlozheniya sel'khozinspektsii po materialam obsledovaniya zemleustroistva. Prilozhenie k protokolu 18.P.2. zasedaniya kollegii HKRKI RSFSR 11 June 1925*, Moscow, 1925.

Narodnyi Komissariat Zemledeliya RSFSR, *Otchet za 1925–6*, Moscow, 1926. *Materialy po perspektivnomu planu razvitiya sel'skogo i lesnogo khozyaistva*, Moscow, 1928.

I. V. Novitski, *Pravo trudovogo zemlepol'zovaniya*, Moscow, no date.

Oganovskii, *Obshchina i zemel'noe tovarishchestvo*, Moscow, 1923.

P. N. Pershin, *Uchastkovoe zemlepol'zovanie v Rossii: khutora i otruby i ikh rasprostranenie za desyatiletie 1907–16 i sud'ba vo vremya revolyutsii (1917–20)*. Novaya Derevnya, Moscow, 1922.

Bibliography

—— *Zemel'noe ustroistvo dorevolyutsionnoi derevni.* Nauchno-Issledovatel'skii Institut Sel'sko-khozyaistvennoi Ekonomiki, Moscow and Voronezh, 1928.

P. Popov, 'Voprosy zemleustroistva na Ukraine', *Na agrarnom fronte*, 1925, no. 5–6.

Prokopich, *Krest'yanskoe khozyaistvo*, Prague, no date.

Shchuleikin, 'Razvitie zemleustroistva', *Na agrarnom fronte*, 1928, no. 2.

S. P. Shvetsov, *Ekonomicheskaya geografiya sel'skogo khozyaistva SSSR*, Leningrad, 1925.

Simferopol (no author given), Documents on land society, no title, bound as a pamphlet.

    Uchreditel'nyi prigovor zemel'nogo obshchestva

    Ustav zemel'nogo obshchestva

    Spisok chlen zemel'nogo obshchestva

    Prigovor zemel'nogo obshchestva

Sukhanov, 'Obshchina v sovetskom agrarnom zakonodatelstve', *Na agrarnom fronte*, 1926, no. 11–12, pp. 98–109.

Tambovskaya guberniya, Statisticheskii byuro i zemel'noe upravlenie, *Materialy po sovremennomu zemlepol'zovaniyu Tambovskoi gubernii*, Tambov, 1926.

I. A. Teodorova (ed.), *Sovetskoe zemleustroistvo i melioratsiya.* Perspektivnyi plan. Trudy zemplana, Moscow, 1925.

Tsentral'noe Statisticheskoe Upravlenie SSSR, *Narodnoe khozyaistvo SSSR*, Moscow, 1925.

—— *Statisticheskii spravochnik SSSR, 1927*, Moscow, 1928.

—— *Sel'skoe khozyaistvo SSSR, 1925–8*, Moscow, 1929.

—— *Narodnoe khozyaistvo SSSR*, Moscow, 1933.

Tsentral'nyi Ispolnitel'nyi Komitet Verkhovnogo Soveta SSSR: 4-yi sozyv. 3-ya sessiya, 7-oe zasedanie, April, 1928. *Otchet.*

—— 4-yi sozyv, 4-ya sessiya, December 1928. *Otchet.*

F. A. Tsylko (ed.), *Materialy issledovaniya kooperativnogo razvitiya krest'yanskogo khozyaistva*, NK RKI SSSR; Soyuz Soyuzov; Nauchno-issledovatel'skii institut sel'skokhozyaistvennoi ekonomiki, Moscow, 1928.

Ural'skoe zemel'noe upravlenie, *Zemlepol'zovanie i perspektivy zemleustroistva na Urale*, Sverdlovsk, 1926.

Voronev, 'Agrarnye ocherki Rybinskogo Kraya', *Na agrarnom fronte*, 1926, no. 1.

Voronovich, *Ob agrarnoi programme RSDRP*, Moscow, 1947.

Bibliography

Votskaya oblast', *Statisticheskii ezhegodnik za 1927*, Izhevsk, 1928.

A. A. Yakovlev, *Derevnya kak ona est'*, Kurak, 1923.

—— *K voprosu o pereustroistve sotsialisticheskogo sel'skogo khozyaistva*, NKRKI, Moscow, 1928.

Zemleustroitel', 1925, nos. 3 and 4.

Zemleustroistvo Samarskoi Gubernii 1927–8 (no author given), Samara, 1928.

Rural soviet and commune

I. F. Akimov, *Novyi zakon o sel'sovetakh*, Moscow, 1930.

Ya. Berman, 'O podgotovke kadrov sovetskikh rabotnikov', *Izvestiya*, 17 February 1930.

N. Bogdanov, *Sovety v raionakh sploshnoi kollektivizatsii*, Saratov, 1930.

D. A. Borodin, 'K voprosu o sel'skikh skhodakh', *Sovetskoe gosudarstvo i pravo*, 1960, no. 12.

Ts. V. Chernyshev, 'Derevenskoe nalogotvorchestvo', *Izvestiya*, 30 October 1926, no. 251.

L. A. Fadayev, 'Iz istorii administrativnogo raionirovaniya v RSFSR', *Istoricheskie zapiski*, 1953, no. 44.

S. T. Ivanovich, *VKP – 10 let kommunisticheskoi monopolii*, Paris, 1928.

M. I. Kalinin, *Voprosy sovetskogo stroitel'stva*, Gosizdat, Moscow, 1958.

A. Karp, *Izvestiya*, 15 December 1927, no. 287.

—— *Sel'sovet – boevoi shtab kollektivizatsii*, 2-oe izd, Moscow, 1931.

V. Kavraiskii and O. Khamarmer, *Sel'sovet i sotsialisticheskoe pereustroistvo derevni*, Sibkraiizdat, Novosibirsk, 1930.

V. Kavraiskii, *Sel'sovet i kolkhoz*, Novosibirsk, 1930.

A. Kazakov, 'Sostoyanie i perspektivy raboty KKOB', *Na agrarnom fronte*, 1926, no. 7–8.

M. Khataevich, 'Partiya v derevne', *Na agrarnom fronte*, 1925, no. 2.

—— 'Predvaritel'nye itogi perevyborov sel'sovetov 1924–5', *Na agrarnom fronte*, 1925, no. 6, p. 66.

—— 'Itogi vypolneniya postanovleniya Oktyabr'skogo plenuma TsK.RKP(b) o rabote v derevne', *Na agrarnom fronte*, 1925, no. 5–6, p. 198.

A. Kirpichev, *Prava skhoda i sel'soveta*, Moscow–Leningrad, 1928.

Bibliography

G. Konyukhov, *KPSS v bor'be s khlebnymi zatrudneniyami v strane 1928–9 gg*, Moscow, 1960.

S. A. Kovalev, *Sel'skoe rasselenie*. MGU, Moscow, 1963.

M. V. Kozhevnikov, *Zadachi sel'sovetov v svyazi so sploshnoi kollektivizatsii i likvidatsii kulachestva kak klassa*, Simferopol, 1930.

I. Kozhikov, 'Zemel'noe obshchestvo i sel'skii sovet', *Na agrarnom fronte*, 1928, no. 5.

Krasnoyarskii okruzhnyi ispolnitel'nyi komitet, *Zadachi sel'sovetov v dele razvitiya i pereustroistva sel'skogo khozyaistva*, Krasnoyarsk, 1929.

T. I. Kruglov, *Osnovnye zadachi vika i sel'soveta*, Moscow, 1925.

—— 'Derevenskie obshchestvennye kapitaly', *Izvestiya* 30 December 1926, no. 251.

O. P. Lapin, *Rukovodstvo dlya raionnykh (volostnykh) i sel'skikh rabotnikov*, Yeniseiskii G.I.K., 1925.

M. Latsis, 'Sostoyanie sel'skogo khozyaistva vo vtorom Donoukruge i zadachi sel'yacheek v dele vosstanovleniya sel'skogo khozyaistva', *Na agrarnom fronte*, 1925, no. 4.

Leningradskii gubernskii ispolnitel'nyi komitet, *Instruktsiya sel'sovetam i vikam o sozyve i reshenii voprosov na osg (skhod)*. (Pamphlet), January 1925.

A. Lepeshkin, *Mestnye organy vlasti sovetskogo gosudarstva 1921–36*, Moscow, 1959.

A. Luzhin, *Ot volosti k raionu*, Moscow, 1928.

—— *Organizatsiya sel'sovetov*, Moscow, 1930.

I. Makarov, 'Ukreplenie sel'skoi partiinoi organizatsii v periode podgotovki massogo kolkhoznogo dvizheniya', *Voprosy istorii*, 1962, no. 3.

A. Martynov, *My i oni litsom k derevne*, Moscow, 1925.

Materialy po istorii SSSR, Tom I, Akademiya Nauk, Moscow, 1955.

Milyutin, 'Krest'yanskie Komitety Vzaimopomoshchi', *Na agrarnom fronte*, 1925, no. 11–12.

Mossovet, *O nizovom sovetskom apparate*, Moscow, 1925.

I. Murugov and A. Kolesnikov, *Apparat nizovykh sovetskikh organov (Po materialam obsledovaniya NK RKI RSFSR 1925)*, Moscow–Leningrad, 1926.

Narodnyi Komissariat Vnutrennykh Del SSSR, *Administrativno-territorial'noe delenie SSSR*, Moscow, 1929.

Bibliography

—— *Administrativno-territorial'noe delenie SSSR*, Moscow, 1930.

—— *Administrativno-territorial'noe delenie SSSR*, Moscow, 1931.

M. Rezunov, *Sel'sovet i zemel'noe obshchestvo*, Moscow, 1928.

K. S. Sladkov, *Sel'skie skhody*, Gosyurizdat, Moscow–Leningrad, 1955.

Sokolova, 'Ukrupnenie raionnykh i sel'skikh sovetov v 1930', *Istoriya SSSR*, 1958, no. 6.

I. M. Sorokhanova, 'Iz opyta deyatel'nosti TsKK i RKI po uluchsheniyu raboty nizovogo sovetskogo apparata', *Nauchnye doklady vysshei shkoly, istoricheskie nauki*, 1961, no. 4.

Spravochnik kommunal'nogo rabotnika, Moscow, 1925.

V. N. Strogy, *Nalogovye platezhi zemledel'cheskogo naseleniya v 1925–6*, Moscow, no date.

Timashev, 'Krest'yanstvo i sovety', *Sovremennye zapiski*, Paris, 1928, XXXIV, 453.

Troitskii okrispolkom, *Sbornik rukovodyashchikh materialov dlya sel'sovetov*, Troitsk, 1929.

Tsentral'nyi Ispolnitel'nyi Komitet Verkhovnogo Soveta SSSR, *Mestnye byudzhety za 1926–7*, Moscow, 1929.

—— *Soveshchanie po voprosam sovetskogo stroitel'stva pri prezidiume TsIKa*, January 1925, April 1925.

—— *Materialy komissii po ukrepleniyu raboty sel'sovetov i vikov*, Moscow, 1925.

M. Ustinov, 'Zemel'noe obshchestvo i sel'sovet', *Izvestiya*, 22 August 1929.

V. Verlinskii and A. Viktorov, 'Sel'sovet i zemel'noe obshchestvo', *Khozyaistvo i upravlenie*, 11–12, December 1927.

A. A. Yakovlev and M. Khataevich (eds.), *VIK i sel'sovet*, Moscow, 1925.

P. Zaitsev, *Printsipy i praktika organizatsii sel'sovetov. Sovetskoe stroitel'stvo*, Sbornik 50, Moscow, 1926.

Zhdanov and Smirnov, *Sbornik zakonov i pravil po finansam sel'soveta*, Gosfinizdat, Moscow, 1936.

The collectivisation process – a brief selection

M. Abramov, *Organizatorskaya rabote partii po osushchestvleniyu Leninskogo kooperativnogo plana*, Moscow, 1956.

I. G. Bulatov, *Kooperatsiya i ee rol' v podgotovke sploshnoi kollektivizatsii*, Moscow, 1960.

Bibliography

N. A. Ivnitskii, 'O nachal'nom etape sploshnoi kollektivizatsii', *Voprosy istorii*, 1962, no. 4.

M. P. Kim (ed.), *Istoriya sovetskogo krest'yanstva i kolkhoznogo stroitel'stva*, Moscow, 1963.

A. Lozovoi, 'MTS i ikh rol' v sotsializatsii krest'yanskogo khozyaist-va', *Na agrarnom fronte*, 1929, no. 4.

V. K. Medvedyev, 'Likvidatsiya kulachestva v Nizhne-Volzhskom Krae', *Istoriya SSSR*, 1958, no. 1.

M. I. Ovchenikov, 'Rol' traktornykh kolonn i MTS v kolkhoznom stroitel'stva na severnom kavkaze v 1929', *Nauchnye doklady vysshei shkoly, istoricheskie nauki*, 1960, no. 3.

F. M. Podchufarov, *Tul'skie kommunisty v periode podgotovki massovogo kolkhoznogo dvizheniya 1924–9*, Tula, 1959.

Saratovskaya partiinaya organizatsiya v periode nastupleniya sotsia-lizma po vsemu frontu – sozdaniya kolkhoznogo stroya. Doku-menty i materialy 1930–2, Saratovskoe knizhnoe izdatel'stvo, Saratova, 1961.

P. N. Sharov, 'God velikogo pereloma v Ts Ch O.', *Istoricheskie zapiski*, no. 41(1952); also 51(1955).

S. P. Trapeznikov, *Borba partii bol'shevikov za kollektivizatsii sel'skogo khozyaistva v godakh pervoi stalinskoi pyatiletki*, Gosizdat, Moscow, 1951.

On workers' brigades and 'twenty-five thousanders', see biblio-graphic footnotes 1 and 2 on p. 202.

Collections of decrees

Direktivy KPSS i Sovetskogo pravitel'stva po khozyaistvennym voprosam, Tom I i II, Gospolizdat, Moscow, 1957.

Istoriya kolkhoznogo prava. Sbornik zakonodatel'nykh materialov 1917–58, Tom I 1917–36, Moscow, 19—.

KPSS v rezolyutsiyakh i resheniyakh s'ezdov, konferentsii i plenumov Ts.K., Tom I–III, Gospolizdat, Moscow, 1954.

KPSS o rabote sovetov. Sbornik dokumentov, Moscow, 1959.

Sbornik dokumentov po zemel'nomu zakonodatel'stvu SSSR i RSFSR 1917–54, Gosyurizdat, Moscow, 1954.

Sobranie uzakonenii i rasporazhenii rabochego i krest'yanskogo pravitel'stva (abbreviated to SU).

Sobranie zakonov i ukazov Prezidiuma Verkhovnogo Soveta SSSR (abbreviated to SZ).

Svod Zakonov Rossiiskoi Imperii, Tom 9, Kn. 1, St-Petersburg, 1910.

INDEX

I   249

Index

Commune: (cont.)
87, 120–6, 177, 187, 211; examples 80, 110–20, 172, 198; legislation 59, 97–109, 152–5, 198–9, 235–7; size 87–97
self-taxation 81, 139, 147–9, 173
settlement and 43, 45, 49, 87–97, 207
size 11, 12, 24–6, 37, 39, 40, 42–5, 48, 51, 52, 55, 166–7, 191
socialist competition 197
taxation 7, 56–7, 180, 208, 211; *see also* Commune, self-taxation
volost executive committee and 100, 101, 105–6, 108, 111, 118, 131–2, 154, 172
women 68–71
Conference on questions of soviet construction 111, 121
Conference of peasant members of All-Union Central Executive Committee 61, 73, 181
Contracting, *see* Commune, contracting
Co-operatives, peasants and 156, 158, 178; *see also* Commune and
Crimean ASSR 25–6, 93, 144–5

Danilov, V. P. 7, 60, 63
Decree on land 57
Don oblast 21, 25–6, 173

Enclosed forms of holding, *see* Farms
Engels 156–7
English pre-enclosure village 6, 7
Enukidze 114, 143

Far North region 24
Farms: enclosed farms generally 11, 18, 19, 21–8, 30–2, 34, 36, 48–9, 51–2, 217, 219
fields only enclosed 21, 22–8, 30–2, 35, 39–40, 46, 49, 159–61, 161–2, 166–7, 170, 217, 221, 226–7
fully enclosed 21, 22, 30, 32, 35, 39–40, 42, 46, 159–61, 161–2, 166–7, 169, 170, 177, 180, 181, 217, 219, 226–7
links with commune remaining 32–3, 50, 75–6, 208
unenclosed, non-redistributable 218, 224, 226–7
see also Land use measures
Fourteenth All-Russian Congress of Soviets 126, 149, 151, 197–9

Gathering: atmosphere of 4, 63, 69
attendance at 67–9
definition of 217, 224
frequency of meeting 76–7
kulak influence alleged 72–3, 108–9, 123, 148, 151, 153, 162–177, 187, 198, 204, 210, 230
matters discussed at 65, 110–20, 121, 138, 142, 147, 194–8
women at 68–71
young people at 68–9
see also General meeting of citizens
General foundations of land holding and land use measures 60, 81, 124–5, 149, 152–5, 184–7, 197
General meeting of citizens 48–9, 72, 80, 99, 108–9, 112, 115, 116, 121, 136, 194–5, 199, 201–5, 214, 217, 220, 224, 236
Gomel guberniya 22
Gosplan areas 16
Guberniya executive committee 67
Guberniya land commission 104–5
Guberniya land organs 103

Hamlet 217, 219, 223; *see also* Settlement
Hindus, M. 6
Hire of inventory 175–6
Hire of labour 175–6

Intermingled strip system 217, 219; *see also* Strips
Ivanovo-Voznesensk guberniya 8, 36–8, 61, 73, 80, 93, 166

Kalinin, M. I. 122
Kaluga guberniya 92
Khutor, *see* Farms, fully enclosed
Kindeev 32, 158, 165, 183
Kiselev 88, 111, 119, 121, 126, 149–51, 199
Korovin 4
Kossior 122
Kostroma guberniya 8, 36, 38, 60, 80, 93, 139, 146
Kubanin 171
Kursk guberniya 22, 39, 61, 73, 107, 118
Kuznets oblast 43–4

Land Code 18, 20, 54, 59, 60, 65, 67, 72, 78, 99, 101, 124, 152, 154, 182, 185, 198, 205

250

Index

Index

Peasant Household: (cont.)
  See also Renting land; Hiring of inventory, labour
Peasant mutual aid society 65–6, 118,
  121, 150, 198, 201, 218–19
Penza oblast 43–4, 60, 118
Pershin, P.N. 19, 49
Poltava guberniya 167
Pskov guberniya 21, 30–2, 34, 61, 183

Raion executive committee 131, 205
Redistribution, see Communal holding
Renting land 9, 174–6, 210
Repair brigades 201–2
Rezunov, M. 77, 113, 125, 132, 138,
  172–4
Rural society 24, 31, 35, 100, 218, 224
Rural soviet: agricultural functions
  106–7, 154, 198
  collectivisation 131, 151, 202–5, 212
  commission for helping grain delivery
    195
  commune end, see Commune, rural
    soviet and
  elections 126–7, 211
  finance 125, 137–52, 212
  frequency of meeting 76–7
  numbers 89
  production conference 198–9, 218
  sections 118, 125, 129–30, 194, 198
  size 87–97, 205
  social differentiation and 72, 128, 172
  staff 80, 81, 127–9
Ryazan guberniya 22, 35, 37, 61, 81, 92,
  114, 123, 141, 144–5

Samara guberniya 9, 21, 22, 42–4,
  174–6
Saratov guberniya 9, 21, 22, 49, 111,
  119, 138, 192, 204
Settlement: commune and 43, 45, 49,
  87–9, 207
  defined 218, 223
  rural soviet and 87–97, 207
  size 33, 37, 39, 43, 48–9, 51, 55, 82,
    97, 191
  see also Land use measures, creating
    new settlements
Sholokhov, M. 71
Siberia 24–6, 52, 61, 123, 144–5, 168,
  188–9
Simferopol land statutes 65, 79–80,
  112–13

Smolensk guberniya 8, 9, 21, 30–2, 92,
  118, 159, 161, 183
South east region 8, 24, 28, 189
South west region 24
Stadnyuk, I. 71
Stalingrad guberniya 48–9, 117, 135
Starosta, see Commune, officials
State farm 11, 23–8, 40, 218, 224, 226–7
Stavropol guberniya 21
Stolypin reforms 18, 53, 66, 75–6, 207
Strips: distance from farm and between
  strips 7, 9, 10, 37, 39, 41, 45, 47–8,
    53, 173, 208, 218–19, 221
  number per household, and excessive
    interlocking 7, 8, 34, 37, 39, 46–9,
      53, 55, 173, 208, 218–19, 221
Sukhanov, N. 125, 160, 177
Syrzan oblast 43–4

Tambov guberniya 22, 39, 60, 76, 91,
  118, 132, 141, 202
Tanuichi, Y. 97
Third All-Union Congress of Soviets
  122
Tractor columns 199–200
Tula guberniya 35, 61, 77, 92, 136,
  144–5, 149, 184, 197, 205
Tver guberniya 8, 9, 22, 38, 92, 118
Twenty-five thousanders 71, 202–4

Udmurt republic 46
Uezd land commission 104–5
Uezd land organs 103
Ufa guberniya 167
Ukrainian republic 24–7, 38, 51–2, 71,
  92, 114, 123, 144–6
Ulyanov guberniya 61, 73, 118
Ulyanov oblast 43–4
Ural oblast 8, 22, 24–6, 46–8, 54–5, 60,
  76, 93, 112, 126, 144–5, 149, 183,
  188–9

Village 218, 223–4; see Settlement
Village executive 218, 224
Village judge 236
Vitebsk guberniya 21, 30
Vladimir guberniya 38, 76, 93, 126,
  140–1
Volga, German republic 81, 93, 114, 143
Volga region 25–7, 38
Volga-Kama region 25–6
Vologda guberniya 22, 76, 92

Index